THE
ULTIMATE
DINOSAUR
BOOK

THE
ULTIMATE
DINOSAUR
BOOK

DAVID LAMBERT

DK

DORLING KINDERSLEY
LONDON • NEW YORK • STUTTGART
in association with
THE NATURAL HISTORY MUSEUM • LONDON

A DORLING KINDERSLEY BOOK

Consultant Editors
Dr Angela Milner (The Natural History Museum, London)
Dr Ralph E. Molnar (Queensland Museum, Australia)
Dr John Ostrom (Peabody Museum, Yale University, USA)

Project Editor
Mary Lindsay

Project Art Editor
Jillian Haines

Editors
Edward Bunting, Fiona Courtenay-Thompson,
Mark Ronan

Designers
Johnny Pau, Anne Renel, Clare Shedden

Editorial Assistant
Jeanette Cossar

Design Assistant
Philip Ormerod

Managing Editor
Ruth Midgley

Managing Art Editors
Philip Gilderdale, Stephen Knowlden

Photographers
Andy Crawford, Lynton Gardiner (USA), Steve Gorton
Colin Keates (The Natural History Museum, London),
Miguel Pereira (Argentina), Tim Ridley

Illustrators
Roby Braun, Simone End, Andrew Hutchinson,
Steve Kirk, Janos Marffy, Andrew Robinson,
Graham Rosewarne, John Sibbick, John Temperton

Model Makers
Roby Braun, David Donkin, Graham High and Jeremy Hunt
(Centaur Studios), John Holmes

Production
Sarah Fuller, Hilary Stephens

First Published in Great Britain in 1993
by Dorling Kindersley Limited,
9 Henrietta Street, London WC2E 8PS

Copyright © 1993 Dorling Kindersley Limited, London
Text copyright © 1993 David Lambert

A CIP catalogue record for this book is available from the British Library

ISBN 0 7513 0047 0

Computer page make-up by
Cooling Brown, Hampton-on-Thames, Middlesex
Reproduced by
Colourscan, Singapore
Printed and bound by
Arnoldo Mondadori, Verona, Italy

CONTENTS

DINOSAUR PROFILES 36

A TO Z OF DINOSAURS 168

With entries for all the currently known dinosaur genera, this dinosaur dictionary also includes cross-references for names not now in standard use.

THEROPODS 38
Bipedal predatory dinosaurs with bird-like legs and feet. Most were armed with fangs as well as toe- and finger-claws.

SAUROPODOMORPHS 82
Chiefly quadrupedal, plant-eating dinosaurs – some of which were immense – with long necks, bulky bodies, and long tails.

THYREOPHORANS 110
Quadrupedal plant-eaters, including the plated stegosaurs and armoured ankylosaurs, with bodies fortified by bony studs and spikes or plates.

ORNITHOPODS 130
Bipedal and bipedal/quadrupedal dinosaurs with distinctive hip bones, bony tendons that stiffened the tail, and jaws and cheek teeth remarkably designed for chewing vegetation.

MARGINOCEPHALIANS 152
Plant-eaters with a ridge or shelf at the back of the skull; within this group were the thick-headed and "parrot-beaked" dinosaurs.

FOREWORD

DINOSAURS ARE among the most popular and – nowadays – familiar of all animals. Few readers will not already have heard of *Tyrannosaurus*. Within these pages, you will also meet some less well-known dinosaurs, perhaps for the first time. The last dinosaurs died out 65 million years ago, something like 64.7 million years before our own species evolved. So why should animals that lived in almost unimaginably remote times in the past be such a source of fascination for us today? One reason is the sheer amount of knowledge that has been built up by careful study of the fossilized bones and teeth. Another is the great diversity of the dinosaurs, and the success with which they reigned over the other animals of the Mesozoic era. New discoveries from around the world, and new ways of looking at old favourites, have revolutionized ideas of what dinosaurs were like. We have come to understand more about their behaviour and social lives, and in doing so we have discerned similar lifestyles to those of modern animals. Our own past, too, is linked with the fate of the dinosaurs. Had they not become extinct, then the mammals – including, ultimately, humans – would never have come to dominate the Earth, and we simply would not be here.

Dr Angela Milner
Head of the Fossil Vertebrates Division
The Natural History Museum, London

THE ESSENTIAL DINOSAUR

 THIS SECTION begins with a definition of the dinosaurs and takes a look at how they evolved. It describes the world they inhabited, examining how they lived and how they may have died out. Finally, it surveys the sequence of events from fossilization to discovery, excavation, study, and reconstruction, resulting in today's magnificently lifelike museum displays.

WHAT IS A DINOSAUR?

I N POPULAR IMAGINATION dinosaurs were just immense, slow-witted, slow-moving prehistoric versions of living reptiles. Certainly some grew as long and heavy as a great whale. Yet there were also dinosaurs no bigger than a chicken, dinosaurs as alert as an ostrich, and dinosaurs as swift as a horse. They came in two-legged, four-legged, clawed, hoofed, fanged, and toothless forms. Some even had beaks. In fact they made up a group almost as varied as – and for about 165 million years much more successful than – mammals. Like mammals, all dinosaurs shared a basic body plan, one that set them apart from every other group of reptiles. Some scientists would even classify the Dinosauria as a subclass, or major subgroup, of the class Reptilia. These pages name the characteristics that enable an anatomist to identify a fossil creature as a dinosaur.

ORNITHISCHIAN PELVIS

This Hypsilophodon *pelvis has the typically ornithischian backward-sloping pubis. The fo pointing part of the pubic bone i*

Ilium

SAURISCHIAN

This Allosaurus p
typically saurisch
pubis. The bro
specific to cer
dinosaurs.
pelvis h
ilium, an

Prepubis

Pubis

Ischium

■ DINOSAUR FEATURES ■

The skull of a dinosaur had long bones known as vomers, which ran from the front of the snout to the level of the antorbital fenestrae (skull holes in front of the eyes). All but maybe the most primitive dinosaurs had at least three sacral vertebrae anchoring the hip girdle to the spinal column. The shoulder girdle had a backward-facing glenoid fossa (the humerus or upper arm bone socket); the humerus had a long, low deltopectoral crest; and the fourth finger of each hand had no more than three phalanges (finger bones). There were also key features in the bones of the hips, thighs, legs, and feet. A dinosaur's hind limbs evolved to hold the body vertical, like the legs of a mammal. They stayed erect because each femur (thigh bone) had a sharply inturned neck and ball-shaped head which slotted into the fully open acetabulum (hip socket). This meant that the shaft of the femur turned down instead of sticking out sideways like a lizard's. A supra-acetabular crest helped to prevent dislocation of

the femur. The shaft of a fourth trochanter (a leg-retracting muscles) greater and a lesser tro knee joint was aligned socket, so that the who could swing to and fro rather than with a spra like a lizard's. The tibia was far larger than the bone) and bore a bony (the cnemial crest). Th the tibia was notched t process arising from th (the main ankle bone). ankle joint formed a si and the elongated foot that dinosaurs walked The middle toe tended longest; some dinosaur short outer toes, or no relatives of dinosaurs s but not all, of these fea

HIND LIMB OF TYRANNOSAURUS
The Tyrannosaurus *hind limb bones (above and right) show key dinosaurian features such as a reduced fibula, an ascending process of the astragalus, and a high ankle joint.*

Pelvic girdle
Acetabulum
Ball-shaped head
Femur
Ischium
Knee joint
Fibula
Tibia
Ankle joint
Foot

Cnemial crest
Fibula
Tibia
Astragalus
Ankle joint
Metatarsal
Phalanx

STANCES COMPARED
The dinosaur and the elephant, walk more efficiently than its bent knees and elbo its sprawling, repti

ORNITHOPOD DINOSAURS

This scene shows Lambeosaurus, Parasaurolophus, *and* Corythosaurus. *These three genera are all hadrosaurs (duckbilled dinosaurs) and belong to the family Lambeosauridae, the suborder Ornithopoda, and the order Ornithischia.*

■ DINOSAUR GROUPS ■

All known dinosaurs are divided into two large groups: Saurischia ("lizard hipped") and Ornithischia ("bird hipped"). Most saurischians had forward-jutting pubes (pubic hip bones) while in ornithischians each pubis slanted back, parallel to the ischium (another hip bone). Some saurischians had pubes aligned like those of ornithischians, but there were other, more consistent differences between the groups. These included the saurischians' elongated neck bones, and the ornithischians' predentary bone at the tip of the toothless lower jaw. There were two major saurischian subgroups: the carnivorous, bipedal theropods, and the plant-eating, mostly quadrupedal sauropodomorphs. Ornithischians (all plant-eaters) were divided into three main groups: bird-like ornithopods, armoured thyreophorans, and horned or thick-skulled marginocephalians. A few kinds of small, early bipedal ornithischians seem to have been more primitive than the other ornithischian groups.

DINOSAURIA

DINOSAUR CLADOGRAM

The cladogram (right) shows the relationships between the key groups of dinosaurs. A clade consists of a group of animals that share uniquely evolved features and therefore a common ancestry. On the far right are shown one suborder, eight infraorders, and two families (names ending in -idae). The dotted line represents an uncertain relationship.

KEY

- ⬤ Order
- ⬤ Suborder
- ◯ Intermediate group
- ••• Relationship uncertain

THEROPODA

HERRERASAURIDAE

CERATOSAURIA

TETANURAE

SAURISCHIA

SEGNOSAURIA

SAUROPODA

SAUROPODOMORPHA

PROSAUROPODA

SCELIDOSAURIDAE

THYREOPHORA

STEGOSAURIA

ANKYLOSAURIA

ORNITHISCHIA

PACHYCEPHALOSAURIA

MARGINOCEPHALIA

CERATOPSIA

CERAPODA

ORNITHOPODA

ORIGINS, ANCESTORS, AND DESCENDANTS

DINOSAURS ORIGINATED from microscopic marine organisms several thousand million years ago. From these evolved true plants and animals. The processes of genetic change and natural selection led to the appearance of new forms of life. In the Palaeozoic era (about 570–248 million years ago) soft-bodied creatures gave rise to fishes with internal bony skeletons. Fishes produced amphibians that walked on land, and in turn gave rise to reptiles. Reptiles dominated land life in later Palaeozoic times. One group of reptiles evolved into archosaurs or "ruling reptiles". Dinosaurs were archosaurs that ruled the Mesozoic era (about 248–65 million years ago). Many scientists believe that modern birds are descendants of the dinosaurs.

THE AGES OF THE EARTH

The spiral ribbon (below) represents the Earth through time. The last 570 million years, which are rich in fossil material, are marked off in geological periods. Seven animals, representing predominant groups, are illustrated close to the periods in which they lived. The conodont animal (the first vertebrate), amphibian (the first tetrapod), and reptile (the first amniote) here represent three major evolutionary innovations that were inherited by the dinosaurs. Dinosaurs themselves are symbolized by a theropod, a sauropod, and a ceratopsian.

JURASSIC PERIOD
208–144 MYA: this was the heyday of the sauropods: huge, plant-eating dinosaurs. Among the largest of all was immense, giraffe-like Brachiosaurus.

TRIASSIC PERIOD
248–208 MYA: new groups of reptiles replaced the older forms. Dinosaurs evolved, diversified and spread. Early kinds included the slim, predatory theropod Coelophysis.

CRETACEOUS PERIOD
144–65 MYA: herds of large, horned dinosaurs, such as Triceratops, multiplied, but so did little mammals. This period saw the end of the Age of Dinosaurs.

CAMBRIAN PERIOD
570–510 MYA: invertebrates and eel-like conodont animals filled the seas. These were possibly the earliest of all known vertebrates (animals with backbones).

PERMIAN PERIOD
290–248 million years ago.

TERTIARY PERIOD
65–2 million years ago.

CARBONIFEROUS PERIOD
362–290 MYA: amniotes in the form of reptiles evolved from amphibians.

SILURIAN PERIOD
438–408 million years ago.

ORDOVICIAN PERIOD
505–438 million years ago.

DEVONIAN PERIOD
408–362 MYA: in this period fishes with lungs and fleshy fins gave rise to amphibians.

QUATERNARY PERIOD
2–0 MYA: Homo sapiens has evolved from Homo erectus. Mammals and birds are now the chief land vertebrates.

PRE-CAMBRIAN
4,600–570 million years ago.

FISHES

VERTEBRATES

AMPHIBIANS

TETRAPODS

SYNAPSIDS
AND MAMMALS

AMNIOTES

TURTLES

SAUROPSIDS

PLESIOSAURS
AND ICHTHYOSAURS

■ EVOLVING ■
VERTEBRATES

Dinosaurs inherited key
features that had evolved
successively in other vertebrates,
such as the fishes' internal
skeleton with jaws. From fishes
came amphibians: the first tetrapods
(four-footed animals with lungs, and
limbs evolved from fins). The eggs of
amphibians had to be fertilized and
laid in water or they dried up. From
amphibians evolved amniotes,
whose eggs were fertilized in the
female's body and developed inside
a waterproof membrane called the
amnion. The first amniotes were
reptiles: cold-blooded animals with
dry, scaly skin. With their waterproof
skin and eggs, reptiles no longer
depended on water, and could live
and breed on land.

DIAPSIDS

LIZARDS AND SNAKES

"THECODONTS"

ARCHOSAURS

CROCODILES

ADVANCED
ARCHOSAURS

PTEROSAURS

ORNITHODIRES

■ EVOLVING AMNIOTES ■

Synapsids were mammal-like reptiles
characterized by a skull opening low
down in the cheek. They dominated
the land in Permian times, giving rise
to true mammals before becoming
extinct. Sauropsids (with two openings
in the roof of the mouth) include
turtles and tortoises. Diapsids (with
two openings in the part of the skull
behind each eye) produced plesiosaurs
and ichthyosaurs, lizards and snakes,
and the archosaurs. Archosaurs have
an extra skull opening in front of each
eye, perhaps to hold an excess-salt-
removing gland. Primitive archosaurs
included a mixed group of thecodont
("socket-toothed") reptiles, some
similar to dinosaurs and crocodilians.

DINOSAURS
AND BIRDS

Certain advanced archosaurs gave rise
to two new groups: true crocodilians,
and the ornithodires ("bird necks").
The ornithodires included pterosaurs,
dinosaurs, and modern birds, all of
which walk on their toes. They have
an ankle joint forming a simple hinge,
a shelf above the hip socket, and thigh
bones with an enlarged ridge (fourth
trochanter). Dinosaurs evolved
distinctive skull, spinal, shoulder,
upper arm, hand, hip, calf, and ankle
bones. Strong similarities between the
bones of predatory dinosaurs and
modern birds suggest that birds may
be feathered dinosaurs with wings.

VERTEBRATE EVOLUTION

Starting with fishes (top of diagram), this
simplified family tree shows the sequence
in which different groups of vertebrates
evolved. The lines of extinct groups end
short. Groups below amphibians belong to
the class Reptilia (reptiles). Birds and
mammals are traditionally placed in classes
of their own. Scientists have worked out the
relationships of dinosaurs to other groups of
animals by comparing key characteristics in
fossil bones. Identifying sets of derived
characteristics inherited from a common
ancestor has enabled scientists to decide
which of these organisms evolved first, and
which are most closely related.

TRIASSIC WORLD

T HE TRIASSIC PERIOD (about 248–208 million years ago) was the first phase of the Mesozoic era ("Age of Middle Life"), often called the Age of the Dinosaurs. All lands formed one supercontinent, known as Pangaea ("all Earth"), of which the northern part is called Laurasia, and the southern part Gondwana. The climate was everywhere mild, warm, or hot. No ice sheets covered polar lands, but deserts spread into inland regions. Flowering plants had not yet evolved: conifers, palm-like cycads, and ferns grew in moist areas. Life on land was dominated by prehistoric reptiles suited to dry conditions. Reptiles also took to the air and seas. In the Late Triassic, many of the older reptiles were wiped out, but new kinds took their place. The most successful of these proved to be the dinosaurs.

Dicroidium *was a Triassic seed fern.*

TRIASSIC SUPERCONTINENT
Black outlines show modern continents superimposed on the Triassic supercontinent Pangaea. Despite an extensive area of water, the Tethys Sea, the north (Laurasia) and south (Gondwana) remained joined.

❋ LANDS ❋

Laurasia comprised North America, Europe, and much of what is now Asia. Gondwana included Africa, Arabia, India, Australia, Antarctica, and South America. The South Pole was located over the ocean. The whole of Pangaea was slowly drifting north as one great landmass. This supercontinent began to show the first signs of a future break-up after the Middle Triassic, when cracks appeared in parts of eastern North America, west and central Europe, and northwest Africa.

❋ PLANTS ❋

The plants that flourished in Laurasia were those adapted to dry climates such as ginkgoes, seed ferns, and somewhat palm-like cycads and cycadeoids. The biggest trees were conifers. Ginkgoes formed a fairly open canopy of medium-sized trees, and cycads ranged from short, squat forms to taller, palm-like species. Tree ferns created an understorey in the forests, and low ferns formed

"savannas" in drier open areas that would be grasslands today. Moist, open land supported dense growths of horsetails. Close to the Equator and in drier regions, patchy conifer and cycad forests thrived. Stands of tall seed ferns formed forests in Gondwana. Later in the Triassic period ferns were replaced by cycadeoids and conifers.

EUPARKERIA
Euparkeria *was a lightly built, agile archosaur. A precursor of crocodiles and dinosaurs, it lived in Early Triassic southern Africa.*

❋ LIFE ON LAND ❋

Reptiles ruled life on land during the Triassic period. Plant-eaters included hippopotamus-like dicynodonts, squat, pig-like rhynchosaurs, and mammal-like herbivorous cynodonts. There were formidable flesh-eating cynodonts as well. Dicynodonts, rhynchosaurs, and most cynodonts died out in the first of two mysterious mass extinctions. The thecodonts that largely took their place died out in the second of these extinctions. Survivors included turtles, land crocodilians, dinosaurs, and tiny mammals. Both of the main dinosaur groups emerged during the Late Triassic. Among saurischian dinosaurs were bipedal,

TRIASSIC DINOSAURS
Herrerasaurus, Staurikosaurus, *and* Coelophysis *were all carnivores.* Mussaurus, Melanorosaurus, Technosaurus, *and* Plateosaurus *typify early plant-eating dinosaurs.*

Mussaurus

Herrerasaurus

Melanorosaurus

Staurikosaurus

TRIASSIC COUNTRYSIDE
*Conifers, palm-like cycads, and ferns flourish in a
well-watered valley. An area
of desert lies beyond.*

EUDIMORPHODON
Eudimorphodon *("true two-form tooth") from
Late Triassic north Italy was one of the earliest
known pterosaurs. It grew about 1m (3ft 3in) long.*

flesh-eating theropods and
quadrupedal prosauropods: the first
big, high-browsing herbivores. Early
ornithischians were small, bipedal
herbivores. With no sea to stop them,
dinosaurs quickly colonized the world.

■ LIFE IN THE AIR ■

Small reptiles with "wings" of skin or
scales took gliding flights from tree to
tree. These "wings" may have been
supported by long ribs, or they may
simply have been feathery scales
growing from arms and legs, or webs
of skin between front and hind limbs.
Late Triassic animals like these may
have given rise to furry-bodied, warm-
blooded "reptiles" called pterosaurs.
These had large heads, short bodies,
and long, skin wings supported by
elongated fourth finger bones. Unlike
their gliding ancestors, pterosaurs
were capable of powered flight.

■ LIFE IN WATER ■

Various reptile groups invaded the
shallow Triassic seas. Sharp-toothed,
fish-eating nothosaurs grew up to
4m (13ft) long and had small heads,
long tails and bodies, and paddle-like
limbs. Seal-like placodonts crushed
shellfish between broad, flat back
teeth. Dolphin-like
ichthyosaurs, up to
15m (about 50ft)
long, were the reptiles
best adapted to the sea. Among their
prey were the big, swimming molluscs
called ammonoids.

Coelophysis

Technosaurus

Plateosaurus

JURASSIC WORLD

T HE JURASSIC PERIOD (about 208–144 million years ago) marked the middle of the Mesozoic era. By this time the supercontinent Pangaea was cracking up in earnest. Rifts in the continental crust produced the Atlantic Ocean. Africa began to split from South America, and India prepared to drift towards Asia. Climates were now warm worldwide, and moist winds from invading seas brought rain to inland deserts. Plants spread into once-barren lands, providing food for abundant and widespread dinosaurs (including the largest of all land animals). Above them flew the first small birds, which themselves may have evolved from small dinosaurs. The seas were shared by new, large swimming reptiles, and bony fishes built on "modern" lines.

Megazostrodon, *a shrew-like mammal.*

JURASSIC CONTINENTS
Black outlines show the modern landmasses, but in Jurassic times. Seas now began to cut into Pangaea and to divide Laurasia from Gondwana.

▪ LANDS ▪

When the Jurassic period began, old mountains had been worn away, but, as Pangaea started splitting up, new ones were formed. Floods of basalt lava oozed from geological rifts that ran all the way from southern Africa through Antarctica into Tasmania. Episodes of mountain building racked western North America, and volcanoes pushed up in the Andes. During the Jurassic, Tibet joined Eurasia, and, as the period ended, Africa brushed against southern Europe, losing chunks of crust that formed portions of land as far apart as Arabia and Spain.

▪ PLANTS ▪

Jurassic lands were generally greener and more lush than they had been in Triassic times, and vegetation types were more uniform worldwide. Tall forest conifers included relatives of today's giant sequoias, pines, and Chile pine (monkey puzzle). Other plentiful trees included ginkgoes, while palm-like

cycadeoids were the main small trees and shrubby plants. In conifer forests tall tree ferns often made up the understorey. The most common low-growing plants were ferns and horsetails. These grew prolifically, and may have been important as a food source for sauropod dinosaurs. No flowering plants had appeared yet.

MARINE REPTILE
Ichthyosaurus *was a sleek, swimming reptile with a long snout, paddle-shaped limbs, and a tall tail fin. It was born and lived in the sea.*

▪ LIFE ON LAND ▪

In the Early Jurassic, the main plant-eating vertebrates were prosauropod and ornithischian dinosaurs, and small, mammal-like reptiles. But, by Late Jurassic times, huge sauropods predominated. These browsed on both high and low level vegetation. Sauropods relied mainly on swallowed stones rather than teeth to pulverize their food. Stegosaurs, the next most abundant plant-eating dinosaurs, had toothless beaks and grinding cheek teeth. There were also early ankylosaurs and ornithopods. Large theropods killed and ate herbivores, but small coelurid and compsognathid theropods chased small game or possibly scavenged.

JURASSIC DINOSAURS
Sauropods like Diplodocus *were the major Late Jurassic plant-eaters. Ornithischians included* Dryosaurus, Stegosaurus *(derived from beasts like* Scelidosaurus*), and* Camptosaurus. *The large theropod* Allosaurus *ate such herbivores.*

Camptosaurus

Diplodocus

Dryosaurus

Allosaurus

JURASSIC COUNTRYSIDE

Tall conifers, relatives of the Chile pine, tower above an understorey of tree ferns, palm-like cycadeoids, and cycads. The ground is covered with a dense undergrowth of ferns and horsetails.

ARCHAEOPTERYX

Archaeopteryx may indicate that there is a link between birds and dinosaurs. It has been suggested that birds are winged theropods.

◼ LIFE IN THE AIR ◼

The skin-winged pterosaurs dominated life in the air. Rhamphorhynchoid pterosaurs had a long tail that served as a stabilizer and rudder; pterodactyloid pterosaurs lacked a tail. Many of these creatures had spiky teeth adapted for spearing fish as they swooped low over water. Early birds also appeared. The best known, *Archaeopteryx*, had bones, teeth, and claws that resembled a small theropod's, but also had feathered wings and tail, and was capable of flight.

◼ LIFE IN WATER ◼

By the Jurassic period, both nothosaurs and placodonts had died out, but ichthyosaurs persisted. They shared shallow seas with a group of marine crocodilians whose limbs had also evolved into flippers, and with teleosts (fishes with a bony skeleton and a suction-feeding mechanism). Other sea creatures included barrel-bodied plesiosaurs, which travelled through the water like sealions, and pliosaurs, which were short-necked plesiosaurs with big heads and strong, sharp teeth. By Late Jurassic times, ichthyosaurs and marine crocodilians were in decline.

Scelidosaurus

Stegosaurus

CRETACEOUS WORLD

T HE CRETACEOUS PERIOD (about 144–65 million years ago) marked the last phase of the Mesozoic era, and the climax of the Age of Dinosaurs. During this period thick chalk beds piled up on the floors of shallow seas that invaded North America and Europe; Laurasia and Gondwana fragmented into the continents that we know today; and colliding slabs of continental and oceanic crust thrust up the Rockies and other mountain ranges. Near the Equator, climates stayed warm but grew drier, and forests became thinner. Elsewhere the seasons grew more marked, and flowering plants began to appear. Animals on the now isolated continents began to evolve separately from each other, explaining why more kinds of dinosaurs appeared in Late Cretaceous times than ever before.

Magnolia: a survivor from the Cretaceous.

CRETACEOUS CONTINENTS
Black outlines show the shapes of modern landmasses in their Late Cretaceous positions. Shallow seas then covered immense tracts of continental crust.

▪ LANDS ▪

Early on in the Cretaceous period a land bridge linked East Asia and western North America, forming one faunal region known as Asiamerica. Gradually over the Cretaceous period a shallow sea split North America in half, and western North America became an island with its own dinosaur genera. A shallow sea separated Euramerica (eastern North America, Europe, and Greenland) from Asia. Also, the southern lands of Africa, Antarctica, India, South America, and Australia gradually drifted apart. With Euramerica, these southern lands shared "old-fashioned" forms of dinosaur, and so all arguably made up one great faunal region, known as the Eurogondwanan region.

▪ PLANTS ▪

Typically Mesozoic plants, such as cycadophytes, ginkgoes, conifers, and ferns, still dominated the land in Early Cretaceous times. But small, weedy flowering plants (angiosperms) also started to appear. As these prolific plants spread from the tropics into cooler regions, some evolved into

CRETACEOUS DINOSAURS
Ornithischians, like Hypsilophodon, Iguanodon, *and* Torosaurus *were replacing sauropod herbivores like* Saltasaurus. *Formidable carnivores included* Deinonychus *and* Tyrannosaurus.

FRESHWATER CROCODILIAN
Sarcosuchus, *an Early Cretaceous crocodilian up to 15m (49ft) long, lived in Africa and South America.*

shrubs and small trees. By the Late Cretaceous, oaks, maples, walnuts, and other trees were competing with the still abundant conifers.

▪ LIFE ON LAND ▪

By the Late Cretaceous, small mammals were diversifying fast and snakes had evolved from lizards, but dinosaurs still dominated life on land. New plant-eating ornithischian

families appeared, equipped with teeth and jaws that were engineered for chewing the new flowering plants. Low-browsing, armoured ankylosaurs multiplied too, but the less well-defended stegosaurs grew scarcer. The great, long-necked sauropods also began to diminish in northern lands, although they still predominated in the south. Cretaceous theropods ranged from bird-like ornithomimids to some of the largest of all land carnivores, the tyrannosaurids.

▪ LIFE IN THE AIR ▪

Winged creatures of Cretaceous times ranged from the world's first tiny moths and small social bees to the biggest animals that ever flew: giant pterosaurs. Among the largest pterosaurs were the

Saltasaurus

Deinonychus

Hypsilophodon

Iguanodon

CRETACEOUS COUNTRYSIDE
Flowering herbaceous plants and shrubby trees have started to colonize this heavily browsed river valley in western North America.

PTERANODON
This toothless pterosaur had wings up to 7m (23ft) across, and soared like an albatross. It ate fishes caught with its long beak.

huge *Quetzalcoatlus* and *Pteranodon*. New finds published in the early 1990s show that birds were also diversifying. By the Early Cretaceous, little *Sinornis* from China and *Concornis* from Spain had keeled breastbones, like modern flying birds. Later, flightless diving and running birds appeared, among them the turkey-sized *Mononykus*, with a keeled breastbone as well as a long, bony, dinosaurian tail core.

◼ LIFE IN WATER ◼

Cretaceous water creatures included immense relatives of vertebrates alive today. The largest freshwater species were crocodilians and the huge, crocodile-like champsosaurs, while the marine turtle *Archelon* outgrew the largest leatherback alive today. Sea-going, flippered lizards, known as mosasaurs, grew to 10m (33ft) in length and swam with undulations of a deep, flattened tail. The flippered, swimming plesiosaurs included short-necked forms (called pliosaurs), like formidable *Kronosaurus* with a head 3m (10ft) long, and long-necked fish-eaters, like *Elasmosaurus*, which had no fewer than 70 cervical (neck) vertebrae. During this period, ichthyosaurs all died out.

Tyrannosaurus

Torosaurus

DINOSAUR ANATOMY

S URVIVING FOSSILS reveal the bony frameworks of dinosaurs. It is possible to guess at the internal anatomy and muscles of dinosaurs by looking at those of living crocodilians, birds, and mammals. These animals also help us to deduce how the dinosaurs' bodies worked. Like those of living animals, dinosaurs' skeletons were largely designed to support muscles used for locomotion; to protect internal organs such as the brain, heart, and lungs; and to house bone marrow, which manufactured blood. Different groups of dinosaurs had specialized bones. For instance, heavy dinosaurs had thick, solid limb bones to support great weight, while lightweight dinosaurs had hollow, thin-walled limb bones. Huge "windows" in big theropods' skulls, and deep cavities scooped out of sauropods' vertebrae, removed unnecessary weight. The digestive systems, teeth, and claws of carnivores and herbivores varied according to diet and methods of attack and defence.

▪ SKELETON ▪

Skull and mandible formed braincase and jaws. Holes in the skull were for muscles, nostrils, and glands. Teeth were specialized according to diet; new teeth replaced old ones, which fell out. Cervical, dorsal, sacral, and caudal vertebrae formed the spinal column which supported the head, body, and tail. Ribs shielded the vital organs. Some dinosaurs also had belly ribs, called gastralia. Limb bones acted as levers worked by muscles. The forelimbs consisted of the scapula and coracoid bones (shoulder bones), the humerus (upper arm bone), the radius and ulna (lower arm bones), and the carpals (wrist bones). The metacarpals and

Troodon *had big eyes and a wide visual field.*

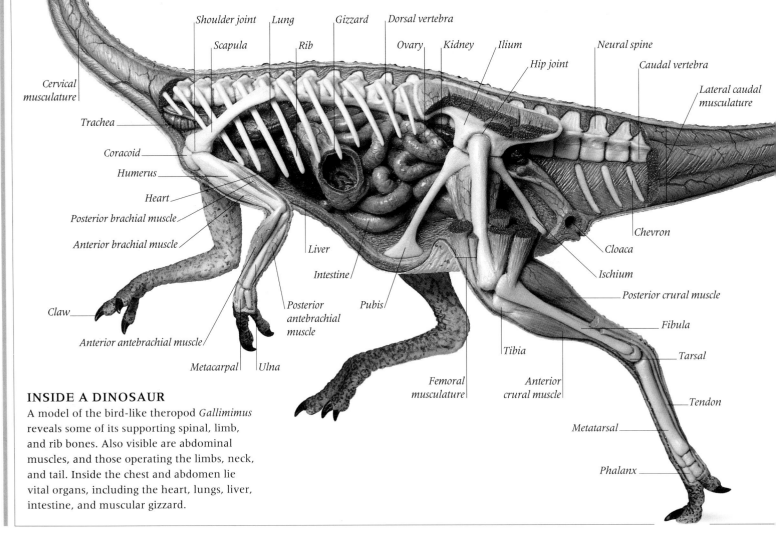

INSIDE A DINOSAUR
A model of the bird-like theropod *Gallimimus* reveals some of its supporting spinal, limb, and rib bones. Also visible are abdominal muscles, and those operating the limbs, neck, and tail. Inside the chest and abdomen lie vital organs, including the heart, lungs, liver, intestine, and muscular gizzard.

Shoulder joint | Lung | Gizzard | Dorsal vertebra
Scapula | Rib | Ovary | Kidney | Ilium | Neural spine
Cervical musculature | Hip joint | Caudal vertebra
Trachea | Lateral caudal musculature
Coracoid | Humerus | Heart | Posterior brachial muscle | Anterior brachial muscle
Chevron | Cloaca | Ischium
Claw | Liver | Intestine | Pubis | Posterior crural muscle | Fibula | Tarsal
Anterior antebrachial muscle | Posterior antebrachial muscle | Tendon
Metacarpal | Ulna | Femoral musculature | Anterior crural muscle | Tibia | Metatarsal | Phalanx

A SKULL AND MANDIBLE

This skull belonged to Plateosaurus, *a prosauropod dinosaur with teeth designed for eating vegetation.*

Antorbital fenestra
Sclerotic ring
Orbit
Paroccipital process
Naris
Maxilla
Serrated, leaf-shaped tooth
Mandible
Infratemporal fenestra

Either way, the mild to hot climate probably meant dinosaurs never cooled enough to become lethargic like ordinary, cold-blooded, reptiles.

▪ CONTROL SYSTEMS ▪

Interacting nervous and hormonal systems coordinated body functions. The brain sent signals to the nerves which operated muscles. Immense sauropods had tiny brains, but some small theropods, like *Troodon*, had brains as big and complex as a bird's. The large theropod *Tyrannosaurus* had a brain well designed to control limb movements and process sight and scent messages, but its cerebrum ("thinking part") was very small.

phalanges formed the "palm" and finger bones. The pelvic (hip) bones were fused to the sacral vertebrae. The structure of the hind limbs was as follows: femur (thigh bone), tibia (shin bone), fibula (calf bone), tarsals (ankle bones), metatarsals (upper foot bones), and phalanges (toe bones).

▪ SOFT ANATOMY ▪

Bones were bound together by ligaments, and muscles were often attached to bones by tendons. Paired, opposing muscles contracted and

relaxed to move limbs to and fro. The digestive system consisted of a convoluted gut. Flesh-eaters would have had a fairly short, simple alimentary tract, but herbivores needed a long, complex intestine to break down fibrous vegetation. Body wastes, sperm, and eggs all left the body through the cloaca.

▪ HEART-LUNG SYSTEM ▪

A dinosaur's heart-lung system may have functioned like those of warm-blooded humans or cold-blooded reptiles. Theropods probably had efficient hearts that kept their body temperatures high, as in birds or mammals. Sauropods might have been warm-blooded in another way: their vast bodies could have stored up enough heat from the sun to keep them warm all through the night.

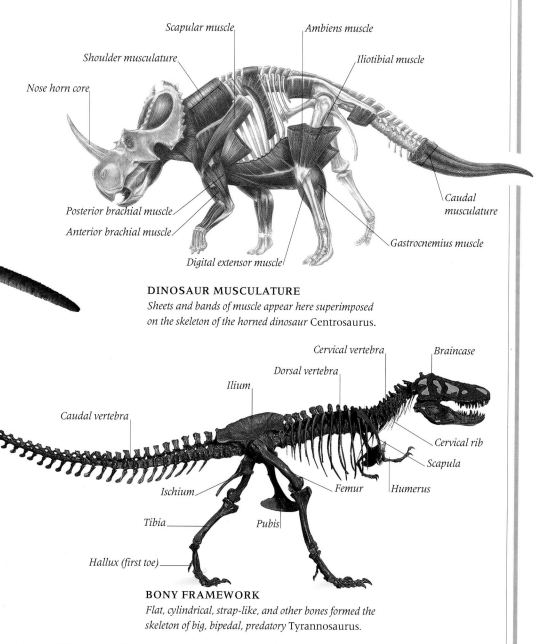

Scapular muscle
Ambiens muscle
Shoulder musculature
Iliotibial muscle
Nose horn core
Posterior brachial muscle
Anterior brachial muscle
Digital extensor muscle
Gastrocnemius muscle
Caudal musculature

DINOSAUR MUSCULATURE

Sheets and bands of muscle appear here superimposed on the skeleton of the horned dinosaur Centrosaurus.

Cervical vertebra
Braincase
Dorsal vertebra
Ilium
Cervical rib
Caudal vertebra
Scapula
Ischium
Femur
Humerus
Tibia
Pubis
Hallux (first toe)

BONY FRAMEWORK

Flat, cylindrical, strap-like, and other bones formed the skeleton of big, bipedal, predatory Tyrannosaurus.

LIFESTYLES

L IKE PRESENT-DAY ANIMALS, dinosaurs lived in a variety of different ways. For example, some species lived in herds or packs whereas others tended to be solitary, and some were plant-eaters while others ate flesh. The variety of dinosaur lifestyles can be seen by looking at how they were adapted for feeding, fighting (attack and defence), and breeding.

▪ FEEDING ▪

Most kinds of dinosaur were either herbivores (plant-eaters) or carnivores (meat-eaters). Among the herbivores, wide-mouthed browsers, such as *Maiasaura* and *Euoplocephalus*, probably snatched mouthfuls of mixed plants, while narrow-mouthed dinosaurs, such as *Edmontonia* and *Stegosaurus,* picked out specific plants. Ankylosaurs had primitive, small teeth with gaps between them. Horned dinosaurs had more advanced and efficient teeth that formed a continuous cutting edge. The vegetation that a dinosaur could eat was limited by the animal's height. Little *Lesothosaurus* and low-slung *Scelidosaurus* cropped ground-hugging plants, although some small plant-eaters may have reared on their hind limbs to browse. In contrast, the long-necked sauropods and prosauropods were tall enough to feed on leafy twigs in the upper levels of trees. Flesh-eating dinosaurs fed on plant-eating dinosaurs and other animals. Large theropods, such as *Tyrannosaurus* and *Allosaurus*, could have picked off plant-eaters that were even larger than themselves. Small predators – *Deinonychus*, for example – mainly hunted small plant-eaters, although by hunting in packs, they may have brought down ornithopods as large as *Iguanodon*. Smaller, more agile theropods, like *Compsognathus*, probably ate small lizards and large insects. A few dinosaurs had extremely specialized diets. "Crocodile-jawed" *Baryonyx* probably ate fishes, while the toothless *Oviraptor* may have fed on

eggs or shellfish, and segnosaurs may have lived mainly on termites.

▪ FIGHTING ▪

Most theropods had sharp teeth and claws for piercing the tough, scaly hides of plant-eating dinosaur prey. Size and mobility largely determined how a theropod attacked. Large theropods, such as tyrannosaurids, may have stalked herds of plant-eaters, rushing in to kill a lagging individual by tearing a hole in its neck. In contrast, dromaeosaurids may have hunted in packs, swarming over their prey and using their

EDMONTOSAURUS SKULL

ALBERTOSAURUS SKULL

SKULLS AND TEETH
The skull of Edmontosaurus *has a toothless beak and batteries of cheek teeth for grinding tough vegetation.* Albertosaurus*'s skull has strong jaws and the large, serrated fangs of a meat-eater.*

STRATEGY FOR ATTACK
Allosaurus, *a large theropod, attacks a much bigger sauropod (right). When hunting such large prey, theropods would have isolated one animal from its herd before attacking.*

second-toe claws to gash open its belly. A small, light hunter, such as *Ornitholestes*, might have sprinted after lizards and seized them in its sharp-toothed jaws or with its clawed hands. All plant-eating dinosaurs had some defence against theropod attacks. Tough hides, some with bony studs or spikes, protected titanosaurid sauropods, stegosaurs, scelidosaurids, and ankylosaurs. However, it was the sheer size of most sauropods, duckbilled ornithopods, and ceratopsid dinosaurs that deterred predators, particularly as large plant-eaters often travelled in herds. When threatened, many large plant-eating dinosaurs could have stood their ground and counter-attacked. Prosauropods, sauropods, and iguanodontids could strike out with their large thumb-claws. Diplodocids and titanosaurids might have lashed out with their whip-like tails. *Shunosaurus* and ankylosaurid dinosaurs could even swing their tails to deliver crushing blows with their bony tail clubs. Less well-protected plant-eaters relied on different survival strategies.

Scelidosaurus, for example, might have crouched down, exposing only its armoured back. Defenceless bipeds, such as the ostrich dinosaurs and the hypsilophodontids, would simply have sprinted away.

▪ BREEDING ▪

Like modern birds, many dinosaurs practised courtship rituals, made nests, laid eggs, and even tended their young. Male duckbills, ceratopsid dinosaurs, and some theropods had crests or horns on their heads that were probably used in courtship rituals. *Pachycephalosaurus* males had head-butting contests to win herds of females. After mating, female dinosaurs laid hard-shelled eggs. In many cases, the eggs were laid in mud nests or hollows scooped in sand, and covered with vegetation or sand. Some dinosaurs grouped their nests in breeding colonies, and certain species returned to the same nesting sites year after year. The mothers of some species stayed by the nests to protect the eggs and the small hatchlings. Most young dinosaurs apparently grew up quite quickly, although young duckbills were probably fed and tended by their mothers for up to several months after hatching. Despite parental care, most young dinosaurs probably fell prey to flesh-eating theropods before reaching adulthood.

DINOSAUR EGGS
The small, horned dinosaur Protoceratops *laid long eggs resembling large potatoes. Each clutch was laid in the form of a ring or spiral in a bowl-shaped hollow dug in the sand.*

COLONIAL NESTING
Maiasaura *mothers here tend their nests, eggs, and young. Nesting in colonies gave these duckbilled dinosaurs mutual protection and improved their offspring's chances of survival.*

AN ARMOURED DINOSAUR'S DEFENCE
Sharp spines stuck out from Edmontonia*'s flanks and shoulders, providing a good defence. A tyrannosaur would have hesitated before attacking such a heavily armoured dinosaur.*

EXTINCTION THEORIES

A FTER 150 MILLION YEARS dinosaurs seemed indestructible. Groups cut off on diverging continents were fast evolving in different directions, and there were now more kinds of dinosaur alive than ever. Yet 10 million years later the creatures we usually think of as dinosaurs were all extinct, as were all land animals heavier than a large dog, marine crocodiles, pterosaurs, plesiosaurs, and many species of marine invertebrates. Scientists dispute why and how scores of groups suddenly died out about 65 million years ago. Various theories, both bizarre and plausible, that have been put forward to explain this mass extinction are described on these pages.

This position was thought to be caused by poisoning, but is the result of drying.

EGG-THIEF
Small, omnivorous mammals like this one could have raided dinosaurs' nests. But egg-stealing did not kill off the dinosaurs.

▪ THE LAST DINOSAURS ▪

The last known dinosaurs lived in western North America. Among these were *Tyrannosaurus* and *Triceratops*, two of the best-known of all. It seems that dinosaurs did not all disappear at once. In one rock formation in Montana, dinosaur genera dwindled from 19 to seven in their last few hundred thousand years. Such declines had happened before, but the next rock formation above holds no dinosaur fossils. In geological terms the Age of Dinosaurs ended abruptly, although the precise timescale is not known. The extinction might have happened in an hour, or could have taken up to 100,000 years.

▪ "SELF-DESTRUCTION" ▪

The least convincing explanations of dinosaur extinction are those that blame the dinosaurs themselves. One suggestion was that vicious carnivores ate all the herbivores, then starved to death. A second notion was that dinosaurs evolved into grotesque, unworkable forms. Horned, crested, and thick-skulled dinosaurs were interpreted as the incompetent products of "racial degeneration". Defective hormones that led to dangerously thin eggshells, and stupidity brought on by shrinking brains, are other unsupported notions.

▪ ENEMY AGENTS ▪

A second group of theories suggests that biological warfare killed the dinosaurs. Perhaps newly evolving flowering plants harboured poisons fatal to the dinosaurs, although the co-evolution of dinosaurs with plants makes that most unlikely. A virus may have caused a fatal pandemic, but no germ was likely to destroy a group as diverse as the dinosaurs. Maybe small, prolific mammals ate all the dinosaurs' eggs. But monitor lizards eat crocodiles' eggs without making crocodiles extinct. None of these theories seems believable.

▪ GLOBAL CHANGE ▪

Harsh changes affecting lands, seas, and climates may possibly have wiped out many dinosaurs and other animals. By the Late Cretaceous, such changes were taking place as a result of continental drift, mountain-building, and sea level changes. As areas of shallow sea disappeared, many marine creatures lost their habitats. Away from the Equator, climates cooled, seasons grew more marked, and hardy plant species evolved. If dinosaurs were cold-blooded, they might have grown too sluggish to survive, and even a small temperature change could have made their eggs all hatch out as one sex, ending future breeding.

ORODROMEUS HATCHLINGS
Colonial nesting casts doubt on beliefs that stressed, overcrowded females laid fatally thin eggs.

▪ VOLCANIC ▪ ERUPTIONS

Climatic change brought about by volcanic eruptions is another strong contender for explaining the demise of the dinosaurs. As they were dying out, vast lava flows were building India's Deccan Plateau, pouring huge amounts of carbon dioxide and acids into the air. Spread around the world by winds, the indirect combined effects of these substances could have been the overheating of the Earth's surface, lethal acid rain, and the destruction of atmospheric ozone that shuts out deadly solar radiation. A different cause for similar effects is concerning us today.

▪ CATASTROPHES ▪ FROM SPACE

The extinction might have been the result of lethal radiation from an exploding star, or solar radiation admitted by a sudden reversal of the Earth's magnetic field which normally deflects it. A far likelier cause is an asteroid or mini-planet hitting the Earth. This impact could have formed a crater up to 200km (124 miles) wide, vaporizing rock and flinging a vast mass of dust and water droplets high into the stratosphere. Strong winds would have dragged this shroud around the planet, causing darkness and cold, stormy weather. Plants would have died, along with

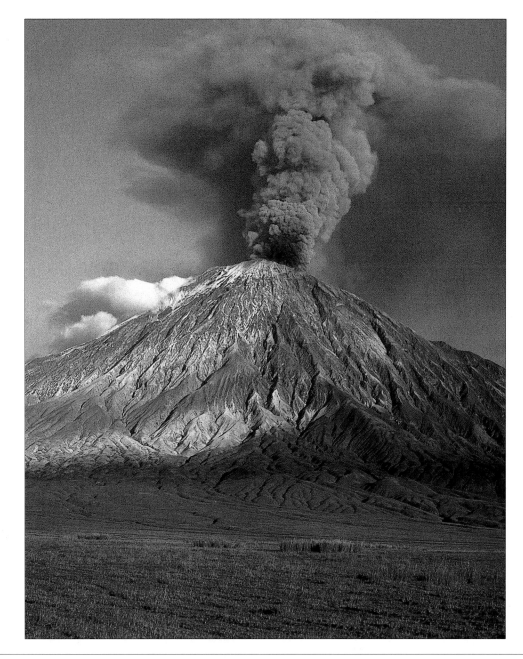

GUNNARITES
All such ammonites (coiled-shell sea molluscs) also died out about the same time as the dinosaurs became extinct.

many animals – especially land animals too large to hibernate. Evidence for this catastrophe, cited in 1979, was a thin, worldwide deposit of the rare element iridium which is frequently found in meteorites. Associated finds included shocked quartz (impact-fractured sand grains) and fossil proof of a sudden loss of flowering plants in North America. In the early 1990s, the discovery in Mexico of Chicxulub, a buried crater 180km (110 miles) across, provided further proof. It now seems likely that asteroids might have caused some other mass extinctions too.

▪ THE SURVIVORS ▪

Most scientists believe the last "true" dinosaurs died out at the end of the Mesozoic era. Dinosaur fossils thought to be from the Cenozoic era (65 mya to present day) have been found in Europe, Asia, and the Americas, but they are just scraps of bone, maybe dislodged from older rocks. Yet birds are arguably winged and feathered theropod dinosaurs. With 8,700 living species, adapted to almost every climate on earth, birds might claim to be the most successful dinosaurs of all.

METEOR CRATER, ARIZONA
A small meteorite punched out this crater (above). That of a big asteroid would have been vast.

VOLCANIC ERUPTIONS
Vast volcanoes erupting for half a million years could have caused catastrophic climatic changes.

FOSSILIZATION

W HEN LAND organisms die their bodies usually disappear, eaten by scavengers, rotted by bacteria, or degraded by the weather. Fossils are exceptions to this rule: they are the remains of long-dead organisms that escaped destruction by being covered up by sediments. The remains turned into fossils while sediments above them hardened into heavy sheets of rock. In time, some of these rock strata were uplifted and eroded to reveal the fossils. Perhaps no more than one dead dinosaur in a million was fossilized, and maybe relatively few of these have so far been exposed. Fossil bones and teeth are our main clues to dinosaur life, but there are also fossil footprints, droppings, eggs, and the remains of prehistoric plants.

A fossilized imprint of a hadrosaur's belly skin.

1 TRICERATOPS ALIVE
A Triceratops drinks from a river flowing through an open woodland of ferns, conifers, and other plants. This scene is set more than 65 million years ago.

2 TRICERATOPS BONES
Killed by disease or drowned by a brief river flood, the Triceratops is now reduced to scattered bones, beside and in the now dried-up river bed.

▪ HOW FOSSILS ▪ FORMED

Fossilization often took place when death occurred in or near water, or in marshland. The soft parts of the dinosaur's body usually soon rotted away. However, the harder bones and teeth took much longer, and sometimes even the skin persisted in dinosaurs that were dried out and mummified by drought. Future fossils tended to be bones or other objects that were quickly cloaked by mud or sand dumped by moving water or wind. This process shut out the oxygen essential to bacteria that cause decay, but let mineral-saturated water percolate into the pores and bigger cavities in bones, filling these with calcite, iron sulphide, silica, or even opal. Permineralization, as this process is called, increased the weight and hardness of the bones. The pressure exerted by the mass of sediments that gradually accumulated overhead often deformed the permineralized bones.

▪ INSIDE THE EARTH ▪

Compacted under their own weight, and bound by natural cement, these sediments hardened, their once-loose particles forming layers of sedimentary rocks. Over many millions of years, thousands of metres of sedimentary rock strata piled up on sagging plains and offshore seabeds. Beneath the weight of these rocks, fragile dinosaur bones collapsed, but fossil teeth and stronger bones endured. In this way, dinosaurs once living on the surface of the land were trapped deep within the Earth's crust. But not irrevocably. The giant jigsaw pieces, or tectonic plates, that form our planet's crust move slowly on convection currents in the Earth's mantle. Where two of these tectonic plates collided, or one overrode another, fossil-rich rock strata became rucked up and tilted into mountain ridges. Attacked by rain, frost, sun, and wind, these mountains slowly crumbled, and their fossil treasures were laid bare.

▪ MOULDS, CASTS, AND ▪ PETRIFICATIONS

Not all fossilized dinosaur bones are heavy and permineralized. Freezing Alaskan rock, for example, has preserved bones that are darkened but lightweight, chemically unaltered since death. At the other extreme, acid-rich groundwater, such as that found in porous sandstones, has completely dissolved bones, leaving only bone-shaped holes, or moulds. Sometimes minerals filled these cavities, creating bone-shaped casts. Bones completely "turned into stone" by mineral replacement are called petrifications.

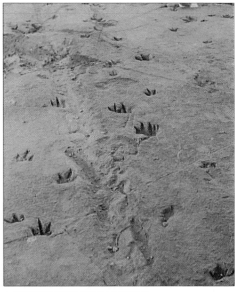

A DINOSAUR TRACKWAY
Spiky footprints in Queensland's Late Cretaceous rocks may show where many small, bipedal dinosaurs fled from a large, predatory dinosaur. This event occurred about 100 million years ago.

COPROLITES
Experts identified these stones as the fossil droppings of a dinosaur. The shape, size, and contents (such as seeds and broken bones) of such coprolites hold clues to the bulk and feeding habits of the dinosaur they came from.

3 LIFE GOES ON

The skull of the drowned Triceratops *lies buried under silt dumped by the river. The rest of the skeleton has been destroyed by animal scavengers, bacteria, and weathering.*

4 BONE TO FOSSIL

Fifteen million years after the Triceratops *died, the same chemicals that helped to cement silt into rock have transformed its buried skull into a stony fossil. The land above is now inhabited by mammals.*

TRICERATOPS AND TAPHONOMY

The scene showing a dead *Triceratops*'s scattered bones (2) is based on taphonomy: the study of what happens to animals after they die and before sediments cover them. Taphonomy shows that big, heavy skeletons held together by strong ligaments break up less readily than small ones. Small dinosaurs quickly decomposed and had their bones crunched up, or dispersed by scavengers or river currents. Rivers even separated the smaller bones of beasts as heavy as *Triceratops*, but fragile forms like *Troodon* tended to persist only as bits of skull or other bones. Few dinosaurs under 50kg (110lb) survive as articulated skeletons.

5 THE ICE AGE

Woolly mammoths roam an Ice Age land 20,000 years ago. Mountain-building Earth movements have brought the skull of the Triceratops *closer to the surface.*

6 TRICERATOPS REVEALED

Frost, ice, rain, sun, and wind have eroded mountain slopes and gnawed deeply into layered rocks formed more than 65 million years ago. The Triceratops *skull is now unearthed by fossil hunters.*

JUMBLED BONES

These jumbled bones (above) belonged to several Coelophysis, *victims of a flash flood.*

PTEROSAUR FOSSILS

One rock (below left) preserves pterosaur bones. The other rock (below right) contains their mould.

■ TRACE FOSSILS ■

Trace fossils are fossils that reveal traces of ancient animal activity. Ichnites are fossil footprints made in soft mud that hardened into rock. Distinctive ichnites are often given names, known as ichnogenera. Fossil footprints can indicate the size, weight, and stance of a dinosaur, and they may identify their maker as a theropod, sauropod, ornithopod, ceratopsian, or ankylosaur. Footprints forming a trackway can show how fast a dinosaur moved (the longer its stride the greater its speed), and parallel tracks may reflect herding habits. Track sites with millions of footprints mark where sauropod herds followed a Late Jurassic shore in western North America. Fossil clues to dinosaur diet include bitten leaves and coprolites (fossilized droppings) some of which still hold traces of food. Evidence of breeding activity comes from broken fossil eggshells, whole eggs, complete clutches, nests, embryos, and young. Proof of injury lies in bones scratched by teeth or broken by a fall (and sometimes subsequently healed). Abnormally swollen or fused bones are clues to bone disease. Fossilized wood, leaves, and old lake and river beds provide clues to the dinosaurs' environments.

DINOSAUR FINDS

I N THE YEAR 1824 the English naturalist and clergyman William Buckland published the first scientific account of a dinosaur – *Megalosaurus*. The following year, amateur palaeontologist Gideon Mantell described the teeth and bones of *Iguanodon*. The comparative anatomist Sir Richard Owen coined the term Dinosauria for the very few dinosaurs then known in 1841, and in 1887 Professor Harry Govier Seeley grouped all dinosaurs into the Saurischia and Ornithischia according to their hip design. While theoretical understanding grew, the hunt for fossil dinosaurs gained impetus and in the course of the nineteenth century the search spread from England to mainland Europe and the Americas. Since 1900, palaeontologists have prized dinosaurs from Mesozoic rocks in every continent, and each year brings fresh discoveries.

EDWARD DRINKER COPE (1840–1897)
Cope gave names to a number of different dinosaurs.

FOSSIL JAWBONE
This Megalosaurus *jawbone formed the basis of the first scientific description of a dinosaur.*

❊ FINDS IN EUROPE ❊

Dinosaur discovery very quickly spread from England and led to exciting fossil discoveries elsewhere in Europe. In 1837, Hermann von Meyer described *Plateosaurus*, a Triassic prosauropod found in Germany, and in 1861 he named *Archaeopteryx*, a bird closely linked to dinosaurs. In 1878, Belgian miners made the dramatic discovery of more than 30 complete *Iguanodon* skeletons in a deep coalmine. Since the 1860s, searchers in southern France have found clutches of large eggs laid by a Late Cretaceous sauropod. Numerous Late Cretaceous dinosaurs have been found across Europe, but England remains the best source of Early Cretaceous dinosaurs.

❊ UNITED STATES FINDS ❊

Early finds of fossil dinosaur bones and footprints in New England went unrecognized. But, in 1856, anatomist Joseph Leidy named *Troodon* from

OTHNIEL CHARLES MARSH (1831–1899)
Marsh (centre back row) funded Wild West fossil hunts and named dozens of dinosaurs.

fossil teeth found in Montana. In 1858, he also named *Hadrosaurus* from New Jersey, the first dinosaur skeleton from the Americas to be described. Discovery began in earnest in 1877, with news of finds of huge fossil bones in Colorado and Wyoming. The rival palaeontologists Othniel Charles Marsh and Edward Drinker Cope hired teams who raced to wrest the remains of sauropods from the Late Jurassic rocks of Morrison and Canyon City,

Colorado, and Como Bluff, Wyoming. Over 20 dinosaur genera, including *Apatosaurus* and *Camarasaurus*, were named by these scientists. Fresh finds by Henry Fairfield Osborn, William J. Holland, and Earl Douglass came in the early 1900s. Since the middle of this century, excavations by Sankar Chatterjee, David Gillette, John Horner, James Jensen, Robert Long, John Ostrom, and many more have thrown light on dinosaurs from all three Mesozoic periods. Finds include *Seismosaurus*, *Deinonychus*, and whole colonies of nesting hadrosaurs. With about 110 genera, the United States led the world by the 1990s.

❋ FINDS IN CANADA ❋

In 1884, Joseph Tyrrell's discovery of the first *Albertosaurus* skull launched a great dinosaur hunt that continues in the badlands beside Alberta's Red Deer River. Thomas Chesmer Weston and Lawrence Lambe prospected for dinosaurs from river boats. In 1910, Barnum Brown competed with Charles Sternberg and sons who were collecting for the Canadian Geological Survey. Work stopped in 1917 but by this time a wealth of Late Cretaceous horned and duckbilled dinosaurs had been found. In the 1980s, Philip Currie and other fossil-hunters renewed the search, and by the 1990s the area of Alberta now known as Dinosaur Provincial Park had yielded more dinosaur specimens than any comparable area on Earth.

❋ FINDS IN ASIA ❋

Chinese dinosaur discovery began in earnest under Young Chung Chien, whose work continued from the 1930s into the 1970s. Since then, further discoveries were made under Dong Zhiming. With 95 named genera in 1990, China ranked second only to the United States. In the early 1920s, American teams of scientists led by Roy Chapman Andrews and Walter Granger revealed Mongolia's Gobi Desert as one of the world's richest sources of dinosaur remains. Since then, Russian, Mongolian, Polish, and American teams have worked this desert. Russian palaeontologists have also opened dinosaur quarries in remote parts of Siberia.

❋ DINOSAURS FROM ❋ GONDWANA

By the early 1900s dinosaur finds had been made in South America, Africa, India, and Australia – the now inhabited parts of Gondwana. Most South American finds were made in Argentina, but Brazil was the site of the major discovery of *Staurikosaurus*. Other

EAST-WEST COLLABORATION
Dong Zhiming (right) and Philip Currie take part in a Sino-Canadian excavation in Inner Mongolia.

SHUNOSAURUS (A CHINESE SAUROPOD)
This skeleton is one of scores of finds that have made China one of the top two sources of fossil dinosaurs.

important finds included the theropod *Carnotaurus*, sail-backed *Amargasaurus*, and *Eoraptor* (the most primitive of all known dinosaurs). The Argentinian palaeontologist José Bonaparte named a number of South American genera. African discoveries began in the early 1900s, and by the 1990s at least 16 nations had recorded dinosaur finds. They included early forms in Morocco and South Africa, sail-backed dinosaurs in the Sahara Desert, and mixed Late

Jurassic dinosaurs in what is now Tanzania. Dinosaur detection in India dates from the 1860s. By the 1990s it had produced a primitive sauropod, the last known stegosaur, and a giant theropod. Organized Australian discovery dates only from about 1980. By the 1990s Ralph Molnar, Thomas Rich, and others had raised Australia's tally to nearly a dozen genera, including *Minmi*.

❋ NEW LOCATIONS ❋

Since 1980, dinosaur fossils have emerged in some unexpected places. In 1980, Ralph Molnar described a theropod vertebra discovered in the North Island of New Zealand. By 1990, Yoshikazu Hasegawa had studied scraps of perhaps nine dinosaur genera unearthed on the Japanese islands of Honshū and Kyūshū, and in 1992, *Wakinosaurus*, a large Kyūshū theropod, was named by Yoshihiko Okazaki. During the 1980s, both Polar regions yielded dinosaur fossils. In 1985, teams from the universities of California and Alaska found many Late Cretaceous bones in the North Slope of Alaska. In 1986, Argentinian palaeontologists noted a dinosaur from Antarctica, and by 1993 Antarctic finds included a sauropod and a horned theropod.

JOSE BONAPARTE
Since the 1960s, the work of this palaeontologist from Argentina has revealed valuable information on South American dinosaurs. Among the dinosaurs named by Bonaparte are Carnotaurus, Riojasaurus, *and* Patagosaurus.

MUSSAURUS
Found in Argentina and named in 1979, this "mouse lizard" was a tiny, young prosauropod.

EXCAVATING DINOSAURS

DIGGING UP DINOSAURS means first finding where their remains are likely to be. Dinosaur-hunters must concentrate on rocks formed from sediments laid down in Mesozoic times. Only certain regions of the world with special kinds of countryside provide rich hunting grounds. Sometimes amateurs discover dinosaurs by chance, but most finds result from palaeontologists' systematic fossil hunts. Once located, a small, isolated dinosaur fossil may be collected single-handed in a few minutes, but prying a big fossil from hard rock can take a large team weeks or months of wielding an arsenal of machines and tools. Excavation is only part of the work; measuring and recording full details of the find are equally important. Once they are excavated, the fragile bones need careful cushioning and labelling before being transported to an often distant museum.

EXCAVATING AN ANKYLOSAUR
A Polish palaeontologist's delicate work with knife and brush lays bare the forepart of Saichania. *This ankylosaur may have been suffocated by a sandstorm in the Gobi desert nearly 80 million years ago.*

■ WHERE TO EXCAVATE ■

The best places for hunting dinosaurs are exposed Mesozoic rocks derived from sediments that accumulated on land or close inshore. This can mean roadside cuttings, quarries, sea cliffs, river banks, and even coalmines. But the most extensive, dinosaur-rich outcrops occur among badlands and remote deserts, such as parts of western North America, the Gobi Desert, Patagonia, and some sandy tracts of the Sahara. Here erosion lays bare great tracts of fossil-bearing Mesozoic rock. Unfortunately much dinosaur-bearing rock can never be explored. It lies deeply buried under other rocks, soil, water, or ice; was deformed by heat and pressure; or was removed completely by erosion.

■ DINOSAUR DISCOVERY ■

This can be accidental or planned. For example, the discovery of *Iguanodon* is said to have begun when a doctor's wife noticed a fossil tooth in a heap of roadside stones. Farmers and people working on roads and railways have made important finds. Amateur and weekend fossil-hunters, often armed with no more than a geological hammer, have also been known to strike fossil "gold",

UNEARTHING OPISTHOCOELICAUDIA
Six workers here use hammers and picks to remove sandy rock from this headless fossil sauropod, discovered in southern Mongolia.

WITH ROCK REMOVED
The tools around this Stegosaurus *skeleton in the Smithsonian Institution were used to free it from its rocky matrix.*

as when Joan Wiffen discovered New Zealand's first known dinosaur, an unnamed theropod; William Walker discovered *Baryonyx*; and Eddie and Vivian Jones located new dinosaurs in Colorado. But a large number of major discoveries have occurred on long-term expeditions to remote regions, usually organized by universities or museums. Teams of palaeontologists set off in trucks loaded with gear for excavating, surveying, and packing fossil finds.

❋ EXCAVATION METHODS ❋

Fossil-hunters usually walk along dry stream-beds and below slopes, scouring the ground for dark, shiny, or otherwise unusual "stones". Such scraps may well be fossil fragments washed down from bones embedded in the rocks above. A single dinosaur bone projecting from a hill may prove an isolated find, or it may lead to an entire skeleton hidden underground. Picks and shovels are used to clear soil and soft rock from around a large fossil skeleton. In some deserts, bones can be exposed by

merely brushing away the uppermost layer of the sand. Large skeletons entombed in hard rock present much bigger problems. To get at a hidden skeleton a team may have to raze half a hillside with explosives, bulldozers, and power drills. Careful work can then be carried out with a variety of tools, including toothbrushes, to free the fossil from its surrounding matrix. Fragile bones are often removed while still embedded in large chunks of rock.

❋ RECOVERING AND ❋ REMOVING

Once the bones lie exposed, scientists can number and photograph them, and plot their position on a plan. Later, this detailed survey may help anatomists to reconstruct the skeleton, and may also help scientists to understand what happened to the dinosaur after its death. Bones are prepared for removal by painting resin on crumbly fossils to stop them from disintegrating. Big bones can be protected with sacking soaked in plaster or with plastic foam.

EXCAVATING COELOPHYSIS
After tunnelling under rock rich in Coelophysis *fossils, members of a Carnegie Museum team protect the fragile rock surface with sacking and plaster.*

TRANSPORTING COELOPHYSIS
Members of the Carnegie Museum team (above) prepare to slide a block of plastered rock containing Coelophysis *fossils down a timber slope. This quarry is at Ghost Ranch, Abiquiu, New Mexico, USA.*

AFTER EXCAVATION
The blocks of solid rock and plaster enclosing a Stegosaurus *skeleton (above) were removed before it was displayed at the Smithsonian Institution (left).*

DINOSAURS IN MUSEUMS

R ECOVERING A DINOSAUR fossil is the first step on a journey of discovery. When a museum laboratory has prepared the specimen, a palaeontologist compares it with known dinosaurs. Differences may indicate a brand-new genus. A description of the specimen appears in a scientific journal. When studies are complete, experts may reconstruct the creature's skeleton and put it on display. These pages show the creation of a major sauropod exhibit for one American museum. Thanks to international collaboration, hundreds of such dinosaur displays have been developed around the world. At least three dozen institutions hold about 500 original specimens from Alberta's Dinosaur Provincial Park alone: area for area perhaps the world's richest "goldmine" of articulated fossil dinosaurs.

❋ IN THE LABORATORY ❋

Work in the museum laboratory begins with freeing a fossil from its rock matrix. The protective jacket is cut away by a preparator, who then strengthens the exposed, fragile bone with chemical solutions. A saw, or hammer and chisel can then be used to remove the outer rock. If that is softer than the fossil it surrounds, shot-blasting (where tiny high-speed plastic pellets bombard the specimen inside a steel and glass cabinet) can be used. If the rock is a limestone, the preparator can use dilute acetic acid to dissolve the rock, leaving the fossil unharmed. Final treatment, though, is often slow, painstaking work with a magnifying glass or microscope and dental drill, dental pick, and needle. Removing a great dinosaur like *Seismosaurus* from rock that is as hard as concrete could take anything up to ten years. Extracting the rock inside a fossil skull or eggshell may be impossible, but X-rays or CAT scans may detect an internal embryo or brain cavity.

WELDING STEEL SUPPORTS
Sparks fly as a welder, wearing a protective mask, fuses metal rods together (above). The rods provide internal support for the tail vertebrae of the mounted Barosaurus *skeleton.*

MOUNTING AN ALLOSAURUS
A team positions an Allosaurus *skeleton in the American Museum of Natural History, New York.*

RECONSTRUCTED BAROSAURUS SKELETON

Among the most ambitious of any reconstructed dinosaurs, this rearing *Barosaurus* skeleton towers over 15m (49ft) above the floor of the American Museum of Natural History. Steel rods concealed inside its bones support their weight, which is substantial, even though the bones are in fact lightweight plastic and fibreglass replicas of the originals. This method of reconstructing dinosaur skeletons is far more effective than earlier methods, where the original, heavy fossil bones were supported by obtrusive scaffolding on the outside of the skeleton.

■ SCIENTIFIC STUDY ■

A palaeontologist first compares the prepared, newly discovered bones with equivalent bones from known dinosaurs. Bones with unusual features may reveal a new dinosaur genus. The palaeontologist draws or photographs these to illustrate a scientific paper in which the bones are described. Details of skull, teeth, limb bones, and vertebrae may help the writer to draw conclusions about the size, appearance, and behaviour of the dinosaur. Finally, the article gives the animal a scientific name unique to that species. Independent experts must pass the description of the new dinosaur before a scientific journal can accept it for publication.

POSITIONING THE LEGS AND TAIL
A museum worker on a mobile lifting platform positions Barosaurus's tail vertebrae. Another lowers the hip girdle and hind limb bones on to a supporting metal framework.

■ RECONSTRUCTION ■

Once scientists have worked out how the dinosaur bones fit together, a museum may want to reconstruct the skeleton for display in a lifelike pose. Skeletons seldom survive intact, but museum staff can make fibreglass models of the missing bones. Heavy, mineralized bones need thick rods and bars to hold them up. Nowadays, most big mounted skeletons are light fibreglass replicas, made as shown on page 35, and supported by slim, metal rods invisibly threaded inside.

■ HIDDEN TREASURE TROVES ■

The dinosaurs the public sees are often a fraction of the fossils held in store. For instance, the Earth Sciences Museum, Brigham Young University, Provo, Utah, has a stockpile of 100 tonnes of big fossilized bones, still encased in plaster. Many a museum basement is similarly crammed with labelled bones, laid on racks or placed in drawers. For years most of these lie there unexamined, waiting for a scientist to study them. Sometimes a palaeontologist identifies a "brand-new" dinosaur from one or two bones found a century ago and left in store, undescribed or misidentified.

BONES IN STORE
Shelves in the basement of the American Museum of Natural History hold the bones of Barosaurus *and of many other dinosaurs.*

■ BACKROOM WORK ■

Much of what we know of dinosaurs springs from backroom work in museum and university laboratories. Once, the only guide to when these creatures lived was the relative ages of fossil-bearing rock layers laid down on top of one another, the youngest layer usually uppermost. Now, radiometric dating can be used in order to pinpoint the age of dinosaurs within a million years or so. In radiometric dating, special instruments are used to measure the radioactive elements in certain rocks. These elements decay into others at known rates, so their relative proportions allow scientists to work out the age of the rock, and thus also the age of the fossils within it.

AN EARLY RECONSTRUCTION
Wooden trestles featured in this early effort to mount a Diplodocus *skeleton in Pittsburgh's Carnegie Museum.*

RESTORATION OF DINOSAURS

W HILE RECONSTRUCTION is the task of piecing together fossil bones to rebuild a skeleton, restoration is fleshing out the bones to show the creature as it would have looked alive. Clues to dinosaur muscles and intestines can be found in rare fossils of soft tissues, from muscle attachment points on fossilized bones, and from living animals. Accurately drawing and modelling a dinosaur is a skill that calls for special understanding of the creature's size, shape, stance, and of details such as whether it had fleshy cheeks, and whether it dragged its tail or carried it aloft. By keeping up-to-date with new discoveries and theories, specialist artists and sculptors have transformed the popular images of many dinosaurs.

DEINONYCHUS AND HYPSILOPHODON
Two modern, lifelike restorations in a museum in Taiwan depict the stiff-tailed, ferocious theropod Deinonychus, *with its sickle claws poised to strike its prey, a terrified, fallen* Hypsilophodon.

"OLD STYLE" HYPSILOPHODON MODEL
Old models show Hypsilophodon *perched in trees. New models depict it as a ground-based sprinter.*

RESTORING GALLIMIMUS

Below are some of the stages in the creation of one of the lifelike model dinosaurs shown in this book. This bird-like theropod was restored with one side of its body dissected to expose bones and internal organs. The other side shows skin colour and texture.

■ RESTORATION ■

A reconstructed skeleton gives artists and model-makers the basis for lifelike restorations of the animal. The anatomies of modern reptiles, birds, and mammals serve as guides that help to indicate the sizes, shapes and positions of the internal organs, and the muscles which give the body bulk. Skin texture is based partly on fossil skin impressions showing non-overlapping scales covering the body, and partly on the scaly skins of the legs of crocodiles and birds. Colour must remain intelligent guesswork, based on what we know of living animals. Big dinosaurs might have been drab like elephants. Smaller

ones could have been striped or spotted as a form of camouflage. Like some modern birds and reptiles, though, breeding males quite possibly had brightly coloured heads and areas of skin. All of these features can be incorporated into models built to any scale. Robotics specialists can even construct life-size, lifelike dinosaurs that move their heads and bellow horribly. Inside the models, pneumatic machinery powers metal skeletons supporting polyurethane bodies. The bodies of these dinosaurs are sheathed in silicone rubber skin painted in convincing colour shades and patterns. Weatherproof models pose realistically in outdoor, wooded situations.

THE SKETCH
A pencil sketch delineates the details of the internal anatomy of Gallimimus. *The muscles and internal organs are based on those of living animals. Next an articulated cardboard "skeleton" is made.*

THE ARMATURE
The armature for the model is made from wire and wood, and based on the reconstructed skeleton. This then forms the framework on which the sculptor will add other substances to build up solid body structures.

BULKING OUT
Modelling clay is used to build the exposed bones on the dissected side of the model. The neck, body, and tail are bulked out with scrim (fabric) and plaster, and sealed with shellac. The claws are cast in resin.

■ DINOSAURS TODAY ■ AND YESTERDAY

Modern restorations incorporate scientific theories of the appearance and behaviour of dinosaurs. Straight thigh bones with sharply in-turned heads indicate that dinosaurs stood with their hind limbs upright, like our own. The ossified (bony) tendons corseting their caudal vertebrae show that most ornithischians had stiffened tails, while teeth set in from the jaw rims indicate that ornithischians had fleshy cheeks. The lack of a tail imprint between their fossil footprints suggests that sauropods did not drag their tails. The restudying of even well-known dinosaurs has led to revelations. We now know that *Tyrannosaurus* walked with its back horizontal and its tail held off the ground, *Iguanodon*'s stiff tail prevented it from standing like a kangaroo, and *Hypsilophodon* ran fast but may not have climbed trees, as was once supposed. Scientific studies even support theories of jousting pachycephalosaurs and head-wrestling ceratopsids.

RESTORING BARYONYX'S SKULL

The biological sculptor John Holmes checks a measurement in this reconstruction of the skull and mandible of *Baryonyx*. Only parts of the actual bones have been discovered. Missing areas are filled in with clay. Careful anatomical drawings of the skull's likely proportions have already been made with reference to other theropod skulls.

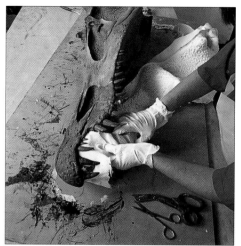

MAKING A RUBBER MOULD

The clay and bone reconstruction of Baryonyx's skull is now used to produce a rubber mould. The skull is first painted with coats of liquid silicone rubber that solidify after adding a catalyst. The resulting rubber mould is then gently peeled away from the skull (above). The next stage is to make a fibreglass cast.

MAKING A FIBREGLASS CAST

The rubber mould of the Baryonyx skull now becomes the basis for making casts. The pale rubber mould is painted with a coat of dark liquid resin (above). Fibreglass mat is embedded in later coats of resin. The complete structure forms a rigid, lightweight facsimile of the original clay skull.

THE CLAY SCULPTURE

To produce a finished clay restoration, the basic shape is built up with small amounts of clay. Skin textures and other details are worked into the surface. A rubber mould is then made from the clay sculpture.

THE RESIN CAST

Using the rubber mould, a cast is made from a special mix of mineral and polyester resin reinforced with glass, metal rods, and carbon fibre. The cast is then cleaned to prepare it for the final stage.

COLOURING THE CAST

The final stage in making a model of Gallimimus involves hand-painting and air-brushing the internal and external features of the model with oil paint. The glass eyes give the final realistic touch.

DINOSAUR
PROFILES

HIS SECTION presents illustrated profiles of 55 different genera selected to represent all the major dinosaur groups. Restorations provide extra realism: some have been made up as models and specially photographed, others are in the form of colour illustrations. Specially commissioned photographs also show skulls, skeletons, and other items from museums around the world.

THEROPODS

T HE BIPEDAL THEROPODS ("beast feet") include all known predatory dinosaurs. Typical examples had bird-like features, such as hollow bones; an S-shaped neck; long, muscular hind limbs; and clawed, four-toed feet, the first toe short and high. Many theropods may have been warm-blooded, and at least some may have had feathers. Small, early forms gave rise to heavy big-game hunters, and to ostrich-like omnivores (and possibly herbivores) with toothless beaks. One group of small, feathered, warm-blooded theropods may have given rise to true birds. Theropods spread worldwide and spanned the Age of Dinosaurs, but many left scanty remains. A number of relationships shown here are open to dispute.

The small, but ferocious theropod Gasosaurus, *found in China.*

DROMAEOSAURUS SKULL

DROMICEIOMIMUS SKULL

ALBERTOSAURUS SKULL

THREE THEROPOD SKULLS
These photographs contrast the skulls of small, sharp-toothed Dromaeosaurus, fanged Albertosaurus, and bird-like, toothless Dromiceiomimus.

■ PRIMITIVE THEROPODS ■

These lacked the distinctive features of the Ceratosauria or Tetanurae. EORAPTOR, from early Late Triassic Argentina, was a primitive theropod no bigger than a large dog. STAURIKOSAURIDAE was a family named after the genus *Staurikosaurus*. It lived in early Late Triassic Brazil. HERRERASAURIDAE, a worldwide Late Triassic/Early Jurassic group, had "old-fashioned" hind limb bones.

■ CERATOSAURIA ■

Ceratosaurs were small to large theropods with a kinked upper jaw, a crested snout, unusual vertebrae, possibly four fingers per hand, bird-like hip bones with rod-shaped pubes, and a stiffened rear half of the tail. NOASAURIDAE contained the Late Cretaceous *Noasaurus*. This small dinosaur had a swivelling toe-claw. ALVAREZSAURIDAE contained the Late

Cretaceous Argentinian genus *Alvarezsaurus*, which resembled the (unrelated) ornithomimids. ABELISAURIDAE included nine or so genera with fused ankle bones and unusual skulls. These big beasts lived in Early to Late Cretaceous times. VELOCISAURIDAE included *Velocisaurus*, a small, Late Cretaceous beast with unusual upper foot bones. CERATOSAURIDAE were big theropods named after *Ceratosaurus* of Late Jurassic North America. COELOPHYSIDAE were lightly built theropods occurring widely from Late Triassic to Early Jurassic times. HALTICOSAURIDAE were primitive, early theropod dinosaurs that may have belonged to the infraorder Tetanurae. MEGALOSAURIDAE were a family of big, robust beasts that may have lived from Early Jurassic

to Late Cretaceous times. EUSTREPTOSPONDYLUS was a big, Middle Jurassic predator from England.

■ TETANURAE ■

Tetanurae had tails that were stiffened for most of their length. There were two main subgroups.

SUBGROUP CARNOSAURIA

ALLOSAURIDAE were large to huge, mainly Late Jurassic theropods with a worldwide distribution. ITEMIRIDAE were a family containing the small, Late Cretaceous *Itemirus*. DRYPTOSAURIDAE included the large, slender-legged *Dryptosaurus* from Late Cretaceous North America. TYRANNOSAURIDAE comprised about nine genera from Late Cretaceous Asia and North America, including some of the largest ever land-based carnivores. AUBLYSODONTIDAE were small, Late Cretaceous hunters of big game. SPINOSAURIDAE were huge, with a tall dorsal "sail". The genus *Spinosaurus*

THREE THEROPODS
Models shown to scale contrast the enormous Allosaurus with the large Gallimimus and the tiny Compsognathus.

lived in Late Cretaceous Africa. **BARYONYCHIDAE,** from North Africa and Early Cretaceous Europe, had long heads and hooked thumb-claws.

SUBGROUP COELUROSAURIA

ORNITHOMIMIDAE were widely distributed, ostrich-like, Late Jurassic to Late Cretaceous theropods.

DEINOCHEIRIDAE came from Late Cretaceous Asia and might have been huge relatives of the Ornithomimidae.

OVIRAPTORIDAE were Late Cretaceous, Asian, bird-like beasts with short, deep heads and strong beaks.

CAENAGNATHIDAE were small, Late Cretaceous, Asian and North American relatives of the oviraptorids.

ELMISAURIDAE were small, Late Cretaceous, Asian and North American beasts with bird-like feet.

THERIZINOSAURIDAE were Asian, Late Cretaceous theropods with scythe-like finger-claws.

TROODONTIDAE were small, alert, Late Cretaceous, northern theropods with a swivelling toe-claw.

DROMAEOSAURIDAE were fairly small, Cretaceous, northern theropods with a "ramrod" tail and a savage, swivelling second-toe claw.

ARCHAEOPTERYGIDAE were a family that contained the genus *Archaeopteryx,* a primitive, Late Jurassic, European bird. (Some scientists believe that all birds are dinosaurs.)

AVIMIMIDAE contained one genus, *Avimimus,* which was a toothless, long-legged, bird-like, running dinosaur from Late Cretaceous Asia.

COELURIDAE were small, Late Jurassic to Late Cretaceous theropods with a worldwide distribution.

COMPSOGNATHIDAE had one genus, *Compsognathus,* a tiny, two-fingered dinosaur that lived in Europe in Late Jurassic times.

ALLOSAURUS HIP BONES

These show a long pubis ending in a broad "foot". The pubis and foot secured the muscles that kept hind limbs close to the body. When Allosaurus lay down, the "foot" might have helped to support its weight.

Ilium

Pubis

Ischium

THEROPOD FAMILY TREE

This diagram shows possible relationships between theropod families (the names ending in -idae), each containing one genus or several genera. Names of individual genera not allocated to a family appear in italics. The infraorders Ceratosauria and Tetanurae are briefly described in the main text. Key subgroups below this level included the Maniraptora: dinosaurs that many scientists now think gave rise to birds. If so, strictly speaking, birds are tetanuran theropods.

THEROPODA

TETANURAE

Coelurosauria

Maniraptora

Ornithomimosauria

Oviraptorosauria

Carnosauria

Abelisauria

CERATOSAURIA

Eoraptor

Staurikosauridae

Herrerasauridae

Noasauridae

Alvarezsauridae

Abelisauridae

Velocisauridae

Ceratosauridae

Coelophysidae

Halticosauridae

Megalosauridae

Eustreptospondylus

Allosauridae

Itemiridae

Dryptosauridae

Tyrannosauridae

Aublysodontidae

Spinosauridae

Baryonychidae

Ornithomimidae

Deinocheiridae

Oviraptoridae

Caenagnathidae

Elmisauridae

Therizinosauridae

Troodontidae

Dromaeosauridae

Archaeopterygidae (Aves: birds)

Avimimidae

Coeluridae

Compsognathidae

KEY

Suborder

Infraorder

Subordinate group

Relationship uncertain

HERRERASAURUS

H ERRERASAURUS ("HERRERA'S LIZARD") is named after Victorino Herrera, the Andean farmer who first stumbled on its skeleton. It is one of the earliest known dinosaurs. A medium-sized, bipedal carnivore, it had sharp teeth, short arms, and three-fingered hands with curved claws. Seemingly "old-fashioned" features of the leg and foot bones made scientists think *Herrerasaurus* more primitive than any in the two main groups, the Saurischia and the Ornithischia. Later, the discovery of a complete skull revealed that it had a sliding lower jaw joint in common with some other theropods. This extra hinge gave killers like *Herrerasaurus* a tenacious bite.

EXTERNAL VIEW
Herrerasaurus's long, agile legs gave this bipedal predator an advantage over slower moving four-legged reptiles also living in early Late Triassic South America.

SKULL
Herrerasaurus's skull was long and narrow, with small nostril holes. A flexible joint in the mandible (lower jaw) let the front half move against the rear half, to give a grasping bite. Similar jaws help some lizards overcome their prey.

Braincase

Infratemporal fenestra

Orbit

Naris

Mandible

Curved, pointed tooth

Scaly skin

Long tail acts as a counterbalance

■ LIFESTYLE ■

Herrerasaurus lived in an upland region where plants grew thickly in the rainy season but died back during the long dry season. The dinosaur may have either ambushed or sought out its prey, striding on bird-like legs through dense riverside vegetation. Tracks that have been found in open sand and among plants were probably those of potential victims. Among these may have been the small, bipedal, plant-eating dinosaur *Pisanosaurus*. But reptiles would have constituted a far more plentiful prey. These included squat, four-legged herbivores, such as the tusked, pig-like rhynchosaurs, as well as a group of armoured, four-legged beasts, the aetosaurs. An adult *Herrerasaurus* could dart in to attack a browsing rhynchosaur, clawing and biting fatal gashes in its hide. A young *Herrerasaurus* might have scavenged from the carcass of a rhynchosaur. There were relatively few species of predatory dinosaur in the Late Triassic, the main predators at this time being the large, crocodile-like rauisuchids. It may be that *Herrerasaurus* and its relatives, with their upright stance, long hind limbs, and clawed, grasping hands, were faster and more dangerous than most of their competitors. Rauisuchids eventually died out, and the theropods dominated predatory life on land for over 150 million years.

COMPETITORS
Two young Herrerasaurus *(left) here vie with a big rauisuchid,* Saurosuchus, *for the remains of a dead rhynchosaur, watched by the small, primitive theropod* Eoraptor *(centre) and by two mammal-like reptiles (right).*

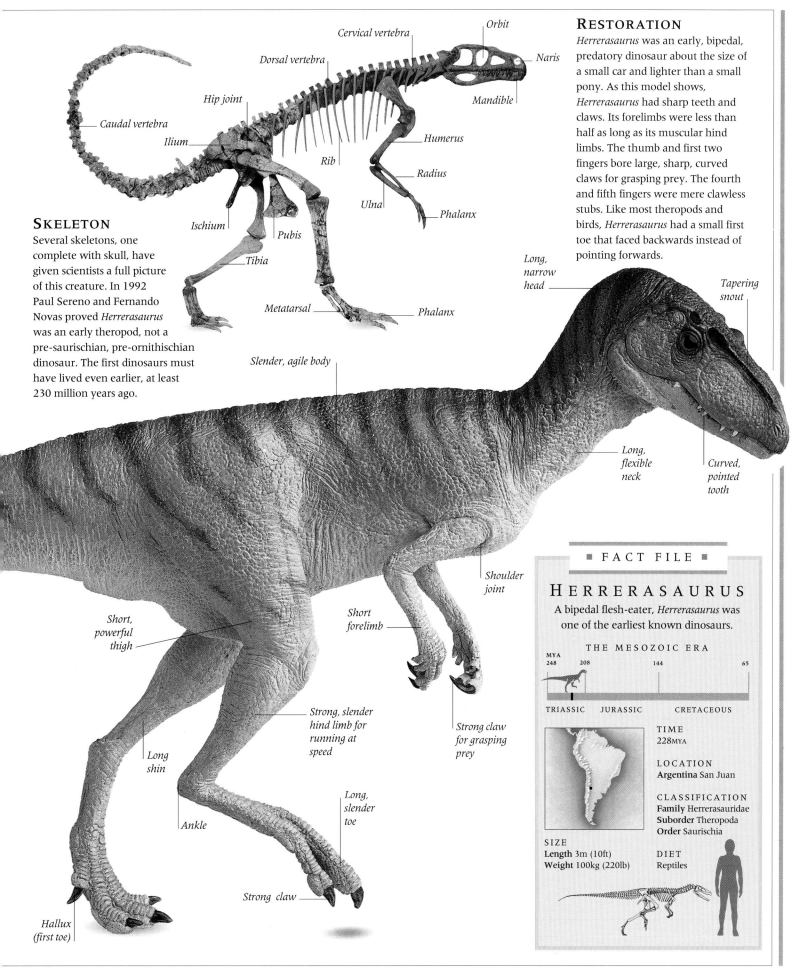

Orbit

Cervical vertebra

Dorsal vertebra

Naris

Hip joint

Mandible

Caudal vertebra

Humerus

Ilium

Rib

Radius

Ischium

Ulna

Pubis

Phalanx

Tibia

Metatarsal

Phalanx

SKELETON

Several skeletons, one complete with skull, have given scientists a full picture of this creature. In 1992 Paul Sereno and Fernando Novas proved *Herrerasaurus* was an early theropod, not a pre-saurischian, pre-ornithischian dinosaur. The first dinosaurs must have lived even earlier, at least 230 million years ago.

Slender, agile body

RESTORATION

Herrerasaurus was an early, bipedal, predatory dinosaur about the size of a small car and lighter than a small pony. As this model shows, *Herrerasaurus* had sharp teeth and claws. Its forelimbs were less than half as long as its muscular hind limbs. The thumb and first two fingers bore large, sharp, curved claws for grasping prey. The fourth and fifth fingers were mere clawless stubs. Like most theropods and birds, *Herrerasaurus* had a small first toe that faced backwards instead of pointing forwards.

Long, narrow head

Tapering snout

Long, flexible neck

Curved, pointed tooth

Shoulder joint

Short, powerful thigh

Short forelimb

Strong, slender hind limb for running at speed

Strong claw for grasping prey

Long shin

Ankle

Long, slender toe

Strong claw

Hallux (first toe)

■ FACT FILE ■

HERRERASAURUS

A bipedal flesh-eater, *Herrerasaurus* was one of the earliest known dinosaurs.

THE MESOZOIC ERA

MYA
248 208   144   65

TRIASSIC   JURASSIC   CRETACEOUS

TIME
228MYA

LOCATION
Argentina San Juan

CLASSIFICATION
Family Herrerasauridae
Suborder Theropoda
Order Saurischia

SIZE
Length 3m (10ft)
Weight 100kg (220lb)

DIET
Reptiles

CERATOSAURUS

T HE LARGEST and in some ways the most primitive of the ceratosaurs, *Ceratosaurus* ("horned lizard") somewhat resembled its more advanced rival *Allosaurus*. Both were powerful, sizeable predators; both had a huge head, vast jaws with curved fangs, a short, thick neck, short arms, and long, muscular legs. But *Ceratosaurus* was probably less heavily built. Its name derives from the bony horn on its snout. Other distinctive features were its unusual hip and hind-limb bones, the small, bony plates along its back, and a heavy tail that stiffened in a way that only let the end half waggle.

Orbit

Nasal horn core

Naris

Premaxilla

Maxilla

Serrated tooth

SKULL FRAGMENT

The lightly built skull was made up of bony struts and sheets. A blade-like horn protruded from the snout and a pair of smaller horns jutted up above the eyes. The fangs were massive.

■ LIFESTYLE ■

Limb design reveals that *Ceratosaurus* could put on a burst of speed to chase fast-running dryosaurid herbivores. Grappling with its teeth and claws, it could have tackled even larger dinosaurs, such as *Camptosaurus* and *Stegosaurus*, and it probably also killed and ate young or sick sauropods. Even a healthy, full-grown *Diplodocus* might have fallen prey if *Ceratosaurus* roamed in packs. However, the few, solitary *Ceratosaurus* fossil finds suggest this was unlikely. Some of the finds were in a quarry, together with more plentiful fossils of *Allosaurus*; however, whether this implies that *Ceratosaurus* was a rarer beast is uncertain. Both lived on the fern savannas and wooded flood plains of Late Jurassic western North America. *Ceratosaurus* might also have roamed similar countryside in East Africa. Two *Ceratosaurus* species have been named from fossils found in Tanzania. One bone certainly resembles the femur of a *Ceratosaurus*. The tibia seems to be very distinctive, and several recognizable examples have been found at Tanzanian sites, making identification reasonably certain. The fossil evidence also suggests that *Ceratosaurus* males were larger and stronger than the females.

Nasal horn core

Orbit

Naris

Braincase

Cervical vertebrae

Dorsal vertebrae

Mandible

Cervical rib

Scapula

Shoulder joint

Humerus

Elbow joint

Ulna

Rib

Pubis

Femur

Metacarpal

Phalanx

SPINE AND FORELIMBS

Ceratosaurus had a strong spinal column, with a short neck, and distinctive dorsal and sacral vertebrae. Sturdy arms bore grasping hands with claws on three digits. The thumb is lacking in this example.

CONFRONTATION
In this illustration, a startled pterosaur is here shown flying away as a snarling Ceratosaurus *confronts a sauropod far larger than itself. However, it seems unlikely that a lone* Ceratosaurus *would have dared to attack a dinosaur as large as this.*

Fibula

Metatarsal

Phalanx

■ FACT FILE ■

CERATOSAURUS

Ceratosaurus was a large, bipedal flesh-eater with blade-like fangs.

THE MESOZOIC ERA

MYA			
248	208	144	65

TRIASSIC   JURASSIC   CRETACEOUS

LOCATION
USA Colorado, Utah,
Wyoming
Tanzania Mtwara

DIET
Herbivorous dinosaurs

SIZE
Length 4.6–6m
(15ft–19ft 6in)
Weight 1 tonne
(1 ton)

CLASSIFICATION
Family Ceratosauridae
Infraorder Ceratosauria
Suborder Theropoda
Order Saurischia

TIME
150MYA

COMBAT BETWEEN RIVALS

Two rival male Ceratosaurus *stand side by side and whack each other with their horned heads. Another possible function of the horns is competitive display: rival males may have harmlessly shown their horns off by nodding their heads vigorously up and down, in the same way as certain lizards do today.*

Ilium

Hip
joint

Ischium

Transverse
process

Ankle joint

Knee
joint

Tibia

Hallux
(first toe)

Caudal vertebrae

Chevron

PELVIS, HIND LIMBS, AND TAIL

Ilium, ischium, and pubis were closely joined,
though not fused together as in birds. The pubis
formed a narrow shaft. We now know its lower
end was not shaped like a foot as pictured in this
skeleton, which is partly based on *Allosaurus*.
Hind limbs were shorter than those of *Allosaurus*,
but the tail was evidently long and deep.

DILOPHOSAURUS

N ICKNAMED "the terror of the Early Jurassic", *Dilophosaurus* ("two-ridge lizard") is the earliest big theropod that is well-known from adequate remains. Partial skeletons of about half a dozen young and adult specimens have been found in Arizona, and the late 1980s brought news of a discovery in China. *Dilophosaurus* was a long, lithe hunter, lighter than its relative *Ceratosaurus*. The build and enormously long tail are reminiscent of *Dilophosaurus*'s smaller cousin *Coelophysis*. Both shared the kinked upper jaw typical of the ceratosaurs. Uniquely, *Dilophosaurus* bore a tall, fragile head crest of two parallel bony ridges that stood like half dinner plates on edge.

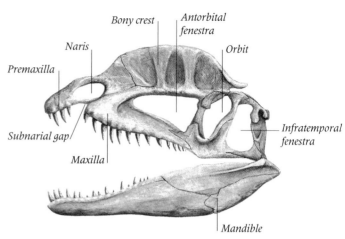

CRESTED SKULL

The light skull was distinguished by its tall, double crest, and by an unusually deep gap in the top jaw between the premaxilla and the maxilla. This is known as a subnarial gap, and a large one is typical of the ceratosaurs, but most notable in *Dilophosaurus*.

▪ LIFESTYLE ▪

Long, agile legs and clawed feet equipped this predator for chasing Arizona's early plant-eating dinosaurs. *Dilophosaurus* probably outsprinted the small, lightly armoured ornithischian *Scutellosaurus* and the bigger, bulkier prosauropod *Massospondylus*. Dashing in upon such prey, *Dilophosaurus* could have savaged them to death with a three-pronged attack: biting with its long teeth as it struck out with the sharp claws on its toes and fingers. *Dilophosaurus* must have aimed at making short, clean kills. Long struggles could have put its slender double crest at risk. So fragile was the crest that some scientists think *Dilophosaurus* fed only on carrion. These sceptics also argue that the jaws were too weak to deliver a lethal bite. (Most scientists disagree.) If the creature killed at all, the sceptics claim, it would have disembowelled its victims by raking their bellies open with its sharp claws. Although a liability in battle, the fragile head crests could have helped prevent fighting between rival males if, as fossil finds suggest, *Dilophosaurus* lived in packs. When males confronted one another, individuals with the smallest crests probably gave way without a struggle. The large-crested winner would then stay to rule a territory and mate with females in his herd. If this was so, the crests may perhaps have been covered with brightly coloured skin for display, like the comb of a farmyard cockerel. It is likely that only the males were equipped with this attractive headgear.

THREAT DISPLAY

A male *Dilophosaurus* might have threatened rivals by performing an open-jawed threat display like this one, or he might have bobbed his head up and down to show off his skull crests. Outright fighting seems unlikely.

SKELETON

The tail was as long as the whole of the rest of the animal, and helped *Dilophosaurus* maintain balance as it raced around after agile prey. The neck was strong but flexible. Each short and sturdy forelimb bore a four-fingered, grasping hand, with sharp claws on the first three fingers. The hind limbs were long and powerful, and ended in three forward-facing, elongated, sharp-clawed toes. As in other ceratosaurian theropods, the pubic hip bones did not end in an expanded "foot".

Skull labels: Naris, Bony crest, Antorbital fenestra, Orbit, Premaxilla, Subnarial gap, Maxilla, Infratemporal fenestra, Mandible

Skeleton labels: Caudal vertebrae, Neural spine, Chevron, Ischium, Ankle joint

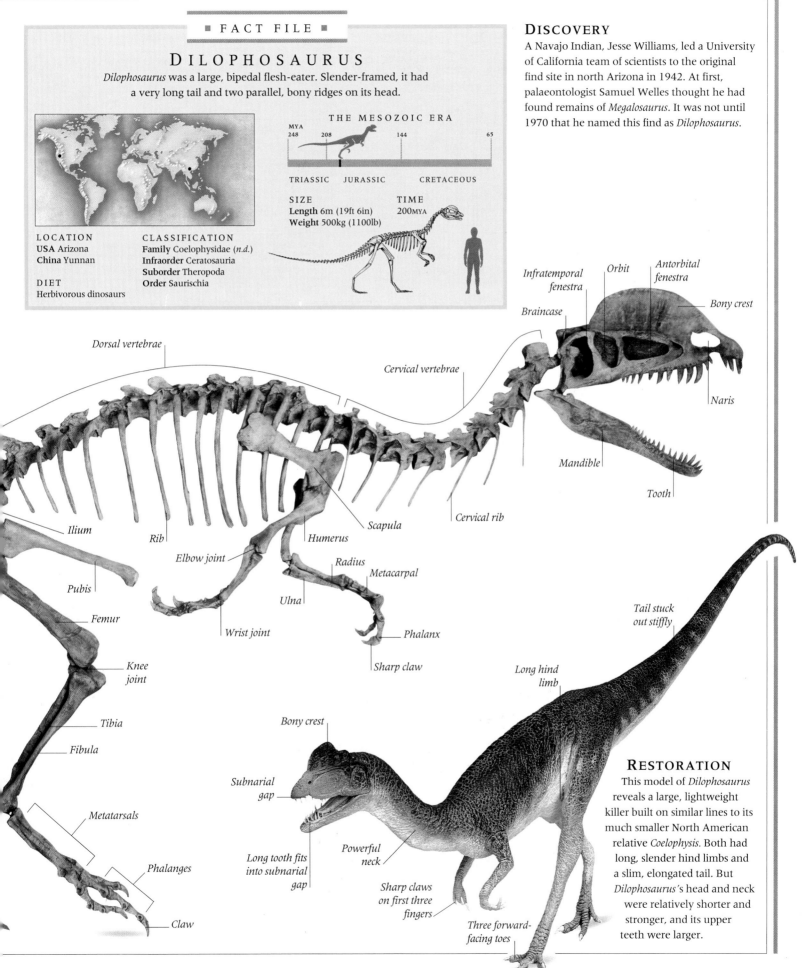

■ FACT FILE ■

DILOPHOSAURUS

Dilophosaurus was a large, bipedal flesh-eater. Slender-framed, it had
a very long tail and two parallel, bony ridges on its head.

THE MESOZOIC ERA

MYA
248   208   144   65

TRIASSIC   JURASSIC   CRETACEOUS

SIZE
Length 6m (19ft 6in)
Weight 500kg (1100lb)

TIME
200 MYA

LOCATION
USA Arizona
China Yunnan

DIET
Herbivorous dinosaurs

CLASSIFICATION
Family Coelophysidae (*n.d.*)
Infraorder Ceratosauria
Suborder Theropoda
Order Saurischia

DISCOVERY

A Navajo Indian, Jesse Williams, led a University
of California team of scientists to the original
find site in north Arizona in 1942. At first,
palaeontologist Samuel Welles thought he had
found remains of *Megalosaurus*. It was not until
1970 that he named this find as *Dilophosaurus*.

Dorsal vertebrae

Cervical vertebrae

Infratemporal
fenestra

Orbit

Antorbital
fenestra

Braincase

Bony crest

Naris

Mandible

Tooth

Cervical rib

Ilium

Rib

Scapula

Humerus

Elbow joint

Radius

Metacarpal

Ulna

Pubis

Femur

Wrist joint

Phalanx

Sharp claw

Tail stuck
out stiffly

Knee
joint

Long hind
limb

Tibia

Fibula

Bony crest

RESTORATION

This model of *Dilophosaurus*
reveals a large, lightweight
killer built on similar lines to its
much smaller North American
relative *Coelophysis*. Both had
long, slender hind limbs and
a slim, elongated tail. But
Dilophosaurus's head and neck
were relatively shorter and
stronger, and its upper
teeth were larger.

Subnarial
gap

Metatarsals

Powerful
neck

Long tooth fits
into subnarial
gap

Phalanges

Sharp claws
on first three
fingers

Three forward-
facing toes

Claw

COELOPHYSIS

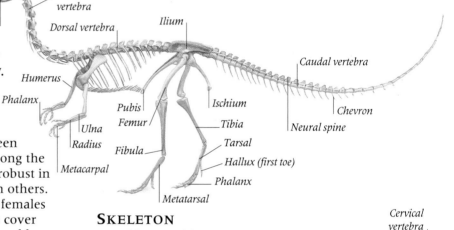

O NE OF THE EARLIEST well-known dinosaurs, *Coelophysis* ("hollow form") was a flesh-eater, built like a large, slender bird, with a narrow, almost stork-like head, an S-shaped neck, a slim body, and long, bird-like legs. Some internal features were also bird-like, including hollow, thin-walled bones, and the fusion of bones at the hips and spine, as well as those of the ankles and upper feet. Other features were unlike those of a bird: the skin was probably scaly, the long jaws bristled with teeth, and the forelimbs were arms with three-fingered hands. A long, reptilian tail balanced the forepart of the body.

RESTORATION

In this restoration, a lightly built, slim *Coelophysis* is propelled forwards by its long, powerful legs. With neck and tail extended, the flesh-eater pursues prey across its open, semi-desert habitat.

■ LIFESTYLE ■

Troops of hunting *Coelophysis* trekked across a red, sandy, semi-desert plain with a distant view of a green fringe of trees and ferns that lined a river bank. Among the animals in each troop, some were noticeably more robust in build, with longer arms and stronger shoulders than others. These may possibly have been the males, while the females could have been the slighter forms. If a lizard broke cover and scuttled away, one of the sharp-eyed hunters would race after it, neck and tail stretched out. With a sudden, snake-like, jabbing movement of the head, the dinosaur would impale the lizard between sharp, saw-edged teeth. *Coelophysis* could manoeuvre a large lizard between its jaws before swallowing it headfirst, as herons handle fish today. If its prey were a larger creature, it might have held the carcass in its clawed hands to tear it apart with its jaws. Jumbled bones discovered in one fossil adult's stomach cavity suggest that *Coelophysis* sometimes turned cannibal and ate its own young, but this probably happened only if food grew scarce. In normal times, the main prey of a hunting pack of *Coelophysis* could have included *Revueltosaurus* and *Technosaurus*, which were small but meaty, early plant-eating dinosaurs. Living in a crowd also gave *Coelophysis* some protection from attack by the large, aggressive reptiles known today as rauisuchids, and from staurikosaurid dinosaurs. But perhaps the most pressing danger of all to *Coelophysis* came from the terrible jaws of parasuchians, otherwise known as phytosaurs. These were crocodile-like carnivores that lurked in rivers and seized reptiles coming down to the water to drink.

Naris
Orbit
Cervical vertebra
Mandible
Dorsal vertebra
Ilium
Caudal vertebra
Humerus
Phalanx
Pubis
Ischium
Femur
Chevron
Ulna
Tibia
Neural spine
Radius
Fibula
Tarsal
Metacarpal
Hallux (first toe)
Phalanx
Metatarsal

SKELETON

Several features of the *Coelophysis* skeleton echo the anatomy of birds: some of the limb bones were hollow with thin walls, and four sets of bones were fused together – the sacral vertebrae, pelvic bones, tarsals (ankle bones), and metatarsals (foot bones).

Cervical vertebra
Claw
Wrist joint
Elbow joint
Dorsal vertebra
Scapula
Humerus
Phalanx
Metacarpal
Radius
Ulna

PREPARATIONS FOR TRANSIT
At a quarry in New Mexico, a rock containing Coelophysis *fossils is protected with plaster and made ready to be moved out on wooden skids.*

■ FACT FILE ■

COELOPHYSIS

Coelophysis was a bipedal flesh-eater with a small head and hollow bones.

THE MESOZOIC ERA

MYA 248	208	144	65

TRIASSIC	JURASSIC	CRETACEOUS

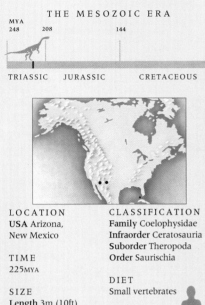

LOCATION
USA Arizona,
New Mexico

TIME
225MYA

SIZE
Length 3m (10ft)
Weight 27kg (60lb)

CLASSIFICATION
Family Coelophysidae
Infraorder Ceratosauria
Suborder Theropoda
Order Saurischia

DIET
Small vertebrates

MINIATURE RELATIVES

Two early theropods no bigger than a songbird chase an insect the size of an modern-day fly. These creatures were shaped like tiny *Coelophysis* but had proportionally bigger heads and larger eyes. Their fossils turned up in Nova Scotia in rocks that date from Early Mesozoic times.

MASS DEATH

Palaeontologists found hundreds of jumbled *Coelophysis* skeletons in the 1940s in northern New Mexico. The herd had apparently drowned when a flash flood poured down a dry desert river bed.

SKELETON IN DEATH POSE

Lying as it fell in death, this fine specimen emphasizes the long, narrow jaws with sharp, curved teeth, grasping hands, long legs, and elongated neck and tail. A cluster of tiny bones near the ribs might be a swallowed baby *Coelophysis*. If so, the adult was at least on one occasion a cannibal.

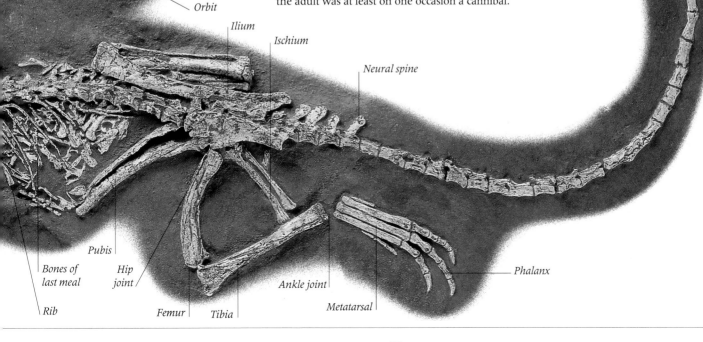

Infratemporal fenestra

Tooth

Naris

Antorbital fenestra

Orbit

Ilium

Ischium

Neural spine

Caudal vertebra

Pubis

Hip joint

Bones of last meal

Rib

Femur

Tibia

Ankle joint

Metatarsal

Phalanx

CARNOTAURUS

EXTERNAL VIEW

Thanks to some good fossilized skin impressions preserved in rock, we have a better idea of what *Carnotaurus* looked like than we have of any other flesh-eating dinosaur. Thousands of non-overlapping, disc-shaped scales covered the body, and rows of similar but noticeably bigger semi-conical scales ran along the back and sides.

Labels (external view): Semi-conical, bony scale; Thick neck; Wing-like horn; Tail; Short forelimb; Hind limb; Foot; Ankle; Claw

I N 1985, Argentinian palaeontologist José Bonaparte announced news of a big, bizarre dinosaur unlike anything described before. *Carnotaurus* ("carnivorous bull") had a deeper, shorter, more bull-like head than other theropods. Most extraordinary were the pointed, wing-like horns above its eyes – perhaps butting weapons used by fighting rivals. Other remarkable features included small, forward-facing eyes, spinal bones with wing-like projections, very short arms, and prominent rows of scales along the back and sides.

■ LIFESTYLE ■

Carnotaurus lived alongside *Chubutisaurus*, a sauropod three times its length. Perhaps it killed and ate *Chubutisaurus* young and hunted moderately-sized adult ornithopods. Short-armed *Carnotaurus* evidently assaulted prey or tackled carrion headfirst.

■ RELATIONSHIPS ■

Carnotaurus proved to belong to the Abelisauridae, a long-lived family of "old-fashioned" theropods that take their group name from *Abelisaurus*, a dinosaur named in 1985. Details of *Abelisaurus* bones prove it was related to *Carnotaurus*, although *Abelisaurus* had no horns, a longer head, and a hooked nose. A third abelisaurid, named *Xenotarsosaurus* ("strange ankle lizard") was described in 1986. A further look at *Genyodectes*, named in 1901, showed it was another South American abelisaurid. Scientists next noted abelisaurid features in skull fragments from South America, India, and France. A pattern appeared to be emerging. The apparent distribution of abelisaurids suggested that they spread across the southern supercontinent Gondwana (which included South America and India) after it separated from the northern supercontinent Laurasia (North America, Europe, and Asia). The French abelisaurid could be explained by the existence of a land bridge where Gondwana briefly touched Laurasia.

JOSE BONAPARTE
This Argentinian palaeontologist has dug up or described dinosaurs that lived in what is now Argentina in all three periods of the Mesozoic.

Labels (internal/cutaway view): Scaly skin; Cervical musculature; Scapula; Lung; Rib; Dorsal vertebra; Small intestine; Trachea; Coracoid; Shoulder joint; Humerus; Heart; Liver; Gizzard; Large intestine; Retroarticular process; Pubis; Hind limb; Hallux (first toe); Toe

Labels (lower jaw): Tooth; Mandible

LOWER JAW

For a beast with a formidably deep, powerful-looking skull that incorporated strong jaw-closing muscles, the lower jaw seems rather slim and perhaps even weakly built. One writer also considers the teeth unusually slender for a big theropod. The combination of deep skull and shallow mandible (lower jaw) makes it difficult to visualize *Carnotaurus*'s likely prey.

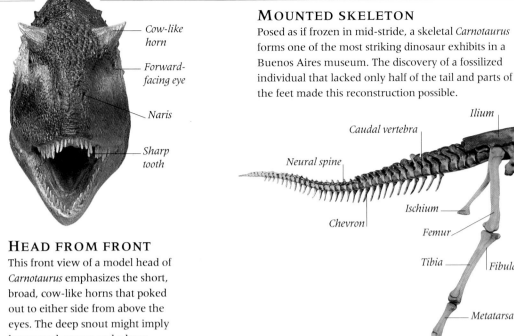

- Cow-like horn
- Forward-facing eye
- Naris
- Sharp tooth

HEAD FROM FRONT

This front view of a model head of *Carnotaurus* emphasizes the short, broad, cow-like horns that poked out to either side from above the eyes. The deep snout might imply large nasal organs and a keen sense of smell.

MOUNTED SKELETON

Posed as if frozen in mid-stride, a skeletal *Carnotaurus* forms one of the most striking dinosaur exhibits in a Buenos Aires museum. The discovery of a fossilized individual that lacked only half of the tail and parts of the feet made this reconstruction possible.

- Naris
- Braincase
- Dorsal vertebra
- Ilium
- Caudal vertebra
- Mandible
- Neural spine
- Cervical vertebra
- Cervical rib
- Chevron
- Ischium
- Humerus
- Femur
- Scapula
- Tibia
- Fibula
- Metatarsal

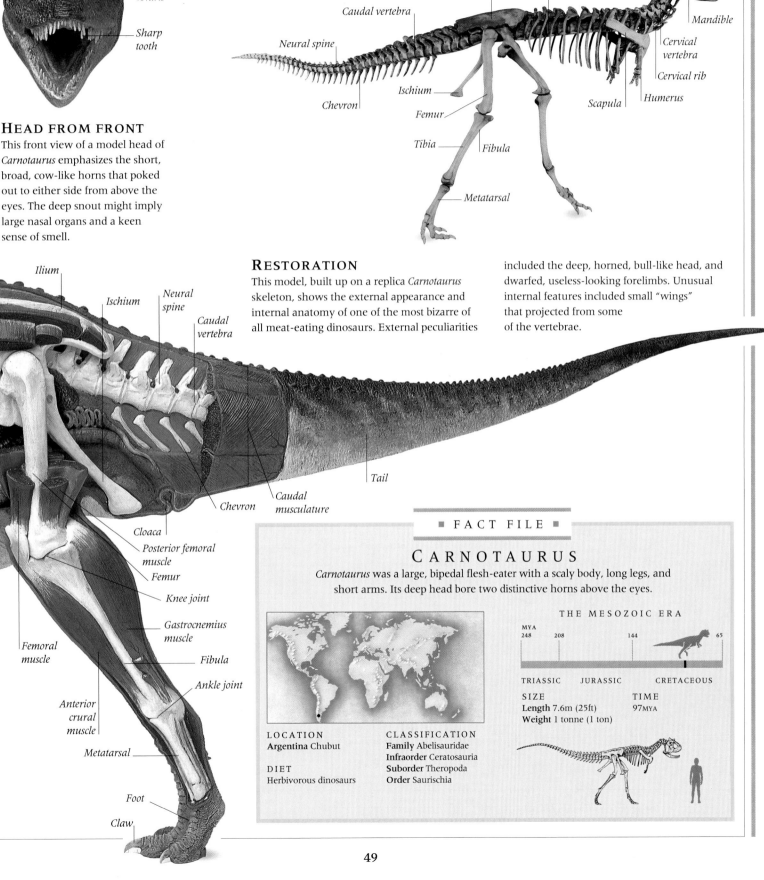

- Ilium
- Ischium
- Neural spine
- Caudal vertebra
- Chevron
- Caudal musculature
- Tail
- Cloaca
- Posterior femoral muscle
- Femur
- Knee joint
- Gastrocnemius muscle
- Femoral muscle
- Fibula
- Ankle joint
- Anterior crural muscle
- Metatarsal
- Foot
- Claw

RESTORATION

This model, built up on a replica *Carnotaurus* skeleton, shows the external appearance and internal anatomy of one of the most bizarre of all meat-eating dinosaurs. External peculiarities included the deep, horned, bull-like head, and dwarfed, useless-looking forelimbs. Unusual internal features included small "wings" that projected from some of the vertebrae.

■ FACT FILE ■

CARNOTAURUS

Carnotaurus was a large, bipedal flesh-eater with a scaly body, long legs, and short arms. Its deep head bore two distinctive horns above the eyes.

THE MESOZOIC ERA

MYA 248	208	144	65
TRIASSIC	JURASSIC		CRETACEOUS

SIZE
Length 7.6m (25ft)
Weight 1 tonne (1 ton)

TIME
97MYA

LOCATION
Argentina Chubut

DIET
Herbivorous dinosaurs

CLASSIFICATION
Family Abelisauridae
Infraorder Ceratosauria
Suborder Theropoda
Order Saurischia

EUSTREPTOSPONDYLUS

T HANKS TO THE DISCOVERY of a fine skeleton in Oxfordshire, England, "well-curved vertebra" was Europe's best-known large, carnivorous dinosaur for many years. It had short arms, thick-walled leg bones, and large, weight-saving "windows" in the skull. Unable to place it in any known family, scientists simply note that a spine on one of its neck bones, and a ridge on the thigh bone, seem typical of carnosaur theropods. Among these, *Allosaurus* displays a possible family likeness in the bones of its skull, neck, and ankle.

RUNNING PREDATOR

This illustration shows bipedal *Eustreptospondylus* running swiftly as though chasing prey. Its victims might have included *Cetiosaurus*, hypsilophodontids, and stegosaurs, all of which lived in Middle Jurassic England.

■ LIFESTYLE ■

Eustreptospondylus shared what is now England with various plant-eaters. This big carnivore was a longer animal than early, plated ornithischians like *Lexovisaurus* and early, armoured ornithischians like *Sarcolestes*. Even a half-grown *Eustreptospondylus*, such as the fossilized specimen found in Oxfordshire which would have been about the size of a lion, could have tackled these inoffensive, plodding herbivores. Sauropods such as *Cetiosaurus* and *Cetiosauriscus* were evidently longer and certainly much heavier than a full-grown *Eustreptospondylus* but they, too, formed potential meals for this large, rapacious theropod.

Long neck

Scapula

Jaw adductor muscle

Sharp tooth

Shoulder joint

Humerus

Short forelimb

Wrist

Pubis

Hand

Elbow

Finger

■ CLASSIFICATION ■

In the early part of the nineteenth century, very few dinosaurs had been discovered or identified, and scientists had the impression that, in western Europe, there had been only one large Jurassic predatory dinosaur. The name *Megalosaurus* (see box opposite) was given to this conceptual animal. For over a century there was considerable confusion because widely differing finds were placed in this genus. In 1964, the British palaeontologist Alick Walker proved that the dinosaur shown on this page could not have been a *Megalosaurus*, and considered the name *Streptospondylus*, which various earlier scientists had proposed. This name turned out to be inadmissible because it had been given, even earlier, to a genus of crocodile. Walker added the prefix *Eu-* ("well"), producing the name *Eustreptospondylus* for the genus, and created the name *oxoniensis* ("from Oxford") for this species.

Metatarsal

Phalanx

Claw

BIRD-LIKE FOOT

Eustreptospondylus had a theropod's three-toed, bird-like foot. The central one of the three metatarsals (upper foot bones) is tapered at the top end, out of this picture. This reflects a change that took place in the course of the evolution of the theropods – by the time *Tyrannosaurus* evolved, the equivalent bone was reduced to a sharp point.

Bird-like foot

Toe-claw

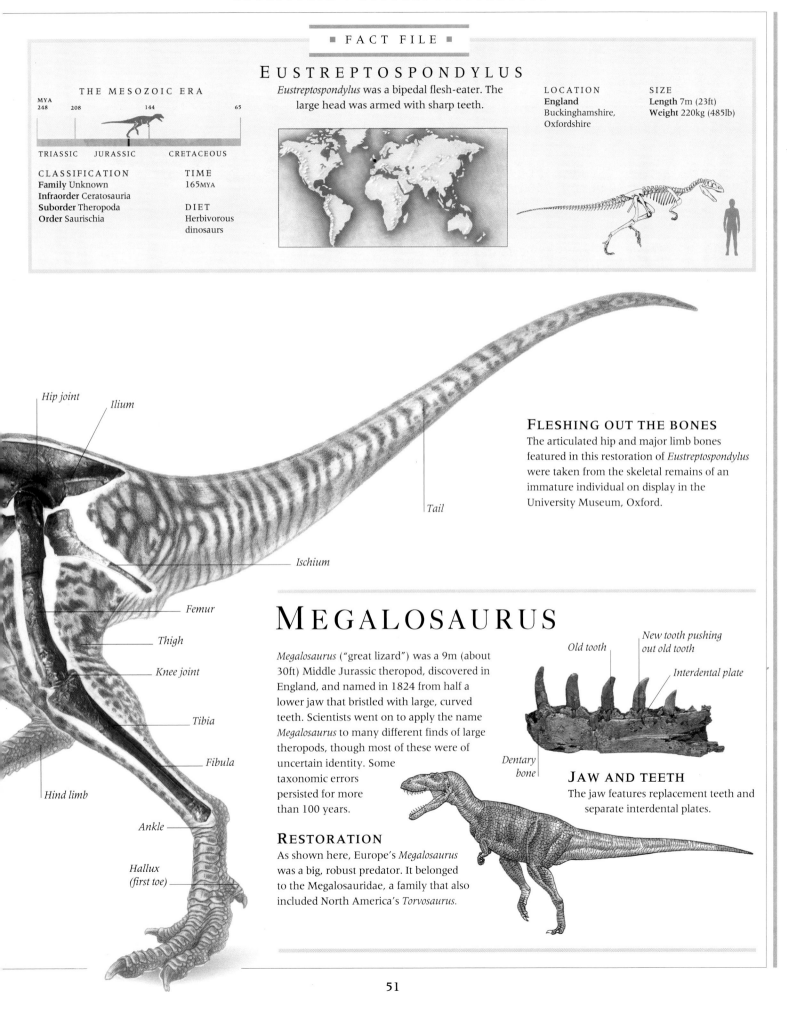

EUSTREPTOSPONDYLUS

Eustreptospondylus was a bipedal flesh-eater. The large head was armed with sharp teeth.

THE MESOZOIC ERA

MYA			
248	208	144	65

TRIASSIC   JURASSIC   CRETACEOUS

CLASSIFICATION
Family Unknown
Infraorder Ceratosauria
Suborder Theropoda
Order Saurischia

TIME
165MYA

DIET
Herbivorous
dinosaurs

LOCATION
England
Buckinghamshire,
Oxfordshire

SIZE
Length 7m (23ft)
Weight 220kg (485lb)

Hip joint

Ilium

Tail

FLESHING OUT THE BONES
The articulated hip and major limb bones featured in this restoration of *Eustreptospondylus* were taken from the skeletal remains of an immature individual on display in the University Museum, Oxford.

Ischium

Femur

Thigh

Knee joint

Tibia

MEGALOSAURUS

Megalosaurus ("great lizard") was a 9m (about 30ft) Middle Jurassic theropod, discovered in England, and named in 1824 from half a lower jaw that bristled with large, curved teeth. Scientists went on to apply the name *Megalosaurus* to many different finds of large theropods, though most of these were of uncertain identity. Some taxonomic errors persisted for more than 100 years.

Fibula

Hind limb

Old tooth

New tooth pushing out old tooth

Interdental plate

Dentary bone

JAW AND TEETH
The jaw features replacement teeth and separate interdental plates.

RESTORATION
As shown here, Europe's *Megalosaurus* was a big, robust predator. It belonged to the Megalosauridae, a family that also included North America's *Torvosaurus*.

Ankle

Hallux
(first toe)

ALLOSAURUS

Supraoccipital crest
Orbit
Antorbital fenestra
Maxillary fenestra
Postorbital bone
Braincase
Naris
Serrated tooth
Infratemporal fenestra
Mandible
Mandibular fenestra

A LLOSAURUS ("OTHER LIZARD") was one of the biggest carnivorous dinosaurs before the tyrannosaurids appeared some 50 million years later. *Allosaurus*'s long, muscular hind limbs supported a body weighing two tonnes or more. The huge but lightweight skull consisted largely of bony struts, with bony ridges above the eyes. The immense, expandable jaws had long, curved, saw-edged teeth. A thick, S-curved neck supported the head, and a long, deep tail counterbalanced the heavy front end of this terrifying theropod. Curved, tapering claws armed the three fingers of each short, strong arm. Each foot had three claw-bearing toes; the short, first toe was turned slightly backwards.

Small, triangular horn

Elastic tissue at corner of mouth

Curved, serrated tooth

■ LIFESTYLE ■

Allosaurus must have been a formidable enemy of medium-to-large plant-eating dinosaurs. A lone *Allosaurus* could have hunted and attacked beasts the size of *Camptosaurus*. The predator probably lurked in dense undergrowth. When an unsuspecting *Camptosaurus* – or any meaty prey – meandered past, the *Allosaurus* might have lunged suddenly forwards onto its victim, grappling with its sharp finger-claws while simultaneously plunging its fang-like teeth deep into its victim's vulnerable neck flesh. Sauropods much larger than the largest *Allosaurus* would have proved more difficult to overcome. Perhaps packs of *Allosaurus* dogged herds of sauropods, singling out and slaughtering any young or sickly individuals that lagged behind the rest. Sauropods like *Apatosaurus* and *Diplodocus* probably went around in herds for mutual protection from gangs of theropods.

SKULL AND HEAD

Allosaurus's great head (above) was less heavy than it appeared. Many skull bones (top) were load-bearing bars that separated "windows" for nostrils, eyes, and muscles. The sturdiest bones supported the teeth and jaw muscles.

Caudal vertebrae

Neural spine

Chevron

Other hints that *Allosaurus* patrolled the land in troops include more than 10,000 disarticulated bones discovered in one quarry in Utah. Usually, the fossil bones of herbivore victims far outnumber the bones of the theropods that preyed upon them. Here, however, it seems that *Allosaurus* greatly outnumbered its prey. Even more intriguingly, the *Allosaurus* bones came from animals of every age and size, including the very young. Some scientists suspect that the theropods had flocked in from far and wide to feast on a few big herbivores trapped in marshy ground; it is possible that the theropods might also have become stuck and died.

HIGH-ANKLED FOOT

Allosaurus's high-ankled, scaly foot looked like that of a gigantic flightless bird, far heavier than any now alive. Three big toes bore the body's weight. The high, tiny first toe was turned back. The toe-claws were bony cores sheathed in horn.

JAW MOVEMENTS

Allosaurus could open its jaws far apart (left), and then expand them (below) to engulf a huge chunk of meat. It bit flesh from its victims by pulling its skull back over its lower jaw so that its narrow-bladed teeth cut through tough, living tissue. Movable joints between the skull bones made all this possible.

Outward movement of jaw

■ FACT FILE ■

ALLOSAURUS

Allosaurus was a large, bipedal predator. It had huge jaws armed with blade-like teeth, a bulky body, muscular hind limbs, and sharp claws.

THE MESOZOIC ERA

MYA				
248	208		144	65

TRIASSIC   JURASSIC   CRETACEOUS

SIZE
Length 11m (36ft)
Weight 1.5–2 tonnes
(1.5–2 tons)

TIME
156–130MYA

LOCATION
USA Colorado, Montana, New Mexico, Oklahoma, South Dakota, Utah, Wyoming
Tanzania Mtwara
Australia Victoria

CLASSIFICATION
Family Allosauridae
Infraorder Tetanurae
Suborder Theropoda
Order Saurischia

DIET
Herbivorous dinosaurs

ALLOSAURUS SKELETON

The skull was long, deep, and narrow. As in other carnosaurs, big neural spines anchored strong neck, back, and tail muscles; there was also a blade-like ilium, a pubis ending in a "foot", and a femur (thigh bone) longer than the tibia (shin bone).

Cervical vertebrae — Braincase — Orbit — Cervical rib — Scapula — Shoulder joint — Serrated tooth — Mandible — Humerus — Radius — Metacarpal — Ulna — Phalanx — Wrist joint

Dorsal vertebrae — Ilium — Femur — Ischium — Tibia — Fibula — Hallux (first toe) — Phalanx — Metatarsal — Pubis

THE FOSSIL RECORD

Allosaurus was named in 1877 from a discovery made in Colorado. Later finds of over 60 individuals came mostly from Utah's spectacular Cleveland-Lloyd Dinosaur Quarry. Other fossils have been found in East Africa and southeast Australia.

Naris — Thick neck — Long tail — Short forelimb — Scaly skin — Hand — Thigh — Hind limb

RESTORATION

This model of *Allosaurus* emphasizes the large head, gaping jaws, thick "bulldog" neck, short back, narrow belly, and long, deep tail. Short arms, with long, three-fingered, claw-tipped hands, contrast with the strong, weight-bearing legs that supported this creature weighing up to two tonnes or even more.

TYRANNOSAURUS

TYRANNOSAURUS ("TYRANT LIZARD") was one of the last, largest, and most powerful of all predatory dinosaurs. Arguably the biggest flesh-eating land animal of any age, this two-legged theropod grew as heavy as an elephant, as long as a tennis court is wide, and tall enough to peer into an upstairs room. Saw-edged teeth armed the mighty jaws of its immense head, 1.2m (4ft) long, and strong claws tipped the three toes of each gigantic, bird-like foot. Compared to its massive legs, the small, two-fingered "hands" and arms no longer than our own appear absurdly puny. Despite its size, *Tyrannosaurus* was lightly constructed, with hollow bones and great windows in the skull.

■ LIFESTYLE ■

Alone, in pairs, or possibly in packs, *Tyrannosaurus* probably trailed migrating herds of horned and duckbilled dinosaurs, picking off the weak, young, and sick. Other tactics might have involved waiting in ambush then charging, jaws wide

open, bringing down its victim with its teeth after a short chase at speeds of 32km/h (20mph) or more. Some experts disagree with this theory. They believe that *Tyrannosaurus* moved more slowly, eating only corpses found already dead; yet no large, land-based carnivore living today survives on carrion alone. *Tyrannosaurus* could have pierced big herbivores' thick hides with its serrated teeth, then twisted its head to and fro to saw off the flesh. Or perhaps the teeth were used to stab smaller dinosaurs that could be eaten whole. The contrast between *Tyrannosaurus*'s huge body and tiny, two-fingered hands long puzzled palaeontologists. Although the forelimbs bore sharp claws, they seemed too puny for use in an attack and too short to bring food to the mouth. We know that the arms were muscular. Perhaps they propped up the front of the animal as it rose from lying to standing, or perhaps the fingers became grappling hooks when *Tyrannosaurus* savaged its victims.

FRONT VIEW OF HEAD

Forward-facing eyes helped *Tyrannosaurus* judge distance well as it moved in to attack, with jaws agape to bare its rows of fangs. The tips of its upper teeth formed a curve like a scalpel blade. When *Tyrannosaurus* bit into a victim, it probably pulled one side of its jaws backwards, so that each sharp-edged tooth cut backwards too. Teeth ploughed through flesh like butchers' knives.

Heavy tail balancing the body

Muscular thigh

DISCOVERY

The first fairly complete *Tyrannosaurus* was found in 1902. In 1905, American palaeontologist Henry Fairfield Osborn described and named the dinosaur. For many years, scientists knew only three partial skeletons. Then, in the 1960s, fresh discoveries shed new light on the animal's anatomy.

HEAD MOVEMENTS
Strobe photography shows the wide range of side-to-side head movements that could have helped Tyrannosaurus *detect prey and also tear flesh from its victims.*

Heel

Toe

RESTORATION

Tyrannosaurus had a massive head, borne on a flexible neck. Forelimbs were short, with clawed, two-fingered hands. The body was deep and broad-chested; the hind limbs were pillar-like, with bird-like ankles. The three big toes of each foot bore robust claws, and a heavy tail counterbalanced the trunk and neck.

Forward-facing eye

Massive head

Neck

Powerful jaws with sharp teeth

Short forelimb

Sharp claws

Two fingered hand

Deep, powerful body

Pillar-like hind limb

Foot with three toes

Heavy claw

TOOTH

Up to 18cm (7in) long, the largest teeth were big and serrated like steak-knife blades. Worn crowns hint that they bit tougher food than rotting meat. This belies the theory that tyrannosaurids had been merely scavengers. As an aging tooth's long root dissolved, the tooth fell out and a new one took its place.

BRAIN CAST

This cast from a *Tyrannosaurus* skull cavity reveals a long, narrow brain. Its olfactory bulb, optic nerve, and auditory nerve were well-developed, which suggests that *Tyrannosaurus* had keen senses of smell, sight, and hearing.

Supraoccipital crest

Orbit

Braincase

Naris

Serrated tooth

Mandible

SKULL

This was deep and massive, with a short snout, narrow jaws, broad cheeks, and a wide braincase. The lower jaw was hinged half way along to increase the gape; the joint between left and right mandibles was movable.

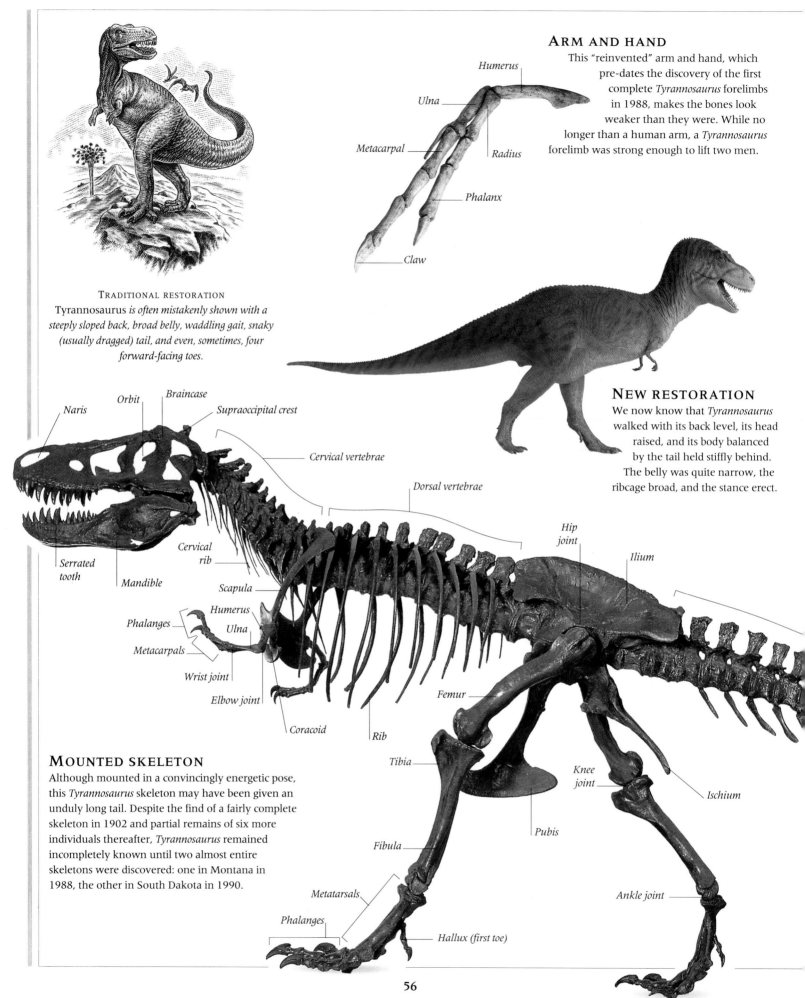

TRADITIONAL RESTORATION
Tyrannosaurus is often mistakenly shown with a steeply sloped back, broad belly, waddling gait, snaky (usually dragged) tail, and even, sometimes, four forward-facing toes.

ARM AND HAND

This "reinvented" arm and hand, which pre-dates the discovery of the first complete *Tyrannosaurus* forelimbs in 1988, makes the bones look weaker than they were. While no longer than a human arm, a *Tyrannosaurus* forelimb was strong enough to lift two men.

Humerus

Ulna

Metacarpal

Radius

Phalanx

Claw

NEW RESTORATION

We now know that *Tyrannosaurus* walked with its back level, its head raised, and its body balanced by the tail held stiffly behind. The belly was quite narrow, the ribcage broad, and the stance erect.

Naris

Orbit

Braincase

Supraoccipital crest

Cervical vertebrae

Dorsal vertebrae

Hip joint

Ilium

Serrated tooth

Mandible

Cervical rib

Scapula

Humerus

Phalanges

Ulna

Metacarpals

Wrist joint

Elbow joint

Coracoid

Rib

Femur

Tibia

Knee joint

Ischium

Pubis

Fibula

Ankle joint

Metatarsals

Phalanges

Hallux (first toe)

MOUNTED SKELETON

Although mounted in a convincingly energetic pose, this *Tyrannosaurus* skeleton may have been given an unduly long tail. Despite the find of a fairly complete skeleton in 1902 and partial remains of six more individuals thereafter, *Tyrannosaurus* remained incompletely known until two almost entire skeletons were discovered: one in Montana in 1988, the other in South Dakota in 1990.

ANATOMY OF THE LEG

Makers of this model of the leg of
Albertosaurus – a relative of *Tyrannosaurus* –
visualized the position of the leg
muscles from grooves and
ridges on the bones.

Femorotibial muscle

Internal tibial flexor muscle

Iliofibular muscle

Femur

Gastrocnemius muscle

Deep digital flexor muscle

Fibula

Tarsal

Toe

Iliofemoral muscle

Iliotibial muscle

Ambiens muscle

Femorotibial muscle

Anterior tibial muscle

Common digital extensor muscle

Metatarsal

Claw

FACT FILE

TYRANNOSAURUS

Tyrannosaurus was a bipedal predator. One of the largest-ever flesh-eating dinosaurs, it possessed huge jaws and sharp claws.

THE MESOZOIC ERA

MYA 248 | 208 | 144 | 65

TRIASSIC   JURASSIC   CRETACEOUS

TIME
68–65 MYA

DIET
Large herbivorous dinosaurs

CLASSIFICATION
Family Tyrannosauridae
Infraorder Tetanurae
Suborder Theropoda
Order Saurischia

LOCATION
Canada Alberta, Saskatchewan
USA Colorado, Montana, New Mexico, Wyoming

SIZE
Length 12m (39ft)
Weight 6.4 tonnes (6.3 tons)

Caudal vertebrae

Chevron

Neural spine

GNAWING BONES

With arms too short to bring food to its mouth,
Tyrannosaurus lowered its great head to gnaw
dismembered bones. Similar huge-jawed
theropods with tiny, two-fingered
forelimbs included Late Cretaceous
Albertosaurus and *Tarbosaurus*.

BARYONYX

BARYONYX ("HEAVY CLAW") takes its name from its murderously large and hook-like thumb-claws. In 1983, the chance find of one of these thumb-claws in southern England led to the discovery of the only known skeleton of this strange, big, predatory dinosaur – the best preserved of any dating from its time (around 120 million years ago). The most unusual features of *Baryonyx* were its long, narrow, crocodile-like jaws filled with sharp teeth. It also had a longer, straighter neck than most big theropods and strong arms and hind limbs; its body was balanced by a stiffened tail.

WILLIAM WALKER
Amateur fossil hunter William Walker with the Baryonyx *thumb-claw he found in a Surrey clay pit in 1983.*

BARYONYX SKULL

CROCODILE SKULL

TWO SKULLS COMPARED

Long, low jaws and sharp, somewhat rounded teeth made *Baryonyx*'s 1.1m (3ft 7in) head less like a flesh-eating dinosaur's than that of a present-day crocodile, a reptile whose jaws were specifically designed to seize and grasp slippery prey. Other notable aspects of *Baryonyx*'s skull are the kinked upper jaw and the position of the nostrils, features that are similar in *Dilophosaurus*.

▪ LIFESTYLE ▪

Baryonyx's homeland was the warm floodplain that stretched from where London now stands, south into France and Belgium. The carnivorous predator prowled through conifer and cycad forests, ferny glades, and horsetail meadows fringing rivers, lakes, and swamps. It probably waded into water and caught big fishes with its great thumb-claws, much as grizzly bears snatch salmon from Alaskan rivers. Or it might have crouched on the shore, its long neck craned out just above the water, seizing passing fishes in its jaws. The long mouth and narrow, pointed teeth would have been ideal for gripping slippery prey. Half-digested fish scales found in *Baryonyx*'s ribcage prove that fish of roughly 1m (about 3ft) in length formed at least part of this creature's diet. However, it has been pointed out that no present-day large land animal eats only fishes, and one scientist has therefore surmised that *Baryonyx* also hunted terrestrial prey. Another possibility is that *Baryonyx* scavenged meat from the corpses of dinosaurs it found already dead, probing deep inside the carcasses with its long, narrow, sharp-toothed jaws.

Stiffened tail acts as a counterbalance

FOSSILIZED SKELETON

Reconstructing a *Baryonyx* skeleton involved making model bones to take the place of bones that were missing. Parts of the skull, ribs, tail, arms, and legs had to be based on other theropods or modelled from bones on the left side of the body, then fitted together.

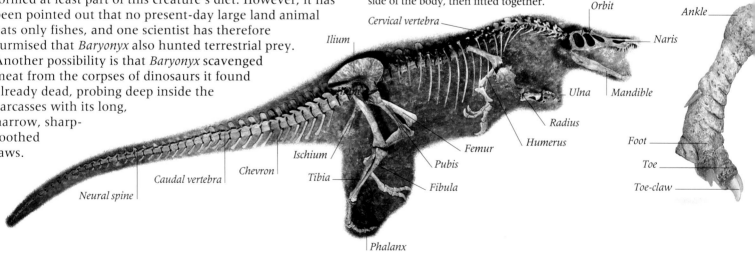

Cervical vertebra
Ilium
Orbit
Ankle
Naris
Ulna
Mandible
Radius
Humerus
Femur
Foot
Pubis
Toe
Ischium
Fibula
Tibia
Toe-claw
Chevron
Caudal vertebra
Neural spine
Phalanx

THUMB-CLAW

Baryonyx's sharp, curved thumb-claw resembled the strong hook on a fisherman's gaff (a tool used to lift heavy fishes out of water). This fossil (right) was reconstructed from fragments that fell out of a large, hard siltstone nodule struck by fossil hunter William Walker's geological hammer. Together with its horny sheath, the claw must have measured 35cm (about 14in).

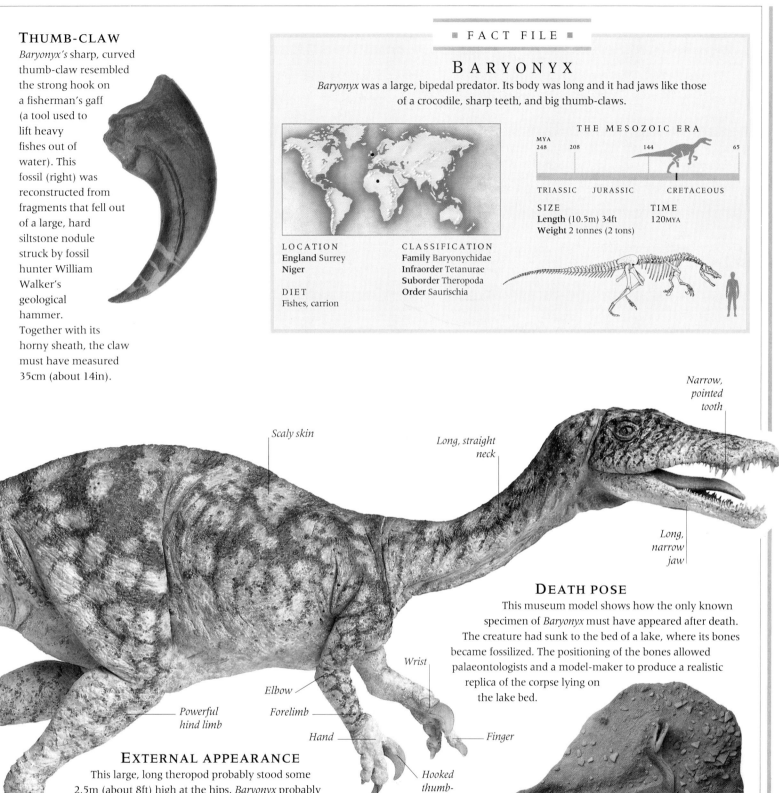

■ FACT FILE ■

BARYONYX

Baryonyx was a large, bipedal predator. Its body was long and it had jaws like those of a crocodile, sharp teeth, and big thumb-claws.

THE MESOZOIC ERA

MYA				
248	208		144	65
TRIASSIC	JURASSIC		CRETACEOUS	

SIZE
Length (10.5m) 34ft
Weight 2 tonnes (2 tons)

TIME
120MYA

LOCATION
England Surrey
Niger

DIET
Fishes, carrion

CLASSIFICATION
Family Baryonychidae
Infraorder Tetanurae
Suborder Theropoda
Order Saurischia

Narrow, pointed tooth

Scaly skin

Long, straight neck

Long, narrow jaw

DEATH POSE

This museum model shows how the only known specimen of *Baryonyx* must have appeared after death. The creature had sunk to the bed of a lake, where its bones became fossilized. The positioning of the bones allowed palaeontologists and a model-maker to produce a realistic replica of the corpse lying on the lake bed.

Wrist

Elbow

Forelimb

Hand

Finger

Powerful hind limb

Hooked thumb-claw

Finger-claw

EXTERNAL APPEARANCE

This large, long theropod probably stood some 2.5m (about 8ft) high at the hips. *Baryonyx* probably prowled around on its hind limbs, with the long, stiffened tail balancing the chest, and the neck and head held low and jutting forwards. (Most other big theropods usually held their necks shaped like a letter S.) The arms were very powerfully built for ambushing fishes and lifting them out of the water, or for tackling carrion. *Baryonyx* probably did not go down on all fours.

SPINOSAURUS

A WORLD WAR II bombing raid destroyed the then few known bones of one of the longest and strangest of all carnivorous dinosaurs. *Spinosaurus* ("thorn lizard") was as long as *Tyrannosaurus*, but less heavily built. Its most unusual feature was a tall skin "sail" which was held aloft by bony "swords" rising up to 1.6m (5ft 6in) from its backbone. Skull and jaw fragments seem to suggest that *Spinosaurus* had a long, low skull and a kinked snout. Similar traits are found in crocodiles, and in the skull of the theropod *Baryonx*.

WARMING UP
Two Spinosaurus *align themselves so that the sun's rays warm up the blood coursing through their tall skin sails.*

■ LIFESTYLE ■

There has been considerable discussion about the shape of *Spinosaurus*'s head. One theory suggests that it had a long, low head and crocodile-like teeth designed for eating fishes rather than killing other dinosaurs. This large theropod may have preyed mainly on big species of freshwater fishes, skewering its victims between its piercing, narrow teeth. Like a heron, *Spinosaurus* may have stood on the banks of lakes and rivers and grabbed prey in its jaws. Or perhaps it stood in shallow water, hooking out fishes by means of long, sharp thumb-claws like those of *Baryonyx*. This is purely guesswork, however, for no *Spinosaurus* claw bones have survived. Scientists disagree as to whether *Baryonyx* and *Spinosaurus* belonged to a single group of predatory dinosaurs. While they show similarities, there are also differences. For instance, *Spinosaurus* seems to have had far fewer teeth, suggesting that it may have scavenged flesh from the decaying corpses of big dinosaurs.

CATCHING FISHES
A Spinosaurus *seizes a slippery catch between jaws armed with piercing teeth like a crocodile's.*

Tail

Lateral caudal musculature

Chevron

■ SKIN SAIL ■

A large skin "sail" makes it unlikely that *Spinosaurus* overpowered and ate large dinosaurs, since a struggling prey could have fractured the sail's bony props. The sail's function is open to debate. If *Spinosaurus* were cold-blooded, the sail might have acted as a solar-heating panel, making *Spinosaurus* warm and active in the early morning, when other cold-blooded dinosaurs were still relatively cold and sluggish. *Spinosaurus* could have attacked them when they were incapable of escaping or fighting back. Alternatively, rival males might have used their sails to try to dominate each other, possibly slightly raising and lowering them for threat displays.

SAIL-BACKED DINOSAURS

Spinosaurus was the largest but not the only theropod to sport a sail on its back. Other sail-backed theropods included *Acrocanthosaurus* and *Becklespinax*, which had much lower sails. Unrelated sail-backed dinosaurs living in North Africa at the same time as *Spinosaurus* were the ornithopod *Ouranosaurus* and the sauropod *Rebbachisaurus*.

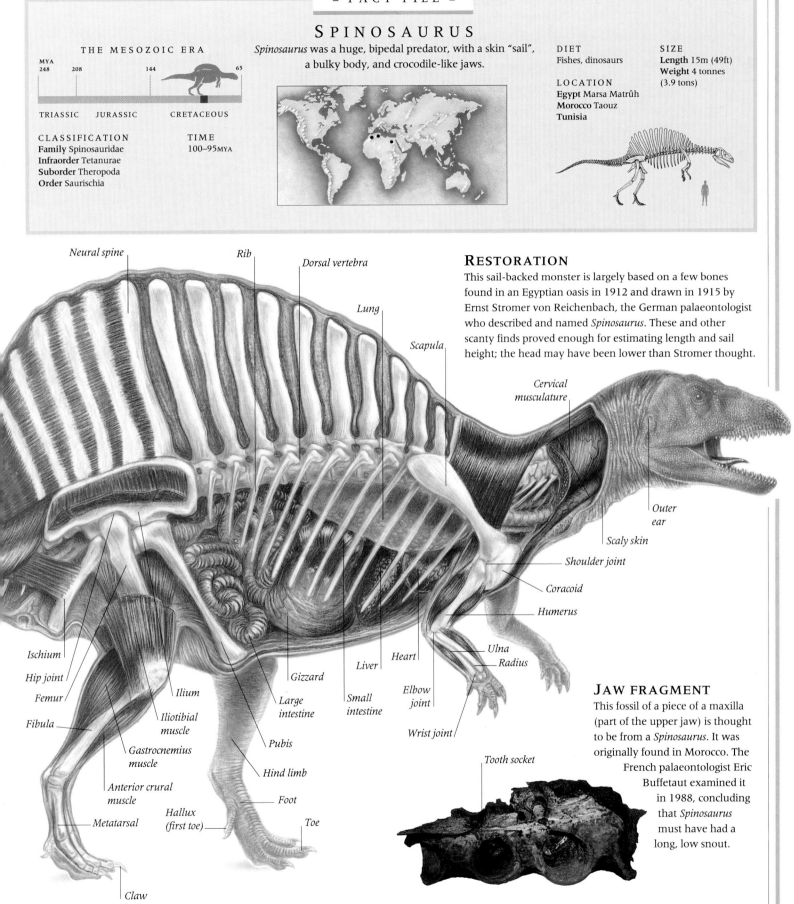

SPINOSAURUS

Spinosaurus was a huge, bipedal predator, with a skin "sail",
a bulky body, and crocodile-like jaws.

THE MESOZOIC ERA

MYA
248   208   144   65

TRIASSIC   JURASSIC   CRETACEOUS

CLASSIFICATION
Family Spinosauridae
Infraorder Tetanurae
Suborder Theropoda
Order Saurischia

TIME
100–95 MYA

DIET
Fishes, dinosaurs

LOCATION
Egypt Marsa Matrûh
Morocco Taouz
Tunisia

SIZE
Length 15m (49ft)
Weight 4 tonnes
(3.9 tons)

Neural spine
Rib
Dorsal vertebra
Lung
Scapula

RESTORATION

This sail-backed monster is largely based on a few bones
found in an Egyptian oasis in 1912 and drawn in 1915 by
Ernst Stromer von Reichenbach, the German palaeontologist
who described and named *Spinosaurus*. These and other
scanty finds proved enough for estimating length and sail
height; the head may have been lower than Stromer thought.

Cervical
musculature

Outer
ear

Scaly skin

Shoulder joint

Coracoid

Humerus

Ischium
Hip joint
Femur
Fibula

Ilium
Iliotibial
muscle
Gastrocnemius
muscle
Anterior crural
muscle
Metatarsal
Hallux
(first toe)

Gizzard
Large
intestine
Pubis
Hind limb
Foot
Toe

Small
intestine
Liver
Heart
Elbow
joint
Wrist joint

Ulna
Radius

Tooth socket

JAW FRAGMENT

This fossil of a piece of a maxilla
(part of the upper jaw) is thought
to be from a *Spinosaurus*. It was
originally found in Morocco. The
French palaeontologist Eric
Buffetaut examined it
in 1988, concluding
that *Spinosaurus*
must have had a
long, low snout.

Claw

GALLIMIMUS

EXCAVATION
Excavation exposes a Gallimimus *pelvis at Altan Ula, in Mongolia. This dinosaur was one of several found in that country in the late 1960s and early 1970s by a joint Polish-Mongolian team of palaeontologists, among whom were Zofia Kielan-Jaworowska and Halszka Osmólska from Poland, and Mongolia's Rinchen Barsbold.*

T HREE NEARLY COMPLETE skeletons from Mongolia's Gobi Desert make "chicken mimic" the best known ornithomimid, or ostrich dinosaur. Over twice the length of a modern-day ostrich, *Gallimimus* was the largest of a group of lightly built, bird-like theropods from Africa, East Asia, and western North America. It had a long, toothless beak, a slim neck, a short body, a stiffened tail, three-fingered hands, and slender legs. It also had a bird's intelligence and big, outward-facing eyes.

Caudal vertebrae

Ilium

Hip socket

Pubis

Chevron

Neural spine

Ischium

Femur

Tibia

Knee joint

Tibia

Ankle joint

Fibula

Metatarsals

Phalanx

HIND LIMBS Although short compared to *Struthiomimus's* legs, *Gallimimus's* slender hind limbs were long and strong, with bird-like metatarsal (upper foot) bones up to four-fifths the length of the femur (thigh bone). The combined length of the tibia and fibula (shin bones) and the metatarsals was greater than that of the femur. This relationship is seen in most fast-running dinosaurs, as well as in modern birds.

▪ LIFESTYLE ▪

Although *Gallimimus* has in the past been thought of as a plant-eating dinosaur, recent work has led to the conclusion that its diet was more carnivorous than herbivorous, and its grasping hand was probably used for catching small animals. *Gallimimus* would have snapped up large insects and their larvae, perhaps small vertebrates, and anything else it could swallow whole. *Gallimimus* lived deeper inland than its North American cousins, in a climate that was drier overall, but in which droughts and rainy seasons alternated. The ornithomimid walked along the banks of rivers, perhaps in company with plant-eating duckbills, armoured dinosaurs, and sauropods. With its head carried high above its narrow shoulders, *Gallimimus* scanned the land, alert to the threat of ambush by such carnosaurs as *Tarbosaurus*. Other enemies perhaps might have included *Deinocheirus* and *Therizinosaurus*, mysterious theropods known only from huge, gangling forelimbs armed with formidable claws. *Gallimimus's* only defence against such large, hungry predators was to accelerate away, increasing its stride as it gained speed – possibly running as fast as a modern ostrich.

DYNAMIC RESTORATION
A restored Gallimimus *is shown here scanning the land for danger, ready to break into a sprint.*

DEATH POSE

Ornithomimids have been found with the head and tail pulled back: they may have died of thirst in deserts or temporary droughts. Dry air would have helped to shrink the ligaments that tugged their necks and tails upwards. Lack of drinking water nearby might also have been the reason why these corpses were preserved in such complete form – few carrion-eaters would survive, who would otherwise have dismembered the corpses and scattered the bones.

Skull

Orbit

Naris

Toothless mandible

Cervical vertebrae

Dorsal vertebrae

SKELETON

This convincing reconstruction of a *Gallimimus* skeleton benefited from the discovery of the remains of several individuals in southern Mongolia. These include two almost complete skeletons, one skeleton complete except for the skull, a skull with other pieces of a skeleton, and bits and pieces from various individuals. Compared to *Struthiomimus*, *Gallimimus*'s small, light skull was longer, its hands were shorter, and its claws were more curved.

Rib

Scapula

Humerus

Radius

Ulna

Wrist joint

Metacarpal

Phalanx

HEAD AND NECK

A *Gallimimus* head and neck in close-up show how the eyes were held: they were high above the ground and their fields of vision did not overlap. This would make it hard to judge distance well, but with one eye on each side of the head and a neck it could twist around, *Gallimimus* would have been able to get an all-round view.

■ FACT FILE ■

GALLIMIMUS

Gallimimus was a bipedal omnivore with a bird-like beak, claws, and long legs.

THE MESOZOIC ERA

MYA 248	208	144	65
TRIASSIC	JURASSIC	CRETACEOUS	

LOCATION
Mongolia Ömnögov

TIME
73MYA

SIZE
Length 6m (19ft 6in)

CLASSIFICATION
Family Ornithomimidae
Infraorder Tetanurae
Suborder Theropoda
Order Saurischia

DIET
Insects, small vertebrates, and possibly fruits and leaves

STRUTHIOMIMUS

S TRUTHIOMIMUS ("ostrich-mimic") is the best-known of North America's large, bird-like, running dinosaurs. A skeleton found in Alberta, Canada, shows striking similarities to that of a modern ostrich (*Struthio*). Both have a small head, large eye sockets, a toothless beak, a long neck, a short back, long legs with longer shins than thighs, elongated upper foot bones, and three large, forward-facing toes with claws. Unlike the ostrich, *Struthiomimus* had gangling arms with clawed, three-fingered hands, and a long tail with a stiffened end; and it probably had bare, scaly skin.

MUSEUM MODEL
A restoration in the Royal Tyrrell Museum, Alberta.

❋ LIFESTYLE ❋

This dinosaur probably ranged over low, open countryside west of North America's great inland sea. Its large eyes and all-round vision gave it early warning of attack. Confronted by a small, hostile theropod, *Struthiomimus* could have delivered powerful kicks to drive it away. However, this would not have deterred larger predators, such as a tyrannosaur or a dromaeosaur pack, and *Struthiomimus* would have had to rely on speed, outrunning its enemies to escape. As it ran, it would probably have had the knack of sharply and suddenly changing direction every now and then, in order to throw off its pursuers, and it would have swung its tail from side to side to maintain balance. Some scientists think *Struthiomimus* might have been able to sprint away almost as fast as a modern horse can gallop. But emergencies demanding this sort of reaction should not have occurred often, for the dinosaur was constantly on the alert for danger.

❋ FEEDING ❋

Most scientists are convinced that *Struthiomimus* was an unfussy feeder. Its long claws – like those of a present-day sloth – were suited to hooking leafy twigs or picking fruits from bushes and low trees; these could then be snipped off by its sharp-edged, horny beak. Extra joints within the skull probably helped this dinosaur to work both halves of the beak, enabling it to manipulate foods held in the mouth, much as parrots dehusk nuts. *Struthiomimus* probably also fed on insects and small animals. By lowering its neck and making sudden lunging movements of its head, it could have snapped up large insects, lizards, and small, shrew-like mammals in the undergrowth.

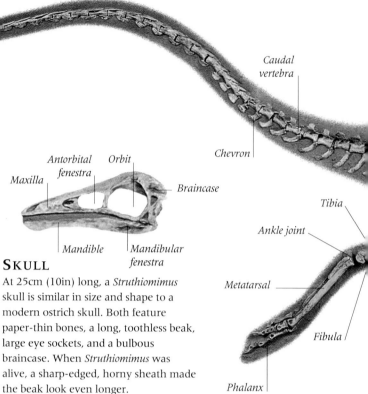

Caudal vertebra

Chevron

Antorbital fenestra · Orbit

Maxilla

Braincase

Tibia

Ankle joint

Metatarsal

Mandible · Mandibular fenestra

Fibula

Phalanx

SKULL
At 25cm (10in) long, a *Struthiomimus* skull is similar in size and shape to a modern ostrich skull. Both feature paper-thin bones, a long, toothless beak, large eye sockets, and a bulbous braincase. When *Struthiomimus* was alive, a sharp-edged, horny sheath made the beak look even longer.

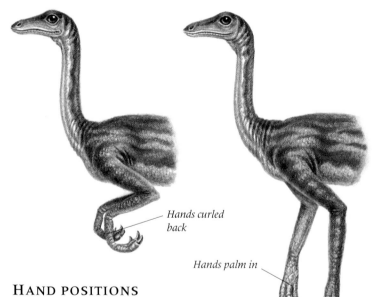

Hands curled back

Hands palm in

HAND POSITIONS
Some scientists believe that *Struthiomimus* and other ornithomimids held their hands curled back (left) and used them when necessary to scrape into the earth to dig up eggs to eat. Further study of the hand bones, however, has more recently persuaded many scientists that the ornithomimids held the hands palm in (right).

Skull

Dorsal
vertebra

Cervical
vertebra

Scapula   Humerus

Radius

Ulna

Rib

Gastralia

Pubis

Ilium

Hip socket

Femur

Ischium

Knee
joint

FOSSILIZED SKELETON

Apart from its long, bony tail and three-fingered hands, the skeleton of a *Struthiomimus* resembles a big, flightless, running bird. After death this individual dried out. As its ligaments shrank, they pulled the cervical vertebrae (neck bones) back into an agonized, unnatural-looking pose.

❊ FACT FILE ❊

STRUTHIOMIMUS

Struthiomimus was a bipedal omnivore. With long legs for running and a slender neck, it resembled an ostrich.

THE MESOZOIC ERA

MYA 248	208	144	65
TRIASSIC	JURASSIC	CRETACEOUS	

TIME
73MYA

DIET
Small animals, plants

CLASSIFICATION
Family Ornithomimidae
Infraorder Tetanurae
Suborder Theropoda
Order Saurischia

LOCATION
Canada Alberta

SIZE
Length 4m (13ft)
Weight 150kg (330lb)

RUNNING ABILITY

Convergent evolution made *Struthiomimus* (far right) a sprinter very like a modern ostrich (right). Studies of its limb bones convinced American palaeontologist Dale Russell that a scared *Struthiomimus* could run very fast indeed. Some experts believe it could reach an ostrich's top speed of 80km/h (50mph). Even at half that speed a *Struthiomimus* would have matched an Olympic 100m sprinter.

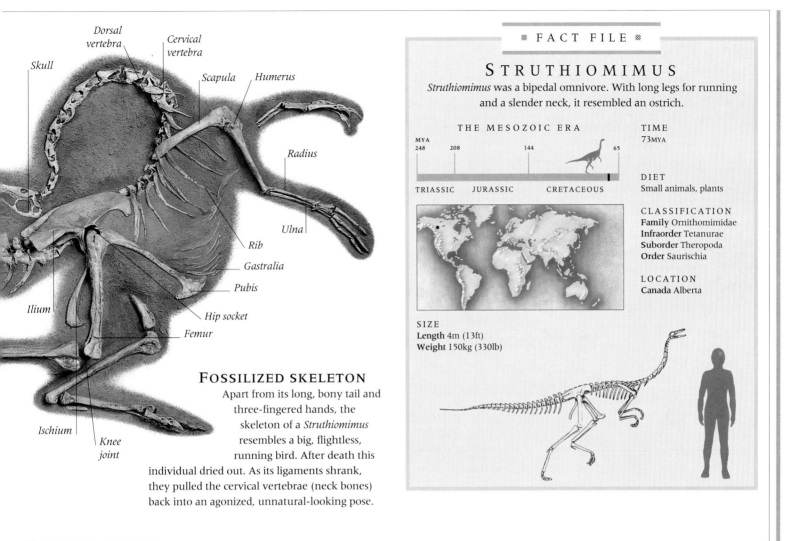

OVIRAPTOR

O VIRAPTOR ("EGG THIEF") was a bird-like
theropod with a bizarrely shaped head.
The strong,
toothless jaws ended in
a horny beak; two
sharp, bony prongs
jutted down from the
roof of the mouth, and the
head was surmounted by a
crest. The rest of *Oviraptor*'s
body was more like that of
a typical theropod, with
muscular arms, clawed, three-fingered hands, long
legs with three-toed feet, and a long, muscular tail.

■ LIFESTYLE ■

This toothless theropod gets its name from the notion
that it stole and ate horned dinosaurs' eggs: the first
Oviraptor philoceratops to be discovered had a smashed skull
and was found lying on a nest of *Protoceratops* eggs.
Oviraptor had strong jaws, and inside its mouth there were
bony prongs with which it could easily have crushed the
hard eggshells of other dinosaurs. A very similar method is
used by egg-eating snakes which use the sharp bones in
their necks to smash eggs. If an *Oviraptor* were surprised at
the nest, running away would have been the best strategy
in the face of its strongly built but less speedy enemies.
Sometimes, though, it seems that a *Protoceratops* stamped an
Oviraptor to death before it could escape or put up a fight.

■ TWO SPECIES ■

There were two *Oviraptor* species, both of which lived in Late
Cretaceous Mongolia. The animal shown in the main picture
on these pages is *Oviraptor philoceratops,* which lived in semi-
desert. In this habitat, eggs could have been important as a
source of moisture as well as nourishment. A second species,

DISCOVERY
*An expedition from the American
Museum of Natural History found*
Oviraptor *in the Gobi Desert in 1923.*

Oviraptor mongoliensis,
had a tall, domed crest,
much larger than that of
Oviraptor philoceratops.
This animal lived near
lakes and rivers rich in
shellfish. One scientist
concluded that it swam
in search of food,
sculling along with its
deep tail, scooping up
shellfish such as cockles
and mussels with its
hands, and crunching
them between its jaws.

OVIRAPTORID SKULL

An oviraptorid's toothless skull was
deep but lightweight. Many of
the skull bones were mere
struts, which enclosed huge
holes for eyes, nostrils, and
jaw muscles. Some
crestless skulls first
attributed to *Oviraptor*
young came from
adults of a different
type of oviraptorid:
Conchoraptor or *Ingenia.*

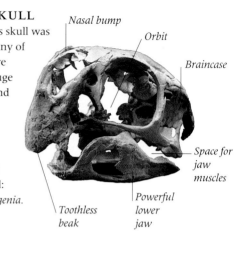

Nasal bump

Orbit

Braincase

Space for
jaw
muscles

Powerful
lower
jaw

Toothless
beak

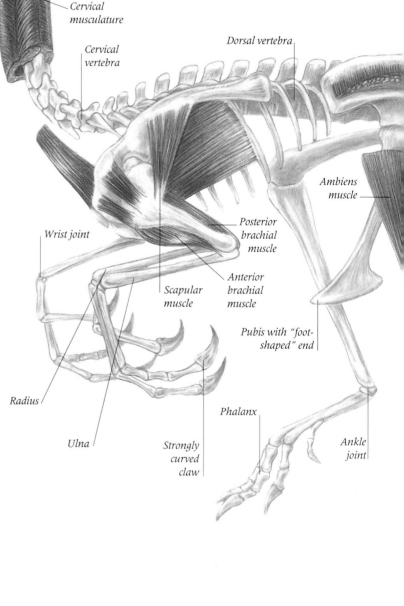

Cervical
musculature

Cervical
vertebra

Dorsal vertebra

Ambiens
muscle

Posterior
brachial
muscle

Wrist joint

Anterior
brachial
muscle

Scapular
muscle

Pubis with "foot-
shaped" end

Radius

Phalanx

Ulna

Strongly
curved
claw

Ankle
joint

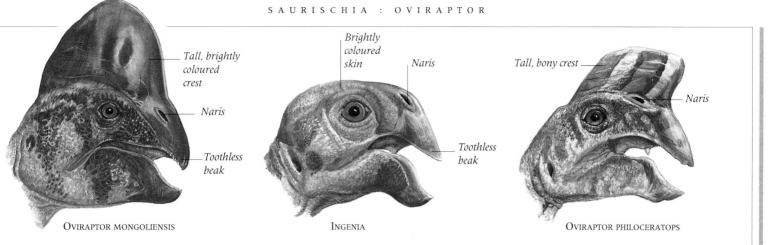

Tall, brightly coloured crest

Naris

Toothless beak

OVIRAPTOR MONGOLIENSIS

Brightly coloured skin

Naris

Toothless beak

INGENIA

Tall, bony crest

Naris

OVIRAPTOR PHILOCERATOPS

HIPS, HIND LIMBS, AND TAIL

As in most theropods, *Oviraptor* had slim hips, and its pubis ended in a "foot". It had elongated shins, and three weight-bearing toes per foot. The long tail's core was formed of 40 caudal vertebrae.

HEADS COMPARED

Crests perhaps sheathed in coloured horn crowned the males' heads in *Oviraptor mongoliensis* and *Oviraptor philoceratops*. They resemble the bony helmet of a cassowary, a bird that butts its way through forest undergrowth headfirst. Oviraptorids like *Ingenia* probably had brightly coloured skin, but no crest.

Bony helmet

Neural spine

Chevron

Caudal vertebra

Ischium

Iliotibial muscle

ARTICULATED SKELETON

Areas of muscle have been added to the neck, limbs, and tail on this illustration of an *Oviraptor philoceratops* skeleton. The fossil skeleton's upper jaw bones protruded beyond the lower jaw, but the latter was probably extended by a horny beak. Hands with "thumbs" shorter than the fingers, and the strongly curved claws, helped convince scientists that *Oviraptor* did not belong in the same group of toothless theropods as ostrich dinosaurs, such as *Struthiomimus*.

Lateral caudal musculature

CASSOWARY

Gastrocnemius muscle

Tibia

Fibula

Digital exterior muscle

Ankle joint

Hallux (first toe)

Phalanx

■ FACT FILE ■

OVIRAPTOR

Oviraptor was a bipedal, bird-like predator. It possessed a deep beak containing two tooth-like bones, strong forelimbs with curved claws, and a long tail.

THE MESOZOIC ERA

MYA				
248	208	144		65

TRIASSIC   JURASSIC   CRETACEOUS

SIZE
Length 2m (6ft 6in)
Weight 33kg (73lb)

TIME
83–73MYA

LOCATION
Mongolia Ömnögov

DIET
Molluscs, eggs

CLASSIFICATION
Family Oviraptoridae
Infraorder Tetanurae
Suborder Theropoda
Order Saurischia

TROODON

N AMED IN 1856 from a small, sharp tooth, the turkey-sized *Troodon* ("wounding tooth") was at first believed to be a lizard, and then a bone-headed dinosaur. *Troodon*'s tooth was not matched with bones until the 1980s. The bones showed that this dinosaur had been a sharp-eyed, bird-like theropod with a bigger brain for its body size than almost any other dinosaur. Its hands could grasp, and they possessed large, sharp, hook-like claws. Its extremely long, slim legs ended in elongated feet with three weight-bearing toes, the second toe armed with a deep, curved claw a bit like that of *Deinonychus*. Despite this similarity, some scientists believe that *Troodon* and *Deinonychus* were not closely related.

Partly forward-facing eye

Naris

Wide mouth

Long, flexible neck

FRONT VIEW OF HEAD

This model stresses *Troodon*'s alert, bird-like head and large, partly forward-facing eyes. The overlapping visual fields of the two eyes may have allowed accurate judgement of distance, helping *Troodon* to pounce upon fast-moving, rat-like mammals and young, agile, hypsilophodontids. Since we cannot observe *Troodon*'s behaviour, we cannot tell for certain if it hunted at night.

Partly forward-facing eye

Long, slim leg

Sharp finger-claw

Large, swivelling second-toe claw

▪ LIFESTYLE ▪

Scientists suspect that *Troodon*'s anatomy made this theropod a deadly hunter of small mammals that ventured out to feed at dusk. Most dinosaurs had eyes on the sides of their heads, but *Troodon*'s large eyes faced partly forwards, more like ours. This would probably have given it binocular vision, making this predator particularly good at focusing upon small, swiftly moving animals no bigger than rats. If the retinas of its eyes were well-endowed with low-light-sensitive rods, *Troodon* could see the creatures even if they scampered around at night, safe from day-active predatory dinosaurs. *Troodon* could have stalked through forest glades, watching for the slightest movement.

▪ TYPES OF PREY ▪

There is much discussion among experts about the prey that this agile theropod might have hunted. If *Troodon* glimpsed a mammal running for cover, it might have darted after it to grasp it between rows of coarsely serrated teeth. *Troodon* also seems to have been fierce enough to have attacked larger animals, which it could have seized with the sharp claws on its hands and feet. But its second-toe claws were not designed to deal such powerful blows as those of *Deinonychus*. Unlike that dinosaur, *Troodon* could hardly kick a big, plant-eating dinosaur to death while clinging to its back. So *Troodon* might not have been a hunter of big game, instead attacking lizards, snakes, mammals and young dinosaurs. Another difference between *Troodon* and *Deinonychus* was that *Troodon* lacked *Deinonychus*'s system of bony tendons that stiffened the tail, making it exceptionally useful as a balancing rod in fast running or in combat.

EXTERNAL FEATURES

Elongated legs allowed *Troodon* to take enormous strides and so to run very fast indeed, probably with its big second-toe claw held well above the ground. Such theropods probably ran faster than any others living at the time, except perhaps for the fleet-footed avimimid dinosaurs of Asia.

Serrated, cutting edge

SAW-EDGED TOOTH

Troodon's small, triangular, saw-edged teeth were flattened from side to side like a knife-blade, and curved along their length. Along their cutting edges they were armed with big, hooked denticles. There were up to 25 teeth on each side of the upper jaw, with precisely 25 on each side of the lower jaw.

TROODON

Troodon was a bipedal predator with keen eyesight and a relatively large brain.

THE MESOZOIC ERA

248   208   144   65

TRIASSIC   JURASSIC   CRETACEOUS

LOCATION
Canada Alberta
USA Montana,
Wyoming

CLASSIFICATION
Family Troodontidae
Infraorder Tetanurae
Suborder Theropoda
Order Saurischia

DIET
Lizards, mammals,
dinosaur hatchlings

TIME
73–65MYA

SIZE
Length 2m (6ft 6in)

TROODON AND DINOSAUROID

In the early 1980s, the American palaeontologist Dale Russell suggested that, had dinosaurs survived, the big-brained, bipedal, bird-like *Troodon* with grasping hands (left), might have given rise to an intelligent and human-looking descendant like the "dinosauroid" (right).

Long head
Partly forward-facing eye
Neck
Shoulder
Knee
Hand
Finger
Horizontal body
Elbow
Tail
Ankle
Large, swivelling claw
Foot
Claw
Toe

Rounded head
Large, forward-facing eye
Shoulder
Hip
Elbow
Hand
Finger
Knee
Toe
Ankle
Foot

SKELETON

Bones in *Troodon*'s skull, wrists, and hands, and the hinged claws on the second toes of its feet, show some similarity to the formidable dromaeosaurid *Deinonychus*. But *Troodon* had no bony tendons to stiffen the tail.

Caudal vertebrae
Hip socket
Ilium
Dorsal vertebrae
Cervical vertebrae
Braincase
Orbit
Neural spine
Cervical rib
Mandible
Tooth
Chevron
Ischium
Scapula
Humerus
Femur
Wrist joint
Knee joint
Shoulder joint
Radius
Claw
Rib
Gastralium
Ulna
Metacarpal
Tibia
Elbow joint
Phalanx
Pubis
Ankle joint
Metatarsals
Phalanges
Claw
Large, swivelling claw

FOSSIL FINDS

Batches of fossilized *Troodon* eggs were found at sites in Montana during the 1980s. Nearby, eggs of a small ornithopod called *Orodromeus* were also found, though the relationship between these two dinosaurs is not certain.

DEINONYCHUS

THE DISCOVERY OF several nearly whole skeletons of this agile killer in the 1960s undermined old notions that dinosaurs were small-brained, sluggish reptiles. *Deinonychus* – "terrible claw" – was no longer than a small car and no heavier than a human, yet for its size it was more formidably armed than almost any other theropod. Large fangs rimmed the powerful jaws. Long, strong arms bore three-fingered, grasping hands with sharp claws. Most fearsome was the scythe-like claw on the second toe of each of its muscular legs.

Blade-like tooth

Grasping hand

Strong arm

"Terrible claw"

Stiffened tail

RESTORATION

This museum model depicts *Deinonychus* striped somewhat like a tiger. We know that the tiger's stripes break up its outline as it hides in long grass or prowls through the dappled sunlight of a forest floor. *Deinonychus* had no grass to hide in, but it would have benefited from camouflage when it lurked among tall ferns or under trees. Its true coloration, though, remains a matter of guesswork.

◼ LIFESTYLE ◼

Scientists suspect that *Deinonychus* scoured the countryside in packs. Each individual would have snapped up any lizards or small mammals in its path, but gang members joined forces to attack large animals. Working together, they could bring down dinosaurs much bigger than themselves, as wolves combine for killing caribou and cape hunting dogs subdue a zebra. One clue to such behaviour is a fossil site containing the remains of four *Deinonychus* and a much larger *Tenontosaurus*. What took place here can only be guessed at, but one interpretation is that a hunting pack of *Deinonychus*, a good deal more than four in number, had raced in upon the horse-sized ornithopod, stiffened tails swinging to balance violent body movements as they leapt to the attack. The deaths of at least four *Deinonychus* suggest that heavy losses may have occurred during incidents of this kind. Scientists think that for large prey, *Deinonychus* probably jumped into the attack, then balanced on one foot and kicked with the other, tearing deep gashes in the victim's belly. Alternatively it could have performed a two-footed, hopping pounce to land on the victim. Threatened by such a gang, a *Tenontosaurus* might have rolled over on to its attackers or turned suddenly to swing at them with its heavy tail. Such tactics may have killed several of the assailants. But meanwhile the rest would have swarmed all over the ornithischian, inflicting other wounds. Weakened from loss of blood, the victim soon collapsed and died.

Bony tendon

STIFFENED TAIL

Deinonychus's long tail stuck out like a ramrod thanks to stiffening devices that locked together all caudal vertebrae (tail bones) except those closest to the body. From above each vertebra, a forked, rod-like, bony tendon overlapped as many as the next eight vertebrae. Below each vertebra, a forward-pointing extension of the chevron interlocked with neighbouring chevrons, further stiffening the tail.

Caudal vertebra

Chevron extensions

A TENONTOSAURUS IS ATTACKED

Three Deinonychus *(shown here with blue-green backs) attack a big ornithopod called* Tenontosaurus. *With their combined assault they could kill creatures several times their size.*

FRONT VIEW OF HEAD

A prey's-eye view of *Deinonychus*'s head shows powerful jaws formidably rimmed with big, saw-edged teeth like curved daggers. *Deinonychus*'s jaws gaped wide, then clamped upon its victim and tugged backwards so that the teeth sliced easily through flesh. The fierce theropod then tore out and ate a chunk of meaty muscle. Meanwhile the rest of the pack would do the same. Like a wildebeest savaged by hunting dogs, the victim rapidly weakened, fell, and died from blood loss and shock.

Naris

Jaw adductor muscle

Saw-edged tooth

DYNAMIC SKELETON

Reconstructed leaping, and balanced by its stiffened tail, this mounted skeleton stresses *Deinonychus*'s agile and aggressive character. The skull was big but lightly built, with large holes for the eyes and jaw muscles. The jaws bore long rows of fangs. As the arms extended, the hands turned palm-down, and their long, curved claws formed effective grasping weapons. The long hind limbs ended in feet with two weight-bearing toes, and another toe that was formidably armed with a big, hinged "sickle claw".

Cervical vertebra

Cervical rib

Coracoid

Scapula

Rib

Dorsal vertebra

Ilium

Chevron

Hip joint

Femur

Pubis

Knee joint

Ischium

Fibula

Tibia

Ankle joint

Metatarsal

Phalanx

Infratemporal fenestra

Orbit

Antorbital fenestra

Shoulder joint

Mandible

Tooth

Claw

Humerus

Radius

Wrist joint

Metacarpal

Elbow joint

Ulna

Claw

Phalanx

"Terrible claw"

FOOT BONES

Deinonychus's foot had a long, swivelling claw on its second toe, known as the "terrible claw". This was typical of dromaeosaurids, the theropod family to which *Deinonychus* belonged. *Deinonychus* could menacingly raise each foot's second toe while supporting itself on the long third and fourth toes.

Sharp claw

Second toe

First toe

Third toe

Fourth toe

Eye faced chiefly sideways

Powerful, sturdy neck

Shoulder

Scaly skin

Powerful jaws capable of a wide gape

Hand turned palm-down

"Terrible claw"

Metatarsal

First toe

Second toe

Enlarged joint

Claw

Third toe

Fourth toe

Phalanx

LIKE A BIRD

Deinonychus could run, swerve, and keep its balance as skilfully as a big, flightless bird. Indeed, this fierce predator was built much like a bird, even having a somewhat backward-angled pubis. But unlike such bird-like theropods as *Troodon*, *Deinonychus* differed from birds in having a full-length third metatarsal (upper foot bone).

Elbow

Hand with claws capable of grasping

SWIVELLING TOE CLAW

Deinonychus probably retracted its long second toe (above) mainly to avoid blunting the sharp claw tip by scraping it on the ground when it walked or ran. Enlarged joints on the phalanges (toe bones) improved the leverage exerted by toe-retracting muscles. An attacking *Deinonychus* swung the toe down and forwards in a slashing arc (right), delivering stabbing blows. For its body size, its swivelling claws were outsize weapons, like the immense canines of an extinct sabre-toothed cat.

Arc of claw movement

"Terrible claw" in flexed position

"Terrible claw"

Third toe

RIVALS IN COMBAT

Deinonychus males might have fought over females or land: leaping to the attack with claws flailing, and tails as stiffly extended as balancing poles. Yet savage combats could have had fatal results. Perhaps rivals used harmless threat displays instead.

SITE OF DISCOVERY

Half way down this barren hill, 60m (200ft) high, John Ostrom of Yale University's Peabody Museum glimpsed the first fossil fragments of Deinonychus one day in 1964. Scientists unearthed several specimens and a Tenontosaurus that had evidently been their intended prey.

Stripes for camouflage

Strongly stiffened tail

JOHN OSTROM

This American palaeontologist's description of Deinonychus in 1969 undermined the old assumption that all dinosaurs had been cold-blooded. Dr Ostrom argued that erect posture pointed to raised body temperature. He also claimed that small, warm-blooded theropods had evolved into birds.

Thigh

Long hind limb for walking or hopping

Foot with three weight-bearing toes

Claw

■ FACT FILE ■

DEINONYCHUS

Deinonychus was a bipedal predator. Although small in stature, it was heavily armed with blade-like teeth and large claws on its hands and feet.

THE MESOZOIC ERA

MYA 248	208	144	65

TRIASSIC   JURASSIC   CRETACEOUS

SIZE
Length 3m (10ft)
Weight 60kg (130lb)

TIME
113MYA

LOCATION
USA Montana, Wyoming

DIET
Herbivorous dinosaurs

CLASSIFICATION
Family Dromaeosauridae
Infraorder Tetanurae
Suborder Theropoda
Order Saurischia

ARCHAEOPTERYX

L ONG FAMOUS as the oldest known bird, *Archaeopteryx* ("ancient wing") is in fact closely related to the dinosaurs. Its hands, hips, legs, and skull were very like those of small theropods, and research has suggested that it probably evolved from these. Unlike modern birds it had teeth, clawed fingers and a bony tail core. It is likely that *Archaeopteryx* is not the direct ancestor of modern birds, but represents an offshoot from the earliest line of birds, branching out soon after the time when birds evolved from the original theropod stock. Some scientists claim that all birds, including *Archaeopteryx*, can be counted as dinosaurs.

■ LIFESTYLE ■

A comparison between the bones of *Archaeopteryx* and those of modern flying birds suggests that it was less capable of powerful, flapping flight than, for example, a pigeon. It has been thought that *Archaeopteryx* took off by running along the ground and leaping into the air, vigorously flapping its wings. This is unlikely since *Archaeopteryx* must have lacked the well-developed breast muscles used by modern birds that take off from level ground. *Archaeopteryx* probably spent a lot of time perched in trees, having hauled itself up the trunks by its finger-claws. From here it would have launched itself out on short, weak, fluttering flights. Low, scrubby conifers were the tallest trees in its habitat, on a group of semi-desert islands in what is now Germany. Other speculations about *Archaeopteryx*'s lifestyle include the suggestion that it swam and fished in lagoons among the islands. The primitive bird is more likely to have roamed the beaches, scavenging the flesh of stranded fish, king crabs, ammonites, and worms, or snapping up insects blown down to the coast by winds heading out to sea. Such winds may also have blown *Archaeopteryx* specimens out to sea, to drown and be preserved as the fossils we know today.

TREE DWELLER
Archaeopteryx *may have perched in trees, using its wings and tail for balance.*

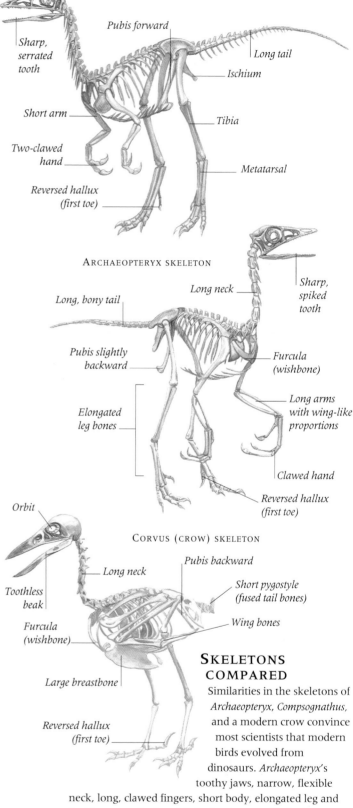

COMPSOGNATHUS SKELETON

Pubis forward

Sharp, serrated tooth

Long tail

Ischium

Short arm

Tibia

Two-clawed hand

Metatarsal

Reversed hallux (first toe)

ARCHAEOPTERYX SKELETON

Long neck

Sharp, spiked tooth

Long, bony tail

Pubis slightly backward

Furcula (wishbone)

Long arms with wing-like proportions

Elongated leg bones

Clawed hand

Reversed hallux (first toe)

Orbit

CORVUS (CROW) SKELETON

Long neck

Pubis backward

Toothless beak

Short pygostyle (fused tail bones)

Furcula (wishbone)

Wing bones

SKELETONS COMPARED

Large breastbone

Reversed hallux (first toe)

Similarities in the skeletons of *Archaeopteryx, Compsognathus,* and a modern crow convince most scientists that modern birds evolved from dinosaurs. *Archaeopteryx*'s toothy jaws, narrow, flexible neck, long, clawed fingers, short body, elongated leg and foot bones, and other details closely resemble features found in small carnivorous dinosaurs like *Compsognathus*. A crow is broadly similar but with some features that represent evolutionary development towards better flight.

MOUNTED SKELETON

A mounted museum skeleton depicts an *Archaeopteryx* on the ground. Like a young hoatzin (a living bird), it might have used its clawed fingers to climb low trees.

FOSSILIZED FEATHER

This fossil feather belonged to *Archaeopteryx*. Its asymmetric primary wing feathers match those of pigeons and prove that *Archaeopteryx* could fly or glide.

FEATHER IMPRESSIONS

Feather impressions plainly show up in a slab of limestone containing a fossil *Archaeopteryx*. Only very fine-grained rock preserves traces of such fragile parts as feathers. This rock comes from a Bavarian quarry.

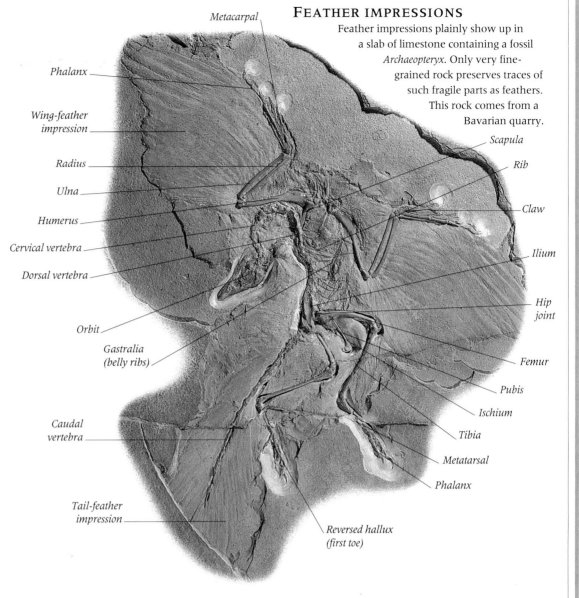

Metacarpal
Phalanx
Wing-feather impression
Radius
Ulna
Humerus
Cervical vertebra
Dorsal vertebra
Orbit
Gastralia (belly ribs)
Caudal vertebra
Tail-feather impression
Scapula
Rib
Claw
Ilium
Hip joint
Femur
Pubis
Ischium
Tibia
Metatarsal
Phalanx
Reversed hallux (first toe)

ARCHAEOPTERYX

A primitive bird closely related to dinosaurs, *Archaeopteryx* had sharp teeth, clawed fingers, and a bony core in its tail. It dated from an early period in the evolution of the class Aves (birds).

THE MESOZOIC ERA

MYA 248	208	144	65
TRIASSIC	JURASSIC		CRETACEOUS

TIME
156–150MYA

SIZE
Length 60cm (2ft)

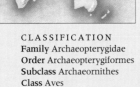

LOCATION
Germany Bavaria

DIET
Insects, small vertebrates

CLASSIFICATION
Family Archaeopterygidae
Order Archaeopterygiformes
Subclass Archaeornithes
Class Aves

TAKING OFF

Archaeopteryx spreads its wings in preparation for flight.

AVIMIMUS

T HE ONLY KNOWN member of its family, "bird mimic" seems to have been a bird-like, running dinosaur. It was a lightweight, long-legged creature with a short, deep head, toothless beak, long, curved neck, well-developed tail, and short forelimbs. No fossil feathers have been found, but the rough ridge on one forearm bone resembles a modern bird's attachment for flight feathers. In the region equivalent to the human wrist, the bases of the metacarpals (palm bones) are fused together in a very bird-like way. *Avimimus* is thought to have been able to fold its wings like a bird.

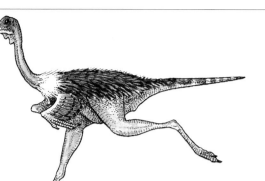

DINOSAUR ROADRUNNER
Avimimus appears here dashing along like a roadrunner: a fast-running, long-legged, ground-dwelling North American cuckoo that snaps up insects, small rodents, and reptiles.

▪ LIFESTYLE ▪

Scientists believe that *Avimimus* shared open plains with harmless dinosaurs, such as the ornithomimid *Gallimimus* and the sauropod *Quaesitosaurus*, as well as with dangerous enemies related to *Deinonychus*. It is likely that *Avimimus* sprinted on its long legs after small animals, darting its head down to seize them in its beak. The beak's partly ridged rim would have gripped wriggling prey too firmly for it to escape. An alternative idea is that *Avimimus* was a herbivore that used its beak for biting off and eating plants. The creature's forelimbs were probably too short to serve as a wing. If feathered, they may have served simply to keep the body warm, although there is another theory that suggests *Avimimus* might have used them for trapping flying insects. One Russian scientist, however, believes that details of its skull and arm bones imply that *Avimimus* could take off and fly short distances. If so, "bird mimic" represents a line of flying dinosaurs quite separate from birds. Most scientists discount that possibility. Some, though, do suspect that many small theropods had a covering of feathers that have left no fossil traces. (Feather impressions survive only in extremely fine-grained rocks, like the limestone that bears the imprints of *Archaeopteryx's* wings and tail.)

SERGEI KURZANOV
The Russian palaeontologist, who named Avimimus *and the* Avimimidae *in 1981.*

DESERT EXPEDITION
Workers rest on a dinosaur hunt in Mongolia's Gobi Desert, where Avimimus *fossils were discovered.*

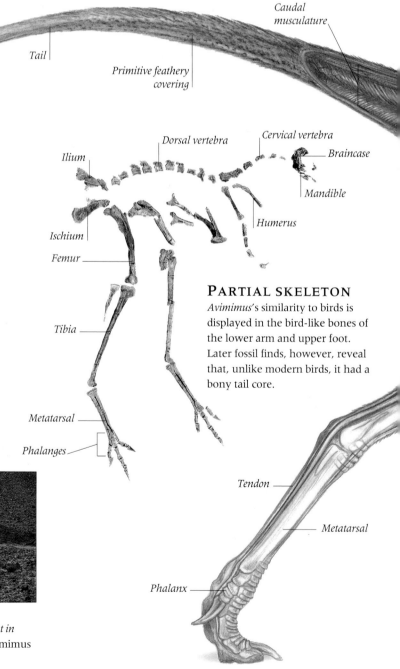

Tail

Caudal musculature

Primitive feathery covering

Dorsal vertebra *Cervical vertebra*

Ilium *Braincase*

Mandible

Ischium *Humerus*

Femur

PARTIAL SKELETON
Avimimus's similarity to birds is displayed in the bird-like bones of the lower arm and upper foot. Later fossil finds, however, reveal that, unlike modern birds, it had a bony tail core.

Tibia

Metatarsal

Phalanges

Tendon

Metatarsal

Phalanx

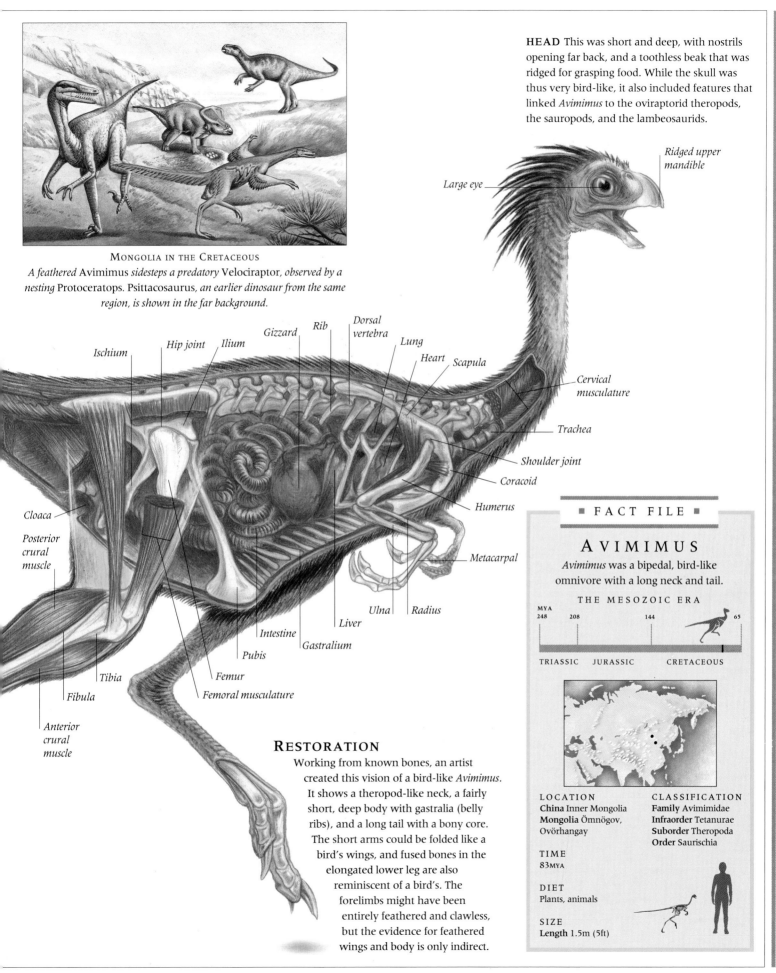

MONGOLIA IN THE CRETACEOUS
A feathered Avimimus *sidesteps a predatory* Velociraptor, *observed by a nesting* Protoceratops. Psittacosaurus, *an earlier dinosaur from the same region, is shown in the far background.*

HEAD This was short and deep, with nostrils opening far back, and a toothless beak that was ridged for grasping food. While the skull was thus very bird-like, it also included features that linked *Avimimus* to the oviraptorid theropods, the sauropods, and the lambeosaurids.

Ridged upper mandible

Large eye

Ischium

Hip joint

Ilium

Gizzard

Rib

Dorsal vertebra

Lung

Heart

Scapula

Cervical musculature

Trachea

Shoulder joint

Coracoid

Humerus

Cloaca

Posterior crural muscle

Metacarpal

Ulna

Radius

Intestine

Liver

Gastralium

Pubis

Femur

Femoral musculature

Tibia

Fibula

Anterior crural muscle

RESTORATION

Working from known bones, an artist created this vision of a bird-like *Avimimus*. It shows a theropod-like neck, a fairly short, deep body with gastralia (belly ribs), and a long tail with a bony core. The short arms could be folded like a bird's wings, and fused bones in the elongated lower leg are also reminiscent of a bird's. The forelimbs might have been entirely feathered and clawless, but the evidence for feathered wings and body is only indirect.

ORNITHOLESTES

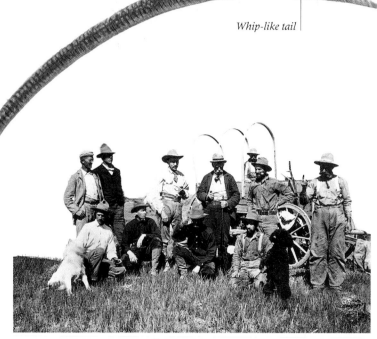

Whip-like tail

A WHIP-LIKE TAIL comprised more than half of *Ornitholestes*'s length. Large individuals probably grew as long as a tall human, yet weighed no more than a medium-sized dog. *Ornitholestes* had a stronger, deeper skull than two other well-known small theropods, *Compsognathus* and *Coelophysis*. Each hand appears to have borne a short, sharp-clawed thumb, and two, long, clawed fingers. Sharp teeth rimmed only the front half of the jaws. Some scientists believe *Ornitholestes* had a nasal crest. The dinosaur is placed in the family Coeluridae, which comprised a number of small theropods.

▪ LIFESTYLE ▪

The scientist who named *Ornitholestes* ("bird robber") imagined the speedy theropod killing and eating the crow-sized early bird *Archaeopteryx*. Both of these creatures lived at about the same time, but it is not certain if they would have lived in the same area. *Ornitholestes* might well have pounced on other early birds, however, and on bird-like dinosaurs and pterosaurs. More often, it probably ate lizards and other small creatures, such as lizard-like sphenodontians, large insects, dinosaur hatchlings, and small mammals. It searched them out as it sprinted through the fern meadows and riverside forests of Late Jurassic Wyoming. Grasping captured prey firmly between its sharp thumb- and finger-claws, *Ornitholestes* brought its victims to its jaws, where it either bit them to death or swallowed them alive.

▪ PACK HUNTER OR SCAVENGER ▪

Another possibility is that *Ornitholestes* was a pack hunter. If this was the case, predatory gangs may have dared to take on ornithopods as big as a half-grown *Camptosaurus*. A third possibility is that *Ornitholestes* fed on carrion. Like jackals at a lion's kill, a pack of *Ornitholestes* might have stolen mouthfuls of flesh from the carcass of a dead sauropod. One after another, agile *Ornitholestes* could have nipped quickly in and out of the huge corpse's body cavity under the noses of its killers, a troop of *Allosaurus* or other large flesh-eaters. These big, heavy dinosaurs, sated with flesh, would have been too slow to stop such small, swift scavengers.

FOSSIL-HUNTERS
Henry Fairfield Osborn, director of the American Museum of Natural History, and other fossil-hunters posed for this photograph in 1899. In 1900, at Bone Cabin Quarry, Wyoming, they found what are still the only known Ornitholestes *skull and jaws. Osborn formally named and described* Ornitholestes *in 1903.*

OLD RESTORATION

NEW RESTORATION

OLD AND NEW RESTORATIONS
Most of the old restorations of *Ornitholestes* show it in a rather sluggish pose, dragging its tail on the ground like a lizard, as in the upper view above. The lower view shows today's concept of this dinosaur as a dynamic predator, with its long tail held clear of the ground to balance its level-backed body, and an S-shaped neck. This restoration is shown with the much disputed nasal crest.

Caudal vertebra

Chevron

Neural spine

Ischium

Ilium

Hip joint

FLESHING OUT THE BONES

A skeleton partly clothed in flesh shows the structure of this long-tailed, short-legged theropod. Scaly skin may have masked any nasal crest. The fairly long arms ended in hands bearing three clawed, grasping digits. Each hind limb had a longer femur than tibia. The pelvis is incomplete and only bits of the feet survive.

Dorsal vertebra

Rib

Scapula

Pointed tooth

Tapering snout

Long, narrow head

Flexible neck

Shoulder joint

Humerus

A SCARCE PREDATOR

Ornitholestes has been called "the only good small theropod" found in the Late Jurassic's Morrison Formation rocks. Few fossils remain, either because small predators were rarer than giants like *Allosaurus* or just because the big theropods' thick bones proved more durable.

Femur

Tibia

Fibula

Hind limb

Knee joint

Radius

Ulna

Wrist joint

Metacarpal

Phalanx

Claw

Hallux (first toe)

Phalanx

■ FACT FILE ■

ORNITHOLESTES

Ornitholestes was a lightweight, bipedal flesh-eater with long claws.

THE MESOZOIC ERA

MYA 248	208	144	65
TRIASSIC	JURASSIC	CRETACEOUS	

LOCATION
USA Wyoming

DIET
Small vertebrates

SIZE
Length 2m (6ft 6in)
Weight 12.5kg (28lb)

CLASSIFICATION
Family Coeluridae
Infraorder Tetanurae
Suborder Theropoda
Order Saurischia

TIME
150MYA

CRANIUM AND MANDIBLE

This reconstruction is based on the theory that *Ornitholestes* may have had a bony crest like *Proceratosaurus*'s nasal horn. *Ornitholestes*, like most small theropods, had large holes for the eyes. Even so, skull bones shielding the bony opening behind the eyes resembled those of big flesh-eating dinosaurs like *Tyrannosaurus*. The lower jaw was strong, downcurved, and rather deep. The front teeth were almost conical; others were small, curved, pointed blades.

Braincase

Orbit

Antorbital fenestra

Bony crest

Naris

Maxillary fenestra

Infratemporal fenestra

Mandible

Sharp pointed tooth

COMPSOGNATHUS

T HE AGILE little predator *Compsognathus* ("elegant jaw") was one of the smallest known dinosaurs. *Compsognathus* was delicately built and bird-like, with a narrow, pointed head, jaws armed with small, sharp teeth, a flexible neck, a compact body, and a relatively long tail. The legs were long and bird-like. Surprisingly, the short arms evidently bore two-fingered hands, like those of the huge tyrannosaurids of much later times. The sharp-toothed jaws and clawed phalanges are typical theropod features, but the short, two-fingered forelimbs and other details place *Compsognathus* in a family of its own.

■ LIFESTYLE ■

Compsognathus lived on the same semi-desert islands (an archipelago now forming part of Europe) as the first known bird, *Archaeopteryx*. The skeletons of the two creatures are so similar that scientists mistook several *Archaeopteryx* fossils for those of *Compsognathus* before they noticed faint feather impressions in the rock that held the fossil bones of *Archaeopteryx*. Only two fossil specimens of *Compsognathus* are known: one from southern Germany is roughly the size of a chicken, and is seemingly half-grown, and the other, about the size of a turkey, from southeast France, has the fully formed bones of an adult. Despite its small size, *Compsognathus* might have been the largest carnivorous land animal on its archipelago. These semi-desert islands would not have had sufficient vegetation to nourish the number of big plant-eaters that larger carnivores would have needed as a meat supply. We can imagine *Compsognathus* stalking through the undergrowth, its keen eyes quick to catch the slightest movement of large insects, lizards, or mouse-like mammals. It could have outrun lizards and might have chased a young *Archaeopteryx* if it surprised one on the ground. In the morning, basking lizards, still sluggish after cooling down at night, would have been easy prey. *Compsognathus* probably bit large victims while gripping them with its hands; the claws were not sickle-shaped weapons for inflicting wounds. Smaller creatures would have been swallowed whole.

AGILE HUNTER
One of the tiniest of all predatory dinosaurs, Compsognathus *used its speed to catch small vertebrates.*

LIGHTWEIGHT SKULL
For a small theropod, the skull of *Compsognathus* was large but low. It tapered to the snout and was lightly built, with huge openings, especially the orbits (eye sockets). The mandible (lower jaw) was slender, and the teeth were sharp, curved, and far apart.

Braincase

Orbit

Antorbital fenestra

Tooth

Mandible

Infratemporal fenestra

Long, narrow head

Tapering snout

Outer ear

Sharp, curved tooth

Jaw adductor muscle

Long, flexible neck

FORELIMBS
These were short but sturdy. Each hand had only two fingers and their claws seem too weakly curved for cutting or piercing. Scientists once mistook the French specimen's forelimbs for the flippers of a swimming animal.

Short forelimb

Hand

Finger

Claw

COMPSOGNATHUS

Compsognathus was a tiny, fast-moving predator with sharp teeth.

THE MESOZOIC ERA

MYA
248   208   144   65

TRIASSIC   JURASSIC   CRETACEOUS

TIME
156–150MYA

LOCATION
France Var
Germany Bavaria

DIET
Invertebrates, lizards

CLASSIFICATION
Family Compsognathidae
Infraorder Tetanurae
Suborder Theropoda
Order Saurischia

SIZE
Length 70cm–1.4m
(2ft 4in–4ft 6in)
Weight 3kg (6.5lb)

Eye

Forelimb

Slender body

Long, thin tail

Foot

TOP VIEW

An overhead view stresses the long, lean appearance of the head, neck, body, and tail. This streamlined shape seems well suited to chasing prey through thick vegetation.

Long tail

Scaly skin

FOSSILIZED SKELETON

After death, shrinking ligaments and tendons raised the tail and pulled back the head of this fossilized *Compsognathus*. Detailed examination of the fossil has revealed a tiny skeleton lying inside the ribcage. This belonged to a long-tailed lizard known as *Bavarisaurus*.

Hip

Cervical vertebra

Short thigh

HIND LIMBS

Compsognathus had the long legs, with longer shins than thighs, and elongated feet typical of speedy dinosaurs. It ran on the second, third, and fourth toes. The short-clawed first toe formed a spur, but the fifth toe had shrunk to a mere sliver of a metatarsal bone.

Caudal vertebra

Orbit

Ischium

Tibia

Long shin

Hallux (first toe)

Ankle

Foot

Claw

Rib

Femur

Phalanx

SAUROPODOMORPHS

T HE SAURISCHIAN suborder Sauropodomorpha ("lizard-feet forms") comprised small to immense, bipedal to quadrupedal herbivores with small heads, long necks, bulky bodies, and long tails. There were two infraorders. Prosauropods evolved from beasts no larger than a human and gave way to sauropods, which included the heaviest and longest land animals ever. Long necks allowed sauropodomorphs to browse both high up and low down on tree leaves and ferns. These dinosaurs often moved in herds. They were the most abundant large, plant-eating dinosaurs from Late Triassic to Late Jurassic times, and long afterwards in southern continents. *Segnosaurus*, also included in this section, was a member of a puzzling group from Late Cretaceous Asia. Despite some prosauropod-like features, the segnosaurs might have been therizinosaurid theropods.

PLATEOSAURUS
This sauropodomorph had a typical prosauropod's relatively small head, bulky body, long neck and tail, and extremely large, sharp, curved thumb-claws.

HOLLOWED VERTEBRAE
Cavities in Diplodocus's *cervical (neck) vertebrae reduced weight without sacrificing strength. Various advanced dinosaurs evolved this engineering stratagem.*

▪ PROSAUROPODA ▪

This early infraorder included seven families of small to large, bipedal and quadrupedal dinosaurs with big, curved thumb-claws. Some were the first large, high-browsing animals. The last died out in Early Jurassic times. THECODONTOSAURIDAE were small, primitive, and bipedal. They lived in Late Triassic Europe and maybe Africa. ANCHISAURIDAE contained *Anchisaurus*, a bipedal/quadrupedal beast, 2.4m (8ft) long, from Early Jurassic North America and maybe Africa and China. MASSOSPONDYLIDAE included a 5m (16ft 6in) dinosaur, *Massospondylus*, whose lower jaw may have ended in a beak. It lived in Early Jurassic southern Africa and North America. YUNNANOSAURIDAE held one genus, *Yunnanosaurus*, from Early Jurassic China. It was 7m (23ft) long, with spoon-shaped teeth.

PLATEOSAURIDAE included more than half-a-dozen genera up to 8m (26ft) long. They lived worldwide during the Late Triassic and the Early Jurassic. MELANOROSAURIDAE contained the first very large dinosaurs: up to 12m (39ft) long. They lived during the Late Triassic and the Early Jurassic in South America, Africa, Europe, and Asia. BLIKANASAURIDAE held *Blikanasaurus*. This had stocky hind limbs, grew 5m (16ft 6in) long, and lived in Late Triassic southern Africa.

▪ SAUROPODA ▪

This infraorder contained about eight families of very large to immense, plant-eating quadrupeds weighing up to 50 tonnes (49 tons) or more. Many had hollowed vertebrae to reduce weight. By the Middle Jurassic, sauropods had replaced prosauropods and spread worldwide. They persisted into Late Cretaceous times. Various family relationships remain unclear. VULCANODONTIDAE, the most primitive sauropod family, included Early Jurassic genera up to 9m (29ft 6in) long, from Africa, Europe, and Asia. BARAPASAURIDAE were the family of *Barapasaurus*, which had distinctive vertebrae, reached 18m (60ft), and lived in Early Jurassic India. CETIOSAURIDAE included about 15 "old-fashioned" genera up to 18m (59ft) long, with blunt heads and rather short necks. They lived worldwide from Early Jurassic to Middle Cretaceous times.

THREE GIANT SAUROPODS
These sauropods (left) were among the largest-ever land animals. The brachiosaurid Brachiosaurus *(centre) attained 25m (82ft). The diplodocids* Supersaurus *(far left) and* Seismosaurus *respectively grew to 30m (98ft) and 40m (130ft).*

DIPLODOCUS SKULL

CAMARASAURUS SKULL

FAMILY TREE
This diagram shows possible relationships between sauropodomorph families (the names ending in -idae), each containing one genus or several genera. Connections between some families are unclear, and some scientists even suspect that sauropods and prosauropods did not share the same ancestor. If this is so, the Sauropodomorpha is an artificial grouping.

KEY

- Suborder
- Infraorder
- "Mainstream" Sauropods
- Relationship uncertain

DIPLODOCUS HIP BONES
The ilium, pubis, and ischium were extremely strong in order to help support Diplodocus. Ilium, pubis, and ischium combined to frame the acetabulum, a socket that held the ball-shaped head of the femur, transmitting its load to one hind limb.

Ilium

Ischium

Pubis

TWO SAUROPOD SKULLS
Diplodocus's low skull and peg-like teeth contrast with Camarasaurus's deep skull and strong, spoon-shaped teeth. Variations in sauropod skull and tooth design may reflect different kinds of diet.

BRACHIOSAURIDAE were about 12 immense, giraffe-like genera. Among the largest, heaviest dinosaurs, they grew to 25m (82ft) long and weighed 50 tonnes (49 tons) or more. They were widespread from Middle/Late Jurassic to Early Cretaceous times.
TITANOSAURIDAE held about 19 genera with distinctive tail bones. They grew from 9m to 21m (29ft 6in to 69ft) long or more, and lived mostly in the southern continents from Late Jurassic to Late Cretaceous times.
CAMARASAURIDAE were six (known) genera with deep skulls, strong teeth, and hollow vertebrae. They grew from 12m to 18m (39ft to 59ft) long, and lived from Late Jurassic to Late Cretaceous times in North America, Europe, Asia and maybe Africa.
EUHELOPODIDAE were a Chinese family of about half a dozen genera. They were 10m to 26m (33ft to 85ft) long and lived from Late Jurassic to Early Cretaceous times. Some of them had extremely long necks.
DICRAEOSAURIDAE contained four or five genera 9m to 21m (29ft 6in to

69ft) long, with high, forked spines. They have been found in rocks from Late Jurassic to Late Cretaceous South America, Africa, and Asia.
DIPLODOCIDAE included 12 known genera with elongated necks and whiplash tails. *Seismosaurus*, at 40m (130ft), is the longest known dinosaur. The group lived from Late Jurassic to Late Cretaceous times in North America, Africa, Europe, and Asia.

PROSAUROPODA

SAUROPODOMORPHA

SAUROPODA

Blikanasauridae

Melanorosauridae

Plateosauridae

Yunnanosauridae

Massospondylidae

Anchisauridae

Thecodontosauridae

Barapasauridae

Vulcanodontidae

Cetiosauridae

Brachiosauridae

Titanosauridae

Camarasauridae

Euhelopodidae

Dicraeosauridae

Diplodocidae

ANCHISAURUS

P ERHAPS THE FIRST dinosaur to be discovered in North America, *Anchisaurus* was rather longer than a human's height. It was among the smallest and most primitive of all prosauropods – plant-eating cousins of the mighty sauropods. The head was slight in comparison with the lengthy neck, back, and tail, and the capacious belly. "Near lizard" often bore its weight on all fours, although its legs were far longer and more powerful than its arms. Like the bipedal *Thecodontosaurus*, it had slender, four-toed feet and five-fingered hands that were mysteriously armed with sickle-shaped thumb-claws.

Cervical vertebra
Dorsal vertebra
Sacral vertebra
Ischium
Pubis
Ilium
Caudal vertebra

REARING-UP POSE

This model suggests how *Anchisaurus* may have looked on the occasions when it reared up, for instance to feed, possibly using its large thumb-claw to grasp branches. It could reach as high as the twigs and foliage of relatively small trees, supporting its body on the hind limbs and tail.

■ LIFESTYLE ■

Anchisaurus lived in what is now the Connecticut Valley. In Early Jurassic times this was a warm, steep-sided trench like the Great Rift Valley that runs through east and central Africa today. *Anchisaurus* moved in search of food along the shores of lakes that filled depressions in the valley floor. Its front-heavy body made it tend to topple forwards at low speeds, so perhaps it stood and sometimes walked on all fours, holding its two thumb-claws off the ground to stop them getting injured. However, *Anchisaurus* often reared up to feed. Then its powerful hip girdle transmitted the weight of the forepart of the body to the long hind limbs and tail. Supported by this sturdy tripod, *Anchisaurus* craned its neck to reach and snip off low-growing tree leaves (probably rather soft ones) with its rather gappy, saw-edged teeth.

■ COMMUNITIES ■

In dry weather, groups of *Anchisaurus* and other creatures walked across the wet mud left behind by shrinking lakes. As the mud dried and began to harden into rock, the tracks of all these animals came to be preserved as fossils, known as ichnites. From these and other fossil clues we know that *Anchisaurus* shared eastern North America with harmless early ornithischians and predatory theropods. If a plodding *Anchisaurus* saw a large theropod approaching, it could have risen and hurried off on its hind limbs. If taken by surprise, the best the otherwise comparatively defenceless creature could do would be to stand at bay and strike out with its sickle claws.

HEAD AND NECK

Anchisaurus's head was surprisingly small for the size of its body. The head was long and narrow, and the skull relatively flat, with a lower crown than that of *Plateosaurus* and most other prosauropods. In addition, the slope of the forehead was more gradual. The model shown here is based on the assumption that *Anchisaurus* had no cheeks. This might be consistent with a mode of feeding based mainly on snatching and gulping, but anatomical evidence suggests prosauropods had cheeks.

CHEEKS

This artist's restoration (left) shows how prosauropods would have looked if they had possessed cheeks, which would have helped to retain food for chewing.

Long tail held off the ground

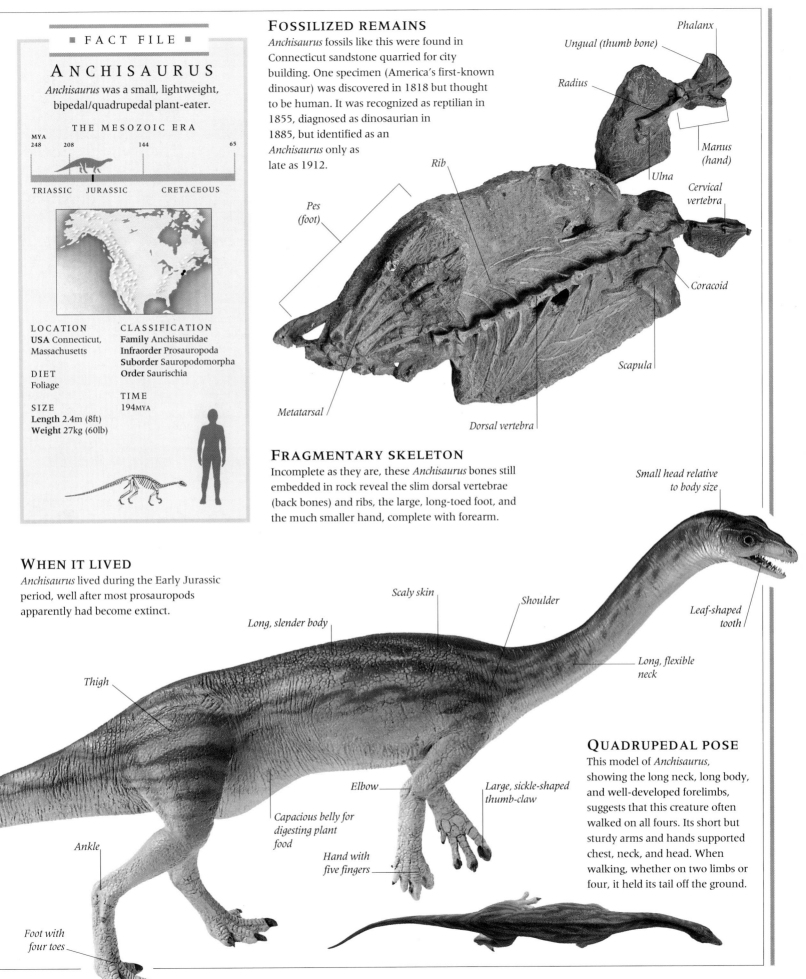

FACT FILE

ANCHISAURUS

Anchisaurus was a small, lightweight, bipedal/quadrupedal plant-eater.

THE MESOZOIC ERA

MYA 248	208	144	65
TRIASSIC	JURASSIC	CRETACEOUS	

LOCATION
USA Connecticut, Massachusetts

DIET
Foliage

SIZE
Length 2.4m (8ft)
Weight 27kg (60lb)

CLASSIFICATION
Family Anchisauridae
Infraorder Prosauropoda
Suborder Sauropodomorpha
Order Saurischia

TIME
194MYA

FOSSILIZED REMAINS

Anchisaurus fossils like this were found in Connecticut sandstone quarried for city building. One specimen (America's first-known dinosaur) was discovered in 1818 but thought to be human. It was recognized as reptilian in 1855, diagnosed as dinosaurian in 1885, but identified as an *Anchisaurus* only as late as 1912.

Phalanx
Ungual (thumb bone)
Radius
Manus (hand)
Ulna
Cervical vertebra
Rib
Coracoid
Pes (foot)
Scapula
Metatarsal
Dorsal vertebra

FRAGMENTARY SKELETON

Incomplete as they are, these *Anchisaurus* bones still embedded in rock reveal the slim dorsal vertebrae (back bones) and ribs, the large, long-toed foot, and the much smaller hand, complete with forearm.

WHEN IT LIVED

Anchisaurus lived during the Early Jurassic period, well after most prosauropods apparently had become extinct.

Small head relative to body size

Scaly skin
Shoulder
Long, slender body
Leaf-shaped tooth
Long, flexible neck
Thigh
Elbow
Large, sickle-shaped thumb-claw
Capacious belly for digesting plant food
Hand with five fingers
Ankle
Foot with four toes

QUADRUPEDAL POSE

This model of *Anchisaurus*, showing the long neck, long body, and well-developed forelimbs, suggests that this creature often walked on all fours. Its short but sturdy arms and hands supported chest, neck, and head. When walking, whether on two limbs or four, it held its tail off the ground.

PLATEOSAURUS

S CORES OF SKELETONS dug up amid central Europe's Late Triassic rocks make this the best-known of the larger early dinosaurs. "Flat lizard" was one of the prosauropods, which were perhaps the ancestors of the sauropods, the largest dinosaurs ever to walk the Earth. It had a small head, long neck, bulky body, huge thumb-claws, and large, powerful hind legs. Its tail, however, was deep, and the narrow skull larger, stronger, and taller than that of *Anchisaurus*, with a deeper snout and more teeth. A ridge on the lower jaw, below the level of the tooth row, anchored the powerful muscles that worked the lower jaw. This arrangement produced a highly effective bite.

▪ LIFESTYLE ▪

Plateosaurus would normally have walked on all fours. Sometimes, however, it could have reared and, with its curved thumb-claws, hooked down twigs and fronds to its mouth. Small cheek pouches would hold the bitten-off leaves as the jaws worked up and down causing the top and bottom rows of flat-sided, leaf-shaped teeth to mesh together, chopping up the mouthful. The shredded mass was then ground up inside its stomach by pebbles that rubbed against each other. Finding enough to eat could have kept each *Plateosaurus* on the move, particularly if it lived in a herd, as seems quite probable. When the herd had stripped an area of tasty, young tree-fern fronds, it would have had to wander off in search of more. But living together would have had advantages. If a big predator confronted them, the prosauropods could have closed ranks, reared, and struck out with their thumb-claws, inflicting wounds and driving off the enemy. At the same time, a great disadvantage would have been that in the event of a natural catastrophe – a sudden flood, for example – the whole herd might be swept away. (This seems actually to have happened in the vicinity of the present-day German town of Trossingen, where numbers of skeletons were found buried close together).

BIPEDAL FEEDING

A *Plateosaurus* rears and cranes its neck to eat leaves that grow beyond the reach of other reptiles. Prosauropods were the first large land animals to feed high above the ground. *Plateosaurus* might also have used its arms to pull branches to its mouth.

ELEVATED TAIL A museum in Tübingen, Germany, shows a *Plateosaurus* skeleton as if briskly striding on two legs, with its tail off the ground. That is how experts now believe it walked when not on all fours: they reject an old notion that it dragged its tail on the ground.

Caudal vertebrae

Ilium

Ischium

Femur

Chevron

Neural spine

Tibia

Fibula

QUADRUPEDAL FEEDING

Preparators in a German museum set up this *Plateosaurus* skeleton as if about to go down on all fours to drink water or eat low-growing vegetation, as it must often have done.

MOUNTED SKELETON

Major features of the *Plateosaurus* body show up clearly in this well-mounted specimen. The rather small skull projects almost straight out from a long, flexible neck of interlocking vertebrae with slim cervical ribs. The deep, lengthy rib cage held a food-filled gut and vital organs, the weight of which made *Plateosaurus* front-heavy. However, long, strong, arm and shoulder bones helped to prop up the forepart of the body when *Plateosaurus* went on all fours. The elongated upper foot bones suggest that *Plateosaurus* walked on its toes.

Cervical vertebrae

Skull

Naris

Cervical rib

Jaw joint

Mandible

Braincase

Orbit

Sclerotic ring

Antorbital fenestra

Infratemporal fenestra

Naris

Maxilla

Jaw joint

Mandible

Coronoid eminence

Serrated, leaf-shaped tooth crown

Dorsal vertebrae

Scapula

Shoulder joint

Humerus

SKULL

This was more powerfully built than that of *Anchisaurus*, with a deeper coronoid eminence on the lower jaw and a depressed jaw hinge for a harder bite. The teeth were numerous and small, with flat-sided, serrated, leaf-shaped crowns. A dentary ridge left room for comparatively narrow cheek pouches that prevented food spilling when *Plateosaurus* ate.

Elbow joint

Radius

HAND BONES

Broad, strong bones helped to form a sturdy, five-fingered hand capable of bearing weight and becoming a weapon for defence. The first three digits were much the longest and strongest, and the first, the thumb, had a large, broad, wicked-looking claw. However, the fourth and fifth digits were short and weak, with only puny metacarpals and phalanges. This made the hand appear somewhat lopsided.

Rib

Ulna

Wrist joint

Phalanx

Pubis

Knee joint

Ulna

Radius

Ankle joint

Wrist joint

Metatarsals

Fifth digit

Thumb (first digit)

Fourth digit

Second digit

Third digit

■ FACT FILE ■

PLATEOSAURUS

Plateosaurus was a long, quadrupedal plant-eater with a bulky body and a small head.

THE MESOZOIC ERA

MYA
248   208   144   65

TRIASSIC   JURASSIC   CRETACEOUS

LOCATION
France Doubs, Jura
Germany Baden-Württemberg, Bavaria
Switzerland Aargau, Baselland

TIME
220MYA

DIET
Leafy plants

CLASSIFICATION
Family Plateosauridae
Infraorder Prosauropoda
Suborder Sauropodomorpha
Order Saurischia

SIZE
Length 6–8m (20–26ft)

MASSOSPONDYLUS

M ASSOSPONDYLUS was a medium-sized prosauropod with a shorter, lower head than *Plateosaurus*, more variation in its teeth, and an unusual, projecting upper jaw. The overshot jaw gave rise to suggestions that the lower jaw ended in a beak, but the anatomy of the rest of the jaw does not support this theory. Some 80 partial skeletons make "massive vertebra" the world's best-known Early Jurassic prosauropod. *Massospondylus* was also remarkably widespread. Most of its fossils were discovered in southern Africa, but in 1985 a *Massospondylus* skull was reported in North America, proving that the genus inhabited both continents when all the world's great landmasses were joined.

■ LIFESTYLE ■

In Arizona, *Massospondylus* shared a wooded flood plain with turtles, pterosaurs, and other creatures. It roamed southern Africa with early theropods and ornithischians, furry, mammal-like reptiles, and tiny, shrew-like mammals. *Massospondylus*, with its tiny, narrow

head and bulky body, was evidently designed for a placid, plant-eating life. In 1981, however, a scientist suggested that this prosauropod and others like it were carnivores.

■ CLUES TO THE DIET ■

Supposed clues to *Massospondylus*'s meat-eating diet included unusually tall, strong, front teeth, ridged a bit like steak-knife blades. In addition, lack of wear on the teeth seemed to indicate that the top and bottom teeth met less effectively for crushing plants than the teeth of *Lesothosaurus*, a small, early ornithischian. Furthermore, *Massospondylus*'s skull was thought too flimsy and its jaw muscles too weak for munching fibrous stems and leaves. An alternative suggestion was that *Massospondylus* tore meat with its strong, serrated front teeth, and chewed plants with the weaker, flatter teeth farther back in its jaws. In 1985 there was a counterclaim from another group of scientists that *Massospondylus* cropped and chewed up leaves as effectively as any modern iguana lizard. Finds of polished pebbles mixed with fossil bones hint that "millstones" in the creature's gizzard helped to mash the swallowed leaves to a pulp, allowing digestion to proceed as enzymes broke down the nutrients locked up inside the plant cell walls.

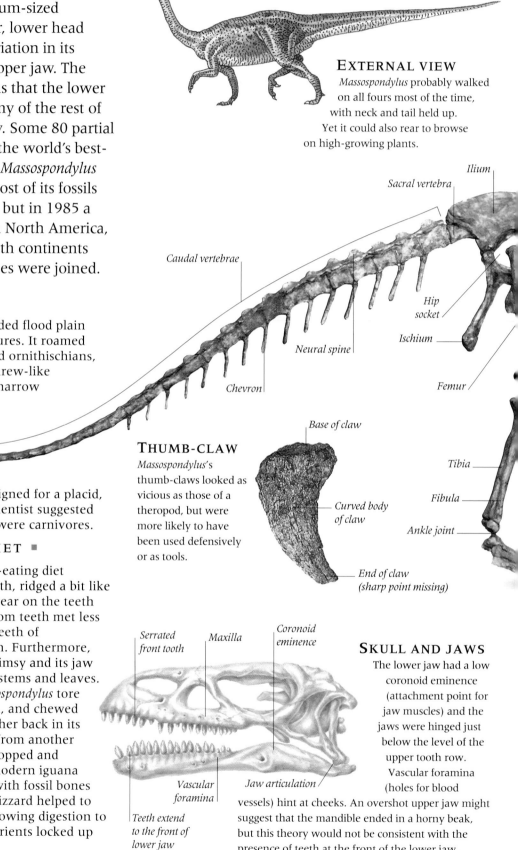

EXTERNAL VIEW
Massospondylus probably walked on all fours most of the time, with neck and tail held up. Yet it could also rear to browse on high-growing plants.

Ilium

Sacral vertebra

Caudal vertebrae

Hip socket

Ischium

Neural spine

Chevron

Femur

THUMB-CLAW
Massospondylus's thumb-claws looked as vicious as those of a theropod, but were more likely to have been used defensively or as tools.

Base of claw

Curved body of claw

End of claw (sharp point missing)

Tibia

Fibula

Ankle joint

Serrated front tooth

Maxilla

Coronoid eminence

SKULL AND JAWS
The lower jaw had a low coronoid eminence (attachment point for jaw muscles) and the jaws were hinged just below the level of the upper tooth row. Vascular foramina (holes for blood vessels) hint at cheeks. An overshot upper jaw might suggest that the mandible ended in a horny beak, but this theory would not be consistent with the presence of teeth at the front of the lower jaw.

Vascular foramina

Jaw articulation

Teeth extend to the front of lower jaw

SKELETAL RECONSTRUCTION

This reconstruction presents *Massospondylus* as an elongated creature with a relatively smaller head, shallower ribcage, slimmer tail, and more slender limbs than bigger, burlier prosauropods like *Lufengosaurus* (right), or the more robustly built European dinosaur *Plateosaurus*. The only known member of its family, *Massospondylus* may represent an evolutionary level between plateosaurids like *Lufengosaurus* and more primitive prosauropods such as *Anchisaurus*.

LUFENGOSAURUS

The worldwide distribution of prosauropods was underlined by the discovery in 1941 of this medium-sized prosauropod in Early Jurassic rocks of the Lufeng Basin, Yunnan, a province of southwest China. *Lufengosaurus* had distinctive skull bones but broadly resembled its European counterpart *Plateosaurus*.

RESTORATION
This dinosaur bore a striking resemblance to Plateosaurus.

SKELETON

This mounted *Lufengosaurus* skeleton rears as if to browse or fend off a theropod. More than 30 whole or partial *Lufengosaurus* skeletons are known.

DIMINUTIVE HEAD Seen with the rest of the skeleton, the head appears incongruously minute. Yet *Massospondylus*'s small mouth must have consumed enough of its low-grade plant food to sustain its relatively bulky body.

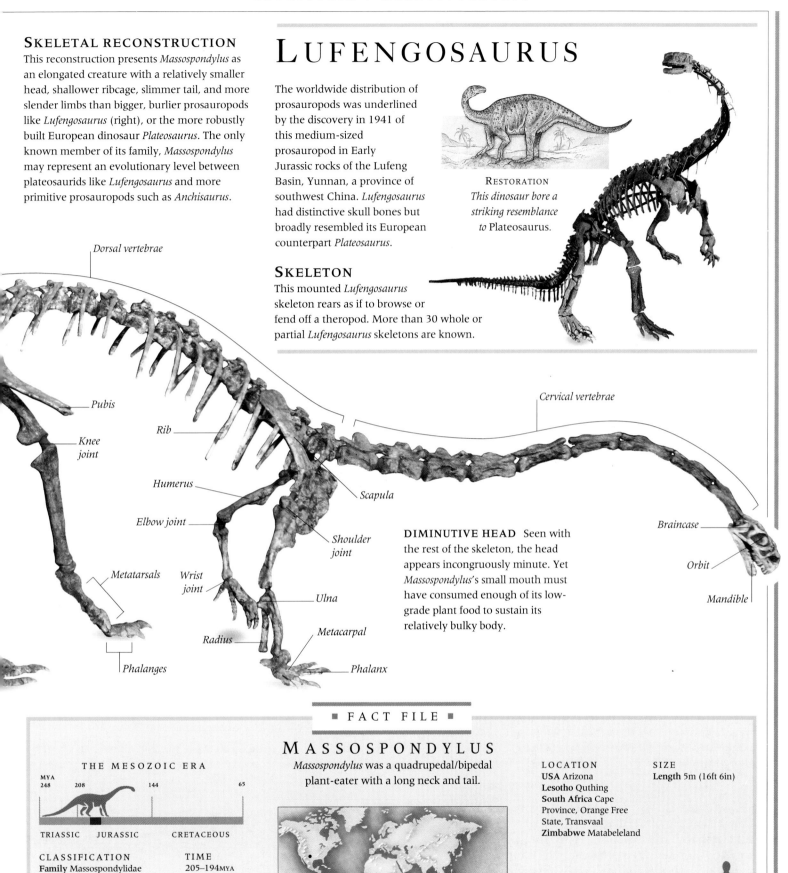

Dorsal vertebrae

Pubis

Rib

Knee joint

Humerus

Elbow joint

Scapula

Shoulder joint

Metatarsals

Wrist joint

Ulna

Radius

Metacarpal

Phalanges

Phalanx

Cervical vertebrae

Braincase

Orbit

Mandible

■ FACT FILE ■

MASSOSPONDYLUS

Massospondylus was a quadrupedal/bipedal plant-eater with a long neck and tail.

THE MESOZOIC ERA

MYA 248	208	144	65

TRIASSIC   JURASSIC   CRETACEOUS

CLASSIFICATION
Family Massospondylidae
Infraorder Prosauropoda
Suborder Sauropodomorpha
Order Saurischia

TIME
205–194MYA

DIET
Foliage

LOCATION
USA Arizona
Lesotho Quthing
South Africa Cape Province, Orange Free State, Transvaal
Zimbabwe Matabeleland

SIZE
Length 5m (16ft 6in)

RIOJASAURUS

R IOJASAURUS ("LA RIOJA LIZARD") had a small head, long neck and tail, massive body, and four elephant-like limbs. This bus-length melanorosaurid prosauropod may have been the largest and heaviest of all land animals before the evolution of the sauropods. In fact, it matched the smaller sauropods in size and weight, and resembled them in build. The vertebrae of this huge dinosaur were made lighter by deep hollows, but its limb bones were massive and solid in order to support the vast body. *Riojasaurus* had relatively longer hands and feet than a sauropod, and more of its digits were tipped with claws.

GASTROLITHS

Like all prosauropods and sauropods, *Riojasaurus* would have swallowed stones such as these to aid digestion. Violent wave-contractions of its gizzard rubbed down and smoothed the edges of the stones while they ground plant material to pulp for biochemical digestion.

Dorsal vertebrae

Sacral vertebrae

Cervical vertebrae

Braincase

Orbit

Mandible

Cervical rib

Pubis

Rib

Femur

Shoulder joint

Knee joint

Humerus

Fibula

Ischium

Elbow joint

Tibia

Radius

Ulna

Ankle joint

Metatarsals

Wrist joint

Metacarpal

Phalanges

Phalanx

■ LIFESTYLE ■

It was once believed that enormous melanorosaurid prosauropods like *Riojasaurus* were carnivores and not herbivores. This misconception arose largely because sharp, pointed teeth were found mixed up with headless melanorosaurid remains. Scientists now think that the old, worn teeth had fallen from the mouths of carnivorous dinosaurs feeding on the prosauropods' corpses. *Riojasaurus* really had leaf-shaped teeth that were designed for shredding plant fibres, not for slicing through flesh. *Riojasaurus*, with its elevated back and long neck, was one of the first land animals capable of browsing on vegetation growing high above the ground. Some scientists believe that large, long-necked plant-eating dinosaurs like this evolved in response to a drying Late Triassic climate. It is thought that lengthening dry seasons would have wiped out lush, low-growing vegetation, but that river valleys would have still held tall, deep-rooted trees: well-stocked larders for creatures tall enough to reach the leaves. This theory of a changing climate might go some way towards explaining why South America's long-necked prosauropods flourished while those once abundant, low-slung, pig-like reptiles, the rhynchosaurs, quickly became extinct. Another benefit of *Riojasaurus*'s enormous size was the protection afforded by sheer bulk against attack from early, large, flesh-eating dinosaurs, or from predatory, carnivorous rauisuchid reptiles.

RESTORATION

Riojasaurus from Argentina was one of a family of heavy, quadrupedal prosauropods: the Melanorosauridae, which included *Melanorosaurus* from South Africa and *Camelotia* from England.

SKULL

Riojasaurus's skull was small for the size of its body, as with other prosauropods. It was shaped like a *Plateosaurus* skull, and the teeth had leaf-shaped crowns similar to those of that European dinosaur.

Paroccipital process

Orbit

Antorbital fenestra

Naris

Infratemporal fenestra

Mandible

Leaf-shaped tooth

■ FACT FILE ■

RIOJASAURUS

Riojasaurus was a quadrupedal plant-eater with massive limbs and a bulky body.

THE MESOZOIC ERA

| MYA 248 | 208 | 144 | 65 |

TRIASSIC   JURASSIC   CRETACEOUS

LOCATION
Argentina La Rioja, San Juan

TIME
219MYA

SIZE
Length 10m (33ft)
Weight 1 tonne
(1 ton)

CLASSIFICATION
Family Melanorosauridae
Infraorder Prosauropoda
Suborder Sauropodomorpha
Order Saurischia

DIET
Tree leaves

MOUNTED SKELETON

Quadrupedal *Riojasaurus* had forelimbs almost as long as its hind limbs, and the limb bones of this Late Triassic giant were longer and stronger than those of any other known prosauropod. *Riojasaurus* represented the climax of a trend to increased size that was matched later, quite separately, by the sauropods of Jurassic and Cretaceous times.

Neural spine

Chevron

Caudal vertebrae

DISCOVERY

This reconstructed skeleton of a *Riojasaurus* stands in a museum at San Miguel de Tucumán in north-west Argentina. More than 20 complete or partial skeletons of the dinosaur have been discovered in that area of the foothills of the Andes.

Large intestine

Caecum

Small intestine

Oesophagus

Small head

Long neck

Hip joint

Ischium

Femur

Pubis

Gizzard

Whiplash tail

INTERNAL ANATOMY

Loaded down with bulky plant food, *Riojasaurus*'s long, convoluted digestive system lay ahead of its obstructive, sloping pubis. Scientists believe that the weight of the internal organs and their contents would have forced *Riojasaurus* to walk on all fours.

CETIOSAURUS

C ETIOSAURUS was the first sauropod to be discovered. This huge plant-eating dinosaur was as long as a great whale. When it was named in 1841, it was the largest known land animal. "Whale lizard" belonged to a primitive family called the Cetiosauridae. Its old-fashioned features included a rather solid backbone unlike the lighter, hollower backbones of most later sauropods. Its head was apparently blunt, with spoon-shaped teeth. *Cetiosaurus* had a moderately long neck, a capacious body, and a relatively short tail. This heavy superstructure was supported on elephantine limbs and feet; thick pads cushioned the toes.

■ DISCOVERY ■

The first hint that colossal dinosaurs had walked the Earth was a probable *Cetiosaurus* tail bone found in Oxfordshire in 1809. In the 1830s, the Oxford University geologist Dean William Buckland received several huge fossil bones dug up in Oxfordshire. The French comparative anatomist Baron Georges Cuvier identified them as whale bones – although fossils of whales were unknown in Mesozoic rocks. Cuvier's British counterpart, Richard Owen, later questioned whether the vertebrae were truly whale-like, and decided their mighty owner had the streamlined body of a water animal that swam by waggling a crocodilian tail. He named it accordingly. Subsequent fossil finds cast doubt on the idea. In 1848, Professor John Phillips discovered a thigh bone as tall as a human. This strongly suggested that its owner had been designed to walk on land. Then, in 1869, from Oxfordshire's same Middle Jurassic rocks, a near-complete skeleton emerged. Thomas Henry Huxley (champion of Charles Darwin and the theory of evolution through natural selection) finally arrived at the correct solution to the mystery of the giant's identity. He discerned that *Cetiosaurus* had simply been a very large, four-legged dinosaur, perhaps as heavy as five modern elephants.

BRACHIOSAURUS VERTEBRA

Zygapophysis

Neural spine

Neural canal

Centrum

CETIOSAURUS VERTEBRA

Neural spine

Zygapophysis

Neural canal

Centrum

COMPARISON OF VERTEBRAE

A *Cetiosaurus*'s dorsal vertebra (above right) was a massive, heavy structure, compared to the weight-saving, scooped-out dorsal vertebra of a more advanced sauropod, such as *Brachiosaurus* (above left). *Brachiosaurus* had a relatively smaller centrum but a more pronounced neural spine and zygapophyses.

Sacral vertebrae

Caudal vertebrae

Ilium

Hip joint

Femur

Ischium

Pubis

Neural spine

Knee joint

Fibula

Tibia

Ankle joint

FOOT BONES

Finds of partial skeletons such as these foot bones sometimes help to complete the missing pieces of a fossil jigsaw puzzle, but it is not always possible to match fossil finds with the dinosaur from which they originated.

Metatarsals

Phalanges

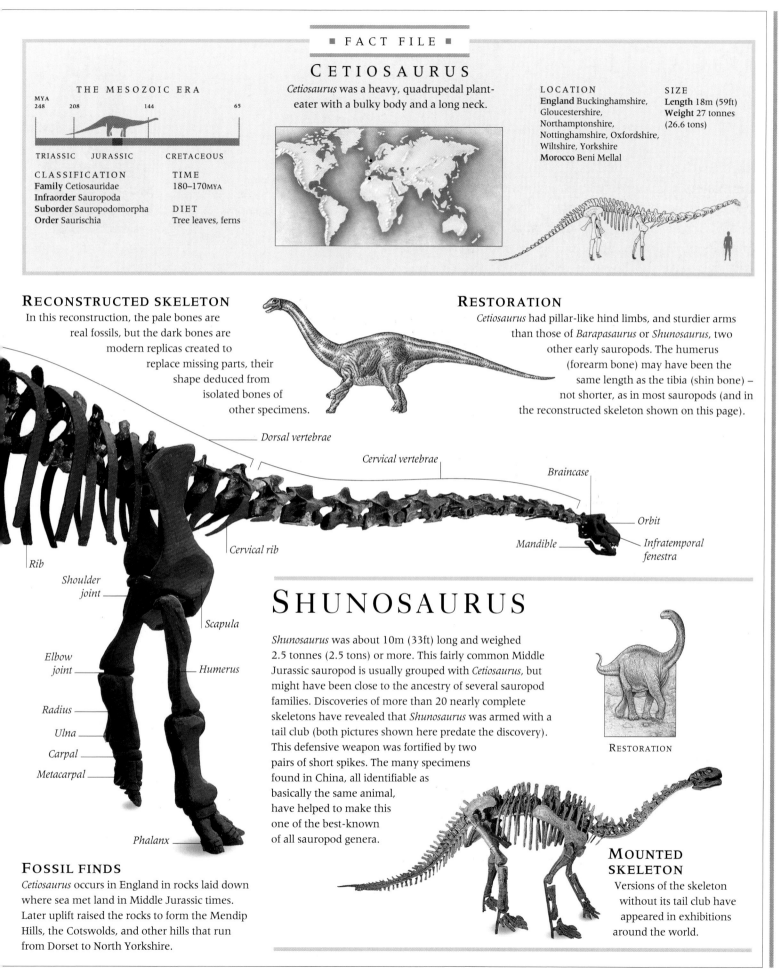

CETIOSAURUS

Cetiosaurus was a heavy, quadrupedal plant-eater with a bulky body and a long neck.

THE MESOZOIC ERA

MYA
248   208   144   65

TRIASSIC   JURASSIC   CRETACEOUS

CLASSIFICATION
Family Cetiosauridae
Infraorder Sauropoda
Suborder Sauropodomorpha
Order Saurischia

TIME
180–170MYA

DIET
Tree leaves, ferns

LOCATION
England Buckinghamshire, Gloucestershire, Northamptonshire, Nottinghamshire, Oxfordshire, Wiltshire, Yorkshire
Morocco Beni Mellal

SIZE
Length 18m (59ft)
Weight 27 tonnes (26.6 tons)

RECONSTRUCTED SKELETON

In this reconstruction, the pale bones are real fossils, but the dark bones are modern replicas created to replace missing parts, their shape deduced from isolated bones of other specimens.

RESTORATION

Cetiosaurus had pillar-like hind limbs, and sturdier arms than those of *Barapasaurus* or *Shunosaurus*, two other early sauropods. The humerus (forearm bone) may have been the same length as the tibia (shin bone) – not shorter, as in most sauropods (and in the reconstructed skeleton shown on this page).

Dorsal vertebrae

Cervical vertebrae

Braincase

Orbit

Mandible

Infratemporal fenestra

Cervical rib

Rib

Shoulder joint

Scapula

Elbow joint

Humerus

Radius

Ulna

Carpal

Metacarpal

Phalanx

FOSSIL FINDS

Cetiosaurus occurs in England in rocks laid down where sea met land in Middle Jurassic times. Later uplift raised the rocks to form the Mendip Hills, the Cotswolds, and other hills that run from Dorset to North Yorkshire.

SHUNOSAURUS

Shunosaurus was about 10m (33ft) long and weighed 2.5 tonnes (2.5 tons) or more. This fairly common Middle Jurassic sauropod is usually grouped with *Cetiosaurus*, but might have been close to the ancestry of several sauropod families. Discoveries of more than 20 nearly complete skeletons have revealed that *Shunosaurus* was armed with a tail club (both pictures shown here predate the discovery). This defensive weapon was fortified by two pairs of short spikes. The many specimens found in China, all identifiable as basically the same animal, have helped to make this one of the best-known of all sauropod genera.

RESTORATION

MOUNTED SKELETON

Versions of the skeleton without its tail club have appeared in exhibitions around the world.

BRACHIOSAURUS

O NE OF THE LARGEST, longest, and possibly heaviest dinosaurs, *Brachiosaurus* ("arm lizard") resembled a massive giraffe. By some estimates its weight was equivalent to ten modern-day elephants, though a recent recalculation has brought this number down to six. *Brachiosaurus*'s forelimbs were much longer than its hind limbs and raised its shoulders far above hip level. The shoulders formed a high base for the neck, which swung the head from side to side and moved it up and down, from higher than a four-storey building down to ground level. Compared to most sauropods, its tail was short.

MOUNTED SKELETON
A Brachiosaurus *skeleton on display in the Humboldt Museum, Berlin.*

■ LIFESTYLE ■

Brachiosaurus seems to have been designed for cropping leaves at high and low levels. Some scientists think it lacked muscles for raising its neck as steeply as a giraffe's and doubt that its heart could have pumped blood to the head if the neck were held high for more than a moment or two. Perhaps this sauropod stood at the edges of woods, swinging its head up, down, and sideways, as its chisel-shaped teeth cut readily through all vegetation in reach, even the low-growing ferns that then carpeted the ground. In its gut, gastroliths ("gizzard stones") probably ground leaves to pulp. Digestion might have depended on bacteria in a specialized hindgut (caecum), such as those in modern, large, plant-eating mammals. If *Brachiosaurus* were warm-blooded, it would have required more than 200kg (440lb) of low-grade conifer and cycad plant food each day, and feeding would have taken up much of its time. If it were cold-blooded, its food needs would have been less. Small herds of these immense sauropods probably spent their lives moving slowly through low-lying riverside forests. Sheer size and weight, together with their sharp claws, probably protected adults against even the largest theropod predators. However, the young would have been more at risk. If *Brachiosaurus* were warm-blooded, the young probably took at least ten years to grow to full size; if cold-blooded, they may have taken more than 100 years to reach adult size.

EXTERNAL APPEARANCE

Long forelimbs and high shoulders raised the base of the long neck high above the ground. Unlike most other sauropods, *Brachiosaurus* sloped down steeply from shoulders to hips and had a relatively short tail.

DORSAL VERTEBRAE

The dorsal vertebrae of *Brachiosaurus* were very large. To reduce their weight without significantly reducing their strength, the dorsal vertebrae had huge cavities in their sides.

Lung

Dorsal vertebra

Neural spine

Small intestine

Ovary

Kidney

Rib

Hip joint

Femur

Cloaca

Thigh musculature

Caudal musculature

Fibula

Ankle joint

Metatarsal

Knee joint

Anterior crural muscle

Gizzard

Large intestine

Digestive caecum

Pubis

Hind limb

Hind foot

Claw

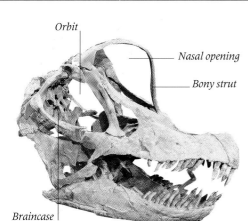

Orbit

Nasal opening

Bony strut

Braincase

SKULL

The skull of *Brachiosaurus* had a low muzzle and strong jaws with chisel-shaped teeth. Light, narrow, bony struts framed the orbits (eye sockets) and the large nasal openings above. Behind the eyes, a tiny braincase held a brain that was no more than one hundred-thousandth the weight of the whole body.

Cervical vertebra

Intercostal muscle

Trachea (wind pipe)

Oesophagus (food pipe)

Scapula

Scapular muscle

Shoulder joint

Humerus

Heart

Posterior brachial musculature

Elbow joint

Radius

Ulna

Posterior antebrachial musculature

Wrist joint

Metacarpal

Cervical musculature

Outer ear

INTERNAL ANATOMY

This cutaway model (left) shows some of the internal structures of *Brachiosaurus*. The girder-like spine supported the neck, back, and tail, and transmitted their weight to the massive limb bones. Ribs protected the heart, lungs, and other internal organs. The long gut included a gizzard, and sausage-shaped caeca for digesting plant food.

MUSCULATURE

This illustration shows how *Brachiosaurus* would have looked with the skin stripped away to reveal the muscles beneath. It is based on an old-fashioned restoration in the Humboldt Museum, Berlin, made in the early twentieth century. Scientists worked out where and how the muscles, ligaments, and tendons were connected to the bones of the Humboldt skeleton.

Cervical musculature

Sheet-like muscles across the abdomen

Old reconstruction with the front limbs in a "bow-legged" posture

---

■ FACT FILE ■

BRACHIOSAURUS

Brachiosaurus was a quadrupedal plant-eater and was one of the largest, longest, and possibly heaviest dinosaurs ever.

THE MESOZOIC ERA

MYA 248	208	144	65

TRIASSIC   JURASSIC   CRETACEOUS

LOCATION
USA Colorado, Wyoming, Utah
Portugal Estremadura
Algeria Wargla
Tanzania Mtwara

CLASSIFICATION
Family Brachiosauridae
Infraorder Sauropoda
Suborder Sauropodomorpha
Order Saurischia

DIET
Conifers, cycads, ferns

TIME
153–113MYA

SIZE
Length 25m (82ft)
Weight 30–50 tonnes
(29.5–49 tons)

CAMARASAURUS

HUGE, WEIGHT-SAVING hollows in its vertebrae gave this sauropod its name, "chambered lizard". No other North American sauropod is known so completely from fossil bones. *Camarasaurus* was more massive than the more famous *Diplodocus* but had a shorter neck and tail, relatively long forelimbs and high shoulders, and stood with its back almost horizontal rather than rising to the hips. Whereas *Diplodocus* had a small, low, horse-like head, *Camarasaurus*'s head was large and deep, with a muzzle more like a bulldog's. Big eye sockets, nostrils, and other cavities reduced some skull bones to lightweight struts. The teeth were strong and spoon-shaped, sited all around its powerful jaws.

E. D. COPE
In 1877 he named Camarasaurus.

Phalanges

■ LIFESTYLE ■

Camarasaurus's teeth seemed designed for cropping vegetation tougher than anything peg-toothed sauropods could tackle. One authority suggests the animal ate not only leaves but rough-barked twigs and branches, and the harsh, fibrous, palm-like fronds of cycadeoid trees. Being an unfussy feeder would possibly have compensated short-necked *Camarasaurus* and its nearest kin for being unable to get at foliage within the reach of the longer-necked sauropods. Big skull cavities for the eyes and nostrils suggest that this sauropod had keen senses of sight and smell that would have helped it find new feeding grounds and detect where dangerous theropods lurked. *Camarasaurus* probably moved around in mixed-age herds. There is no proof for this, but without adults to protect it, a young *Camarasaurus* would have been vulnerable to any hungry *Allosaurus* or *Ceratosaurus*. Even the great size, tough hide, and sharp thumb-claws of a solitary adult might not have saved it from a hunting pack of big, flesh-eating dinosaurs. *Camarasaurus* bones have been discovered deeply scored with the characteristic teeth-marks of *Allosaurus* and *Ceratosaurus*. It is possible, however, that these predators were eating beasts they had not killed but found dead.

SKELETON PRESERVED AS FOUND
Preserved as it lay after death, a fossilized *Camarasaurus* reveals key anatomical features. These include a short, deep skull; a dozen short cervical vertebrae (neck bones) with long, slim ribs; a dozen deeply hollowed-out dorsal vertebrae (back bones); about 50 short caudal vertebrae (tail bones); robust limb bones (each humerus was almost as long as a femur); and short, weight-bearing digits.

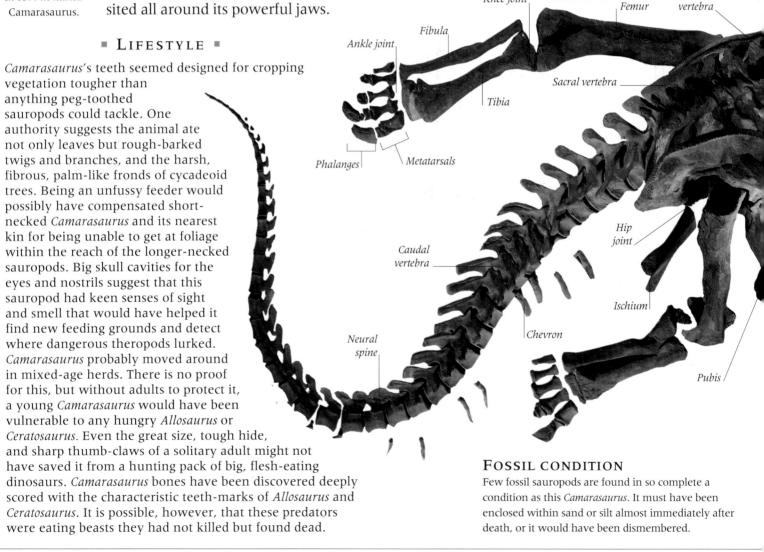

Knee joint
Femur
Dorsal vertebra
Fibula
Ankle joint
Sacral vertebra
Tibia
Phalanges
Metatarsals
Hip joint
Caudal vertebra
Ischium
Chevron
Neural spine
Pubis

FOSSIL CONDITION
Few fossil sauropods are found in so complete a condition as this *Camarasaurus*. It must have been enclosed within sand or silt almost immediately after death, or it would have been dismembered.

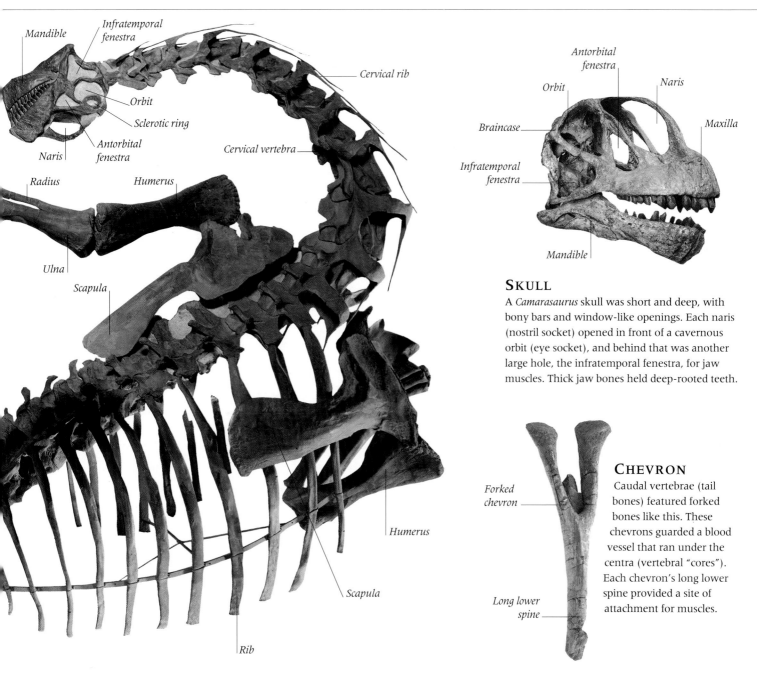

Mandible

Infratemporal fenestra

Orbit

Sclerotic ring

Naris

Antorbital fenestra

Cervical rib

Cervical vertebra

Radius

Humerus

Ulna

Scapula

Humerus

Scapula

Rib

Antorbital fenestra

Orbit

Braincase

Infratemporal fenestra

Naris

Maxilla

Mandible

SKULL

A *Camarasaurus* skull was short and deep, with bony bars and window-like openings. Each naris (nostril socket) opened in front of a cavernous orbit (eye socket), and behind that was another large hole, the infratemporal fenestra, for jaw muscles. Thick jaw bones held deep-rooted teeth.

CHEVRON

Forked chevron

Long lower spine

Caudal vertebrae (tail bones) featured forked bones like this. These chevrons guarded a blood vessel that ran under the centra (vertebral "cores"). Each chevron's long lower spine provided a site of attachment for muscles.

■ FACT FILE ■

CAMARASAURUS

Camarasaurus was a quadrupedal plant-eater with long forelimbs.

THE MESOZOIC ERA

MYA
248   208   144   65

TRIASSIC   JURASSIC   CRETACEOUS

CLASSIFICATION   TIME
Family Camarasauridae   155–150MYA
Infraorder Sauropoda
Suborder Sauropodomorpha
Order Saurischia

DIET
Tree leaves, ferns

LOCATION
USA Colorado, Utah, Wyoming
Portugal Estremadura

SIZE
Length 18m (59ft)
Weight 20 tonnes (19.7 tons)

BAROSAURUS

A N IMMENSELY LONG SAUROPOD, "heavy lizard" resembled its near relative *Diplodocus*. Both had a bulky body that stood highest at the hips. Their hind-limb bones appear identical, and other bones suggest that *Barosaurus*'s skull (which has not yet been discovered) was long and sloping like that of *Diplodocus*; but their neck and tail proportions were different. *Barosaurus*'s tail was relatively short but balanced by an extremely elongated neck that projected 9m (about 30ft) beyond its shoulders, making *Barosaurus* taller than almost any other North American dinosaur.

EARL DOUGLASS
In 1912 he led the team that excavated a Barosaurus *skeleton at the Carnegie Quarry in Utah.*

■ LIFESTYLE ■

Barosaurus's long neck seems designed for feeding at high elevations, like a giraffe's. Some researchers have calculated that pumping blood up to the brain demanded an amazingly large 1.6 tonne (1.6 ton) heart. But the bigger a heart, the slower it beats. In 1992, scientists at Columbia University argued that a heart that size would pump so slowly that blood forced up the neck by one heartbeat would pour back down before the next. They suggested instead that *Barosaurus* had eight hearts – two major hearts in the chest and three pairs of lesser hearts spaced out along the neck; each heart was only big enough to pump blood to the next, but all worked together as a relay team. The Columbia scientists also theorized that the resultant high blood pressure made this dinosaur prone to arterial disease and early death from a heart attack or stroke. Sceptics disagree: they believe *Barosaurus* managed with one moderately large heart aided by arterial valves in the neck to stop backflow, and waves of muscular contractions to push blood to the brain.

Whip-like tail

REARING FOR DEFENCE

Rising on her hind limbs, a *Barosaurus* towers 15m (49ft) high as she guards her vulnerable young against attack from a hungry allosaurid theropod. This lively tableau in New York's American Museum of Natural History suggests that sauropods were more active and caring than people once thought. However, we can only speculate on *Barosaurus*'s actual behaviour. It is possible, for example, that although the animal was capable of rearing up to a great height, it spent much of its time browsing on ferny undergrowth.

Barosaurus *mother rearing up in defence*

Attacking allosaur

Young Barosaurus *sheltering behind the tail*

TAIL The structure of the tail tip remains unknown, but other tail bones lead scientists to think the tail ended in a flexible whiplash, like that of *Diplodocus*. Flexible or not, the whole tail would need to be heavy enough to counterbalance the long neck.

Hind limb

AFRICAN SPECIES

Fragments of the skulls, jaws, limb bones, and other bones of a dinosaur relative of *Diplodocus* that were discovered in Tanzania have been attributed to *Barosaurus*.

Claw

Long, low,
sloping head

BAROSAURUS

Barosaurus was a huge, quadrupedal plant-eater with an extremely long neck,
a low head, and a bulky body. It was among the longest of the dinosaurs.

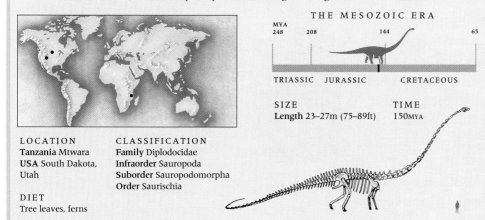

THE MESOZOIC ERA

MYA 248	208	144	65
TRIASSIC	JURASSIC	CRETACEOUS	

SIZE
Length 23–27m (75–89ft)

TIME
150MYA

LOCATION
Tanzania Mtwara
USA South Dakota,
Utah

DIET
Tree leaves, ferns

CLASSIFICATION
Family Diplodocidae
Infraorder Sauropoda
Suborder Sauropodomorpha
Order Saurischia

HEAD The model restores
Barosaurus's head as long, low
and sloping, with nostrils opening
above the eyes. This is guesswork
based on matching parts of the
skeleton with bones from similar
sauropods. More than a century
after Othniel Marsh named it in
1890, no *Barosaurus* skull has
been found in North America.

RESTORATION

A lifelike model restores *Barosaurus* with an immensely long
neck. Supporting this were 16 or more vertebrae. Some of
these vertebrae were a metre (3ft 3in) long, and bore long,
strut-like cervical ribs, but were deeply hollowed out to save
weight. Without this weight reduction the enormously long
neck would have been too heavy to raise. In modern-day
terms, if *Barosaurus* reared and craned its neck it could have
nibbled leaves from treetops as high as a five-storey building.

*Elongated, heavy neck
supported by large,
ribbed vertebrae*

HAZARDOUS WORK
*Earl Douglass and intrepid colleagues
explore a fossil-rich cliff face
at the Carnegie Quarry.*

Elbow

Forelimb

HUNTING DINOSAURS
*A 1922 archive
photograph shows chief
preparator Arthur
Coggeshall filming the
setting up of a camp at
the Carnegie Quarry.
This site was to yield
three nearly entire*
Barosaurus *skeletons.*

DIPLODOCUS

T HE LONGEST COMPLETE dinosaur skeleton found so far is that of *Diplodocus* ("double beam"). This massive diplodocid sauropod resembled a walking suspension bridge and was longer than a tennis court. Four trunk-like limbs, the hind limbs longer than the forelimbs, supported the body. Cantilevered from the forward end of this structure was a long, snaky neck and a small, horse-like head. At the rear end, great muscles linking pelvic bones and vertebrae helped hold aloft an even longer tail that tapered to a flexible, whiplash tip. Despite this animal's tremendous length, deep, huge cavities within its vertebrae suggest that *Diplodocus* possibly weighed no more than two or three present-day elephants.

ANDREW CARNEGIE
(1835–1919)
This American industrialist-philanthropist gave various museums Diplodocus casts.

■ LIFESTYLE ■

Diplodocus could have browsed on tall tree ferns, cycadeoids, ginkgo trees, conifers, and on the ferns and other vegetation that formed the meadows of their age. Certain scientists believe this dinosaur reached treetops by rearing, propped up on the tripod formed by its hind limbs and its tail. Concave bones along the underside of part of the tail (the double beams that gave *Diplodocus* its name) perhaps prevented blood vessels from being crushed when the tail was pressed against the ground. Peg-shaped teeth in the front of its mouth could have combed tree leaves and fern fronds from their tough stalks. However, this dinosaur possessed no back teeth for chewing. Instead, inside a muscular stomach like a bird's crop, gastroliths (swallowed stones) mashed up the leaves. The leaves passed on through the gut, probably to specialized "fermenting vats" where bacteria completed the process of digestion. Fossil footprints indicate that such dinosaurs as *Diplodocus* migrated to new feeding grounds once they had exhausted the food supply in one area. It is likely that they travelled in herds, which would have afforded some protection from predators. Massive as *Diplodocus* was, it had evolved to do little more than eat vast quantities of foliage, and had few defences other than its whiplash tail and perhaps its front limbs. Although older models and mounted skeletons depict *Diplodocus* dragging its tail, this is not supported by the fossil evidence. The absence of drag marks in fossil tracks suggests that it held its tail well off the ground.

Orbit
Braincase
Infratemporal fenestra
Naris
Mandible
Maxilla
Peg-shaped tooth
Antorbital fenestra

SKULL

Diplodocus's skull, seen here from the front (left) and side (above) was small and sloping, with a proportionally tiny brain. The fact that the nostrils were so far back (above the eyes) has prompted suggestions that *Diplodocus* had a trunk. The teeth grew only at the front of the mouth.

Underside of chevron

Concave surface

"DOUBLE BEAM" CHEVRONS

In the middle section of the tail's length, "double beams" are seen on the chevrons (the downward projections of the vertebrae). The "beams" are front and rear extensions of the chevron and may have protected the tail when pressed against the ground.

WHIPLASH TAIL

The tail contained at least 70 and possibly over 80 vertebrae. Cavities lightened the first 19 of these. Towards the tip, the vertebrae diminish into no more than simple rods, supporting the whiplash tail-tip.

Simple, rod-like vertebra

Caudal vertebrae

Chevron with "double beams"

Unextended chevron

SUSPENSION BRIDGE STRUCTURE
Diplodocus's limbs were like supporting piers; the body below its spine was like a roadway held up by cables.

❊ FACT FILE ❊

DIPLODOCUS

One of the longest dinosaurs, *Diplodocus* was an immense, quadrupedal plant-eater.

THE MESOZOIC ERA

MYA 248	208	144	65
TRIASSIC	JURASSIC	CRETACEOUS	

CLASSIFICATION
Family Diplodocidae
Infraorder Sauropoda
Suborder Sauropodomorpha
Order Saurischia

TIME
150MYA

DIET
Tree leaves, ferns

LOCATION
USA Colorado,
Utah, Wyoming

SIZE
Length 27m (89ft)
Weight 12 tonnes
(11.8 tons)

DISCOVERY

Fossil hunter Samuel Williston found partial *Diplodocus* remains in Colorado in 1877. The first good articulated skeleton came from Wyoming in 1899. These and other finds helped palaeontologists to identify four species.

SKELETONS OLD AND NEW

Diplodocus skeletons used to be mounted with their tails apparently dragging on the ground. The picture on the left shows the original mounting of a cast that was presented by Andrew Carnegie to the Natural History Museum in London. Today the cast is displayed in the same location, but with a raised tail, having been remounted in 1993. The other skeleton (below) is also based on a modern interpretation and is on display at the Senckenberg Museum in Frankfurt, Germany.

Orbit

Cervical vertebrae

Sacral vertebrae

Dorsal vertebrae

Mandible

Scapula

Coracoid

Ilium

Rib

Humerus

Femur

Ischium

Elbow joint

Tibia

Radius

Fibula

Metatarsals

Phalanges

Ulna

Wrist joint

Ankle joint

Metacarpals

FOOT BONES

Diplodocus's pillar-like hind limbs rested on broad, five-toed feet supported by fibrous "heels". Only the first three toes bore claws. An exception to this sauropod rule was the diplodocid *Dyslocosaurus*, with four or maybe five claws per foot.

Tibia

Fibula

Ankle bone (astragalus)

Metatarsal

Claw bone

Phalanges

APATOSAURUS

A BOUT TWELVE skeletons, representing three species, make this one of the best-known sauropods. *Apatosaurus* constituted a sturdier, heavier, but rather shorter version of its close relative *Diplodocus*. The creature had a small, low, horse-like head with peg-shaped teeth; a long, muscular neck; a deep, heavy body; pillar-like limbs with short, elephantine toes; and a whiplash tail containing 82 bones – even more than *Diplodocus*. *Apatosaurus* grew nearly as long as a tennis court, stood higher at the hips than an elephant, and weighed as much as four or even five elephants.

RESTORATION

Restored in line with current thinking, an *Apatosaurus* walks with its tail held clear of the ground. This stopped other sauropods treading on its tail, and may also have prevented hunting groups of small theropods from seizing it.

THE CARNEGIE SKELETON

The *Apatosaurus* skeleton pictured on these pages stands in Pittsburgh's Carnegie Museum, which was founded by the Scottish-born, philanthropic steel magnate Andrew Carnegie (1835–1919).

■ LIFESTYLE ■

Apatosaurus herds ambled across the glades and forested riverbanks of Late Jurassic western North America, adults browsing on high treetops. It is a puzzle how *Apatosaurus*'s small jaws could have consumed enough nourishment to power its immense body. The creature probably had to eat almost all the time, stopping only to wallow in water to cool off and to kill skin parasites. At night, *Apatosaurus* might have slept standing on their feet. In the case of carnosaur attack, big, tough-skinned bulls could lash out with their immense, whip-like tails, knocking over and badly injuring a predator. Or they might have reared up on their powerful hind legs, to bring their clawed forefeet crashing thunderously down on the enemy. Solidly heavy as the creature was, many of its bones – especially those of the spine – were honeycombed in structure for lightness. But even so, the creature was too massive to outrun predators. Defence was a matter of staying in herds and, probably, of a system of alarm calls that alerted the big males to come to the fore and confront the danger. Females and the younger dinosaurs would have congregated in a circle behind a wall of males.

MISTAKEN IDENTITY

In 1883 this "*Apatosaurus*" tail became part of the first reconstructed sauropod skeleton. It is in fact the shorter tail of a *Camarasaurus*.

Caudal vertebra

Short tip

Chevrons extend almost to the tail-tip

■ NAME CHANGE ■

Many people know *Apatosaurus* ("deceptive lizard") better by its old name *Brontosaurus* ("thunder lizard", from the supposed sound of its heavy tread). The name was changed when "*Brontosaurus*" fossils proved identical with those of a dinosaur that had been named previously – *Apatosaurus*.

HIGH-LEVEL BROWSING

Apatosaurus was capable of lifting its head high enough to browse on treetops, but probably more often ate fronds of low-growing ferns.

Caudal
vertebrae

Sacral
vertebrae

Dorsal
vertebrae

FEATURES OF THE SKELETON

The cervical vertebrae (neck bones) and limb bones were thicker and heavier than those of *Diplodocus* but both had a long, whip-like tail and a low head with peg-like teeth. *Apatosaurus*'s skull was identified in 1975, nearly a century after the animal was named.

Cervical vertebrae

Ilium

Chevron

Ischium

Knee
joint

Pubis

Femur

Fibula

Tibia

Ankle
joint

Metatarsals

Phalanges

Rib

Ulna

Radius

Metacarpals

Coracoid

Humerus

Elbow joint

Wrist joint

Cervical rib

CLAWED THUMB

In many restorations, sauropods are shown with two or even three large claws on their massive "hands". In fact, only the thumb had a claw. These fossil thumb bones are from the thumb of an *Apatosaurus*. In life, the curved bone at the tip of the thumb was the inner core of a large, horny claw.

Metacarpal

Phalanges

Ungual phalanx
(claw bone)

■ FACT FILE ■

APATOSAURUS

Apatosaurus was a massive, quadrupedal plant-eater with a long tail and neck.

THE MESOZOIC ERA

MYA
248   208   144   65

TRIASSIC   JURASSIC   CRETACEOUS

LOCATION
USA Colorado,Utah,
Oklahoma, Wyoming
Mexico Baja California

TIME
156–150MYA

SIZE
Length 21m (69ft)
Weight 25 tonnes

CLASSIFICATION
Family Diplodocidae
Infraorder Sauropoda
Suborder
Sauropodomorpha
Order Saurischia

DIET
Tree leaves, ferns

DEFENSIVE POSTURE

As shown below, *Apatosaurus* might have reared up on to its hind legs to threaten a large, marauding theropod that was endangering its young. But not all scientists believe that sauropods adopted tactics like this. Perhaps these enormous creatures intimidated their enemies by closing their ranks and relying on sheer size and tough hides for protection.

MAMENCHISAURUS

A LARGE DINOSAUR from China, "Mamen Brook lizard" had more cervical vertebrae than any other sauropod, and the longest neck of any animal ever. Some individuals may have had necks 15m (49ft) long. Yet the neck was comparatively light: some areas of bone were eggshell thin. Each cervical vertebra (neck bone) had two rod-like ribs to stiffen the neck, as in other sauropods. Some features of the spine are reminiscent of *Diplodocus*. Skull fragments found in the 1980s suggest *Mamenchisaurus* had a taller, blunter snout than *Diplodocus*, and teeth that were sturdier and more spoon-shaped.

▪ LIFESTYLE ▪

Scientists disagree about how this dinosaur used its ultra-long neck. Some artists have illustrated *Mamenchisaurus* with its neck jutting out almost parallel with the top of its back. This fits in with a theory that the sauropod stood in lakes, its neck floating on the water and swinging from side to side as its mouth cut a swathe through the soft-leaved water-plants. Most experts now reject this theory and claim that *Mamenchisaurus* lived on land and raised its neck to browse on branches high above. This appears more probable for four main reasons. First, if the dinosaur did have strong, spoon-shaped teeth, it seems unlikely that they would have been needed for cropping soft-leaved waterplants. Second, the neck was lighter than it looked and should not have been difficult to lift. Third, two dorsal vertebrae near the neck apparently met at an angle that would tend to make the neck curve up from the shoulders. Elephantine limbs provide a fourth indication that *Mamenchisaurus* lived on land. This dinosaur would have lived in herds, the adults guarding the young from such hungry carnosaurs as *Szechuanosaurus* and *Yangchuanosaurus*, which occur in the same Chinese rock formation. Scientists conjecture that *Mamenchisaurus* might have belonged to a uniquely Asian family of dinosaurs, together with two other long-necked sauropods known from Late Jurassic China: *Omeisaurus* and *Euhelopus*.

SKELETON EXPOSED

Our restoration is based on a skeleton that lacked a skull. (The head and teeth are depicted as if they resembled those of *Diplodocus*.) As many as 19 cervical vertebrae – more than any other sauropod's – supported the enormously long neck. The forelimbs were relatively longer and sturdier than those of *Diplodocus*, and the bones of the hind limbs were robust. The tail's chevron bones bore fore-and-aft extensions similar to the tail skids of *Diplodocus*; the long tail may have ended in a whiplash.

Cervical vertebra

Dorsal vertebra

Rib

Cervical rib

Scapula

Coracoid

Humerus

Forelimb

Elbow joint

Radius

Ulna

Wrist joint

Forefoot

EXCAVATING A SKELETON
This photograph was taken during an excavation in 1957. Scientists from Beijing and from Chonquing in Sichuan took three months to remove this colossus from the site.

Long, flexible
neck

Naris situated
high up on
the head

Mandible   Tooth

■ FACT FILE ■

MAMENCHISAURUS

Mamenchisaurus was an immensely long, quadrupedal plant-eater. It had the longest known neck of all dinosaurs, and probably a blunt snout and strong teeth.

THE MESOZOIC ERA

MYA 248	208	144	65
TRIASSIC	JURASSIC	CRETACEOUS	

SIZE
Length 25m (82ft)
Weight 27 tonnes
(26.6 tons)

TIME
160MYA

LOCATION
China Sichuan,
Gansu, Xinjiang

DIET
Tree leaves

CLASSIFICATION
Family Euhelopodidae
Infraorder Sauropoda
Suborder Sauropodomorpha
Order Saurischia

EUHELOPUS SKULL

Mamenchisaurus's missing skull might have looked more like *Euhelopus*'s short, steep-snouted skull than *Diplodocus*'s long, low one. *Euhelopus* had larger teeth than *Diplodocus* and these grew from the sides of the jaws as well as from the front.

Orbit

Antorbital fenestra

Naris

Maxilla

Infratemporal
fenestra

Tooth

Mandible

AQUATIC RESTORATION
An old picture shows two Euhelopus *snorkelling and browsing under water. Experts no longer believe that sauropods needed water to support their heavy bodies.*

Femur

Whiplash tail

Knee joint

Fibula

Tibia

Ankle
joint

Hind limb

Tarsal

Claw

CARING PARENTS
Adults are thought to have cared well for their young, guarding them against attack by the dangerous theropod dinosaurs, *Szechuanosaurus* and *Yangchuanosaurus*.

SALTASAURUS

B EFORE PALAEONTOLOGISTS in Argentina identified *Saltasaurus* ("Salta lizard") in 1980, they had assumed that its bony armour, long known from fossil finds in their country, had belonged to ankylosaurs, for these were thought to be the only dinosaurs with armour. The discovery of *Saltasaurus* proved that some sauropods grew armour too. Close-packed bony nodules and ridged, bony plates as big as a human palm fortified its back and sides. A fairly small sauropod, *Saltasaurus* had stocky limbs, a sturdy tail tapering to a slender, diplodocid-like whiplash, and distinctively shaped vertebrae characteristic of the titanosaurids.

▪ LIFESTYLE ▪

Like other sauropods, *Saltasaurus* would have walked on land and could have raised its long neck to feed on vegetation out of reach of smaller herbivores. This titanosaurid may also have been able to rear up on its hind limbs, supporting its body with its tail, in order to reach even less accessible sources of food. *Saltasaurus*'s relatively small size made it more vulnerable than larger sauropods to attack by big carnivorous dinosaurs. But any animal that tried to leap upon *Saltasaurus*'s back would have stubbed its claws and snapped off teeth when it tried to sink them into the rock-hard armour in *Saltasaurus*'s tough hide.

▪ LOCATION ▪

The same Late Cretaceous rock formations in which *Saltasaurus* bones were discovered also contain the skeletons of other titanosaurids like *Antarctosaurus*, *Argyrosaurus*, and *Laplatasaurus*. Very likely, most or all of these had armour plating too. Superior defence may be only part of the explanation why big saurischian herbivores continued to exist in South America long after all sauropods had died out in North America. According to one theory the North American sauropods suffered from competition with duckbilled and horned dinosaurs, which may have been largely confined to the northern continents by a sea barrier. Another possibility is that the new flowering plants, appearing in the north at that time, were not suitable for sauropods to eat. Whatever the cause, one titanosaurid (*Alamosaurus*) did succeed in crossing from South to North America, and survived there.

ARMOURED SKIN
The 1980 description of fossil scraps of *Saltasaurus*'s skin, with its bony, pea-sized lumps, supported what one scientist had suspected as long ago as 1896: that titanosaurids had been armoured sauropods.

TAIL Used as a support when the animal reared, *Saltasaurus*'s long tail had interlocking bones with ball-and-socket joints.

Thick, muscular tail

LATE CRETACEOUS SCENE
Three Saltasaurus, *four duckbilled dinosaurs, and a small theropod,* Noasaurus, *visit a river in what is now Salta province in northwestern Argentina.*

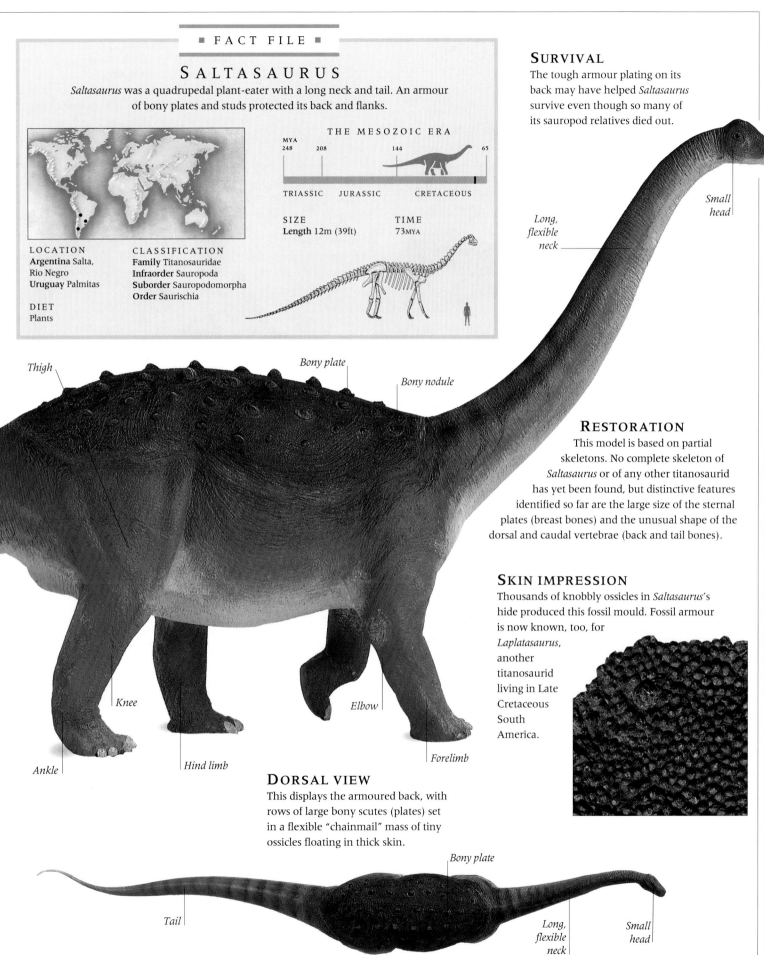

■ FACT FILE ■

SALTASAURUS

Saltasaurus was a quadrupedal plant-eater with a long neck and tail. An armour of bony plates and studs protected its back and flanks.

THE MESOZOIC ERA

MYA
248   208   144   65

TRIASSIC   JURASSIC   CRETACEOUS

SIZE   TIME
Length 12m (39ft)   73MYA

LOCATION
Argentina Salta,
Rio Negro
Uruguay Palmitas

DIET
Plants

CLASSIFICATION
Family Titanosauridae
Infraorder Sauropoda
Suborder Sauropodomorpha
Order Saurischia

SURVIVAL

The tough armour plating on its back may have helped *Saltasaurus* survive even though so many of its sauropod relatives died out.

Small head

Long, flexible neck

RESTORATION

This model is based on partial skeletons. No complete skeleton of *Saltasaurus* or of any other titanosaurid has yet been found, but distinctive features identified so far are the large size of the sternal plates (breast bones) and the unusual shape of the dorsal and caudal vertebrae (back and tail bones).

SKIN IMPRESSION

Thousands of knobbly ossicles in *Saltasaurus*'s hide produced this fossil mould. Fossil armour is now known, too, for *Laplatasaurus*, another titanosaurid living in Late Cretaceous South America.

Thigh

Bony plate

Bony nodule

Knee

Elbow

Ankle

Hind limb

Forelimb

DORSAL VIEW

This displays the armoured back, with rows of large bony scutes (plates) set in a flexible "chainmail" mass of tiny ossicles floating in thick skin.

Bony plate

Tail

Long, flexible neck

Small head

SEGNOSAURUS

A HEAVY-BODIED BIPED as long as the largest modern crocodile, "slow lizard" is often thought of as having a small, narrow skull with a shallow lower jaw, a toothless beak, rather sharp yet prosauropod-like cheek teeth, and fleshy cheek pouches. *Segnosaurus* had muscular arms, and its three-fingered hands probably bore huge, curved claws. Between its broad back and bulky belly, the pubic hip bones slanted backwards. Other peculiarities included short, possibly webbed, feet with four clawed toes.

▪ LIFESTYLE ▪

Segnosaurus belongs to the segnosaurs, an unusual group of saurischians with features that are reminiscent of theropods, prosauropods, and ornithischians. Few other dinosaurs have posed greater puzzles to scientists in their attempt to build up a picture of a particular creature's way of life. One possibility is that *Segnosaurus* might have used its strong arms and hands, probably equipped with long, sharp claws, to rake open termites' nests to feed on the insects. The great anteater, which lives in South America today, wields its claws in this way. Powerful arms and talons could also have served as defensive weapons. Some people believe that *Segnosaurus* swam in lakes or rivers, catching fish to eat – a notion that derives from the discovery, near a find of *Segnosaurus* bones, of fossil tracks preserving a series of four-toed, web-footed imprints. Yet *Segnosaurus*'s mouth seems ill-designed for gripping slippery water animals. Instead, it may have been an animal with a toothless beak, ridged teeth, and roomy cheeks, well equipped for nipping off leaves and biting them into smaller pieces. *Segnosaurus*'s hip structure also suggests a plant diet since the back-turned pubis would have made room for the great gut needed to digest large quantities of low-grade plant material.

▪ UNUSUAL THEROPOD ▪

If the third possibility is true, it might make *Segnosaurus* into a dinosaur oddity – a plant-eating theropod. Its jaw and hip structure would be similar to those of many plant-eating dinosaurs, but no other theropod had these features. The limb bones indicate that *Segnosaurus* might have managed only a brisk walk or a slow run. Certainly, with longer thighs than shins, and short, broad feet, *Segnosaurus* would have moved around too slowly to pursue and catch active prey in the manner of most ordinary theropods.

TERMITE-EATER

Segnosaurus is shown using its immensely strong arms and long, clawed hands to rake open a nest mound teeming with blind, white, ant-like termites (these insects are now known to have existed as long ago as the Late Triassic). *Segnosaurus* might have lapped them up by the mouthful with a long, sticky tongue.

Small, narrow head

Fleshy cheek pouch

Long, flexible neck

Shoulder

Thigh longer than the shin

Knee

Strong, muscular arm

Huge, curved claw

Three-fingered hand

Short, broad foot

FISH-EATER

A second scenario portrays *Segnosaurus* as a fish-eater. Mongolian scientist Altangerel Perle, who named *Segnosaurus* in 1979, thought this dinosaur capable of swimming in lakes or rivers and seizing fishes in its beak. But a toothless beak might have been a clumsy fish-catching device compared to the long, narrow, pointed teeth of fish-eating crocodiles.

PLANT-EATER

American palaeontologist Gregory Paul made the third suggestion: that *Segnosaurus* had evolved for eating plants. Segnosaurs are now seen by some scientists as bizarre plant-eating theropods.

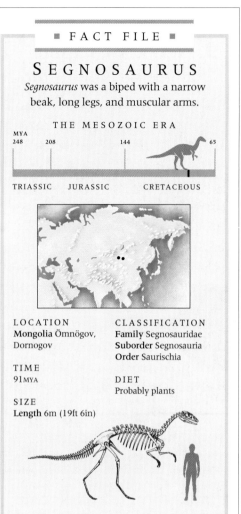

■ FACT FILE ■

SEGNOSAURUS

Segnosaurus was a biped with a narrow beak, long legs, and muscular arms.

THE MESOZOIC ERA

MYA 248	208	144	65

TRIASSIC JURASSIC CRETACEOUS

LOCATION
Mongolia Ömnögov, Dornogov

CLASSIFICATION
Family Segnosauridae
Suborder Segnosauria
Order Saurischia

TIME
91MYA

DIET
Probably plants

SIZE
Length 6m (19ft 6in)

EXTERNAL APPEARANCE

Segnosaurus is depicted here as a heavy-bodied, bipedal theropod. However, other artists sometimes show segnosaurs as having walked on all fours. By the early 1990s, *Segnosaurus* was known only from three partial specimens. The various remains included the lower jaw with teeth, some limb bones, and hip bones, but no skull. The limited scope of the finds meant that the exact appearance of *Segnosaurus* and other segnosaurs remains a matter for speculation.

Scaly skin

Hind limb

Ankle

Hallux (first toe)

SEGNOSAURUS

Ilium

Hip socket

Ilium

Ischium

Pubis

ADASAURUS

Ilium

Hip socket

Ischium

Pubis

HYPSILOPHODON

Ilium

Hip socket

Ischium

Pubis

HIP BONES COMPARED

The scientists who found segnosaurs thought their mixture of features represented a third dinosaur group, between the saurischians and ornithischians. In *Segnosaurus* the pubis sloped back against the ischium, in the same way as in the ornithischian *Hypsilophodon*. Most saurischians' pubes sloped forwards or down, but there were a few exceptions, for instance *Adasaurus*.

THYREOPHORANS

T HYREOPHORANS ("SHIELD BEARERS") were a diverse group of mainly quadrupedal, armoured ornithischians, with small cheek teeth, distinctive cheek bones, heavy limbs, and rows of protective bony studs, plates, or spikes down the back. All of them probably browsed on low-level vegetation. These dinosaurs were primitive ornithischians with simpler teeth and jaws than ornithopods or marginocephalians. The most primitive of all thyreophorans were relatively small, Early Jurassic forms: *Scelidosaurus* and *Scutellosaurus*, and possibly the poorly known genera *Tatisaurus* and *Echinodon*. The rest are grouped together in the infraorders Stegosauria (chiefly Jurassic beasts) and Ankylosauria (which replaced stegosaurs), both of which contained beasts that grew up to 10m (33ft) long.

An ankylosaurid tail club could have broken a tyrannosaurid's ankle.

SCELIDOSAURUS AND MINMI
Scelidosaurus *(top) was an early thyreophoran close in ancestry to ankylosaurs such as* Minmi *(above).* Minmi *was so well-protected that bony armour guarded even its belly.*

NODOSAURID SPINE
This broad-based, sharply pointed, bony spine stuck up from a nodosaurid's shoulder. In life, a horny sheath made the spine more formidable.

✻ SCELIDOSAURIDAE ✻

This family contained *Scelidosaurus*, a 4m (13ft) long quadruped, with a small head and rows of small, bony studs shielding its body. This early thyreophoran is known from Early Jurassic English rocks, and also lived in Arizona and Tibet. *Scutellosaurus*, *Tatisaurus*, and *Echinodon* shared some features with *Scelidosaurus*. All four may be close to stegosaur and ankylosaur ancestors.

✻ STEGOSAURIA ✻

These dinosaurs were medium to large quadrupedal herbivores. Most had long, thick, strong hind limbs giving them an arched back highest at the hips. Some palaeontologists believe stegosaurs could have reared to browse higher up. The low head was small, with a beak and cheek teeth. The most distinctive features were two rows of tall, bony plates and/or spikes jutting up from head to tail, and at least two pairs of long tail spines. Some stegosaurs had shoulder spines too. Despite their size, the largest stegosaurs had a brain no bigger than a dog's. A large centre in the hip region (often misnamed a "second brain") helped to control hind limbs and tail. Both known families of stegosaurs probably arose in China in Early Jurassic times. One family later spread to Africa, Europe, India, and North America. Stegosaurs were an important group of dinosaurs in the Late Jurassic. Several genera survived into the Early Cretaceous, but only India's stegosaurs seem to have persisted into the Late Cretaceous. HUAYANGOSAURIDAE formed the more primitive family of stegosaurs, with a deep, short snout, a beak with upper teeth, fairly long forelimbs, and distinctive bones in the skull and hips. The family is known only from *Huayangosaurus*, a Middle Jurassic genus 4.5m (15ft) long from China. STEGOSAURIDAE basically resembled *Huayangosaurus*, but they had entirely toothless beaks. Some kinds had two rows of paired plates and/or spines jutting up from the neck, back, and tail. In *Stegosaurus* the plates alternated instead of growing side by side. Reputedly the largest stegosaur, *Stegosaurus* grew up to 9m (29ft 6in) long. Altogether, there were about 15 stegosaurid

STEGOSAUR PLATES
The plates and spines of Huayangosaurus tabaii *(left) might have been weapons, or mating signals to others of its species seeking a mate.* Stegosaurus*'s big plates may have contained blood vessels that adjusted body temperature by absorbing and releasing heat.*

genera. This family lived from the Middle Jurassic to the Late Cretaceous. Its members occurred in Africa, Asia, Europe, India, and North America.

❋ ANKYLOSAURIA ❋

Ankylosaurs were relatively low-slung dinosaurs with broad heads; rather short necks; heavy, barrel-shaped bodies supported by four sturdy, erect limbs; and fairly long, muscular tails. Instead of tall plates or spines, these armoured ornithischians depended upon bands of bony studs or plates, some sheathed in horn, to protect the body. These covered the neck, back, and flanks (and in at least some specimens, the belly). Bony plates reinforced the broad, low skull, closing four "windows" left open in most other dinosaurs. A tail club or shoulder spines served as counter-offensive weapons. Ankylosaurs were replacing stegosaurs by the Early Cretaceous, and became the most abundant, low-browsing, quadrupedal dinosaurs. They are chiefly known from fossils found in North America and Asia, but Australian discoveries prove that they also spread to southern continents. There were two ankylosaur families: the Nodosauridae and the Ankylosauridae.

NODOSAURIDAE were the more primitive ankylosaurs. Their skulls had an unusual palate in the shape of an hourglass. Nodosauridae lacked a tail club, but some bore dangerously long, sharp, shoulder spines. There are more than 20 named genera, ranging from 1.6m to 7.6m (about 5ft to 25ft) long. Nodosaurids lived from Middle Jurassic to Late Cretaceous times, and occurred in Asia, Australia, Europe, North America, and probably Antarctica.

ANKYLOSAURIDAE had skulls at least as broad as they were long, with pointed "corners" at the back, and intricate breathing passages. These dinosaurs lacked long shoulder spines but had a tail ending in a heavy, bony club. This tail club could be swung as a powerful weapon against attack by predatory dinosaurs such as the tyrannosaurids. Ankylosaurids ranged from about 5.5m to 10m (18ft to 33ft) long. They include more than a dozen named genera. This dinosaur family flourished from Early to Late Cretaceous times, in Asia and North America.

THYREOPHORAN FAMILY TREE

This diagram shows relationships between thyreophoran families (the names ending in -idae), each containing one genus or several genera. All thyreophorans had distinctive cheek bones and rows of bony studs, spikes, or plates running down the back. They were among the most primitive ornithischians, with teeth and jaws less well evolved for slicing up or pulping vegetation than almost all the rest. Small, early, rather lightly armoured forms, here represented by the Scelidosauridae, gave rise to two families of stegosaurs and two families of ankylosaurs. Stegosaurs had rows of tall plates or spikes on the neck, back, and tail. The heavily armoured ankylosaurs were built like "walking armoured cars".

KEY

⬤ Suborder

⬤ Infraorder

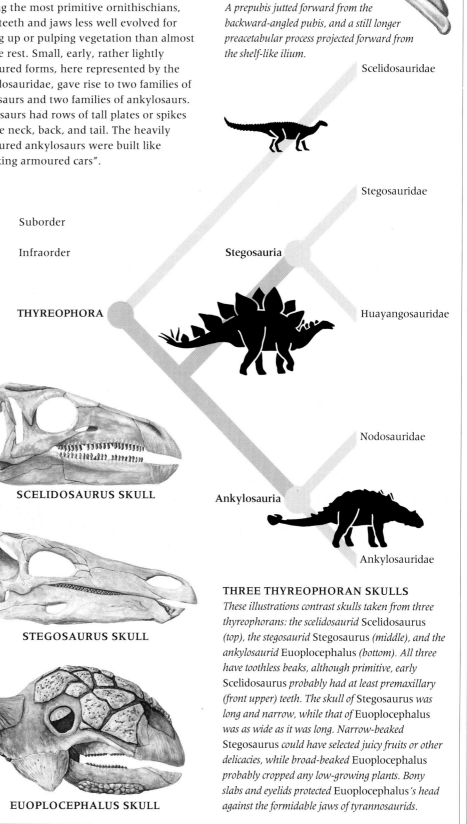

STEGOSAURUS HIP BONES
A prepubis jutted forward from the backward-angled pubis, and a still longer preacetabular process projected forward from the shelf-like ilium.

THYREOPHORA

Stegosauria

Ankylosauria

Scelidosauridae

Stegosauridae

Huayangosauridae

Nodosauridae

Ankylosauridae

SCELIDOSAURUS SKULL

STEGOSAURUS SKULL

EUOPLOCEPHALUS SKULL

THREE THYREOPHORAN SKULLS
These illustrations contrast skulls taken from three thyreophorans: the scelidosaurid Scelidosaurus (top), the stegosaurid Stegosaurus (middle), and the ankylosaurid Euoplocephalus (bottom). All three have toothless beaks, although primitive, early Scelidosaurus probably had at least premaxillary (front upper) teeth. The skull of Stegosaurus was long and narrow, while that of Euoplocephalus was as wide as it was long. Narrow-beaked Stegosaurus could have selected juicy fruits or other delicacies, while broad-beaked Euoplocephalus probably cropped any low-growing plants. Bony slabs and eyelids protected Euoplocephalus's head against the formidable jaws of tyrannosaurids.

SCELIDOSAURUS

L IGHTLY ARMOURED ("LIMB LIZARD") was a herbivore no longer than a car. It had a small head on a neck that was relatively long for an armoured dinosaur, and a long, heavy body that was highest at the hips and underpinned by four sturdy limbs. Bony tendons probably strengthened and stiffened the tail. The hip bones and armoured skin recall those of the primitive North American ornithischian *Scutellosaurus*. The teeth resemble those of stegosaurs. Above all, the rows of ridged, bony plates and studs running down the neck, back, and tail seem prototypes for the more formidable defences of the ankylosaurs. *Scelidosaurus* might have been an ancestor of these fellow thyreophorans.

Skull roof *Orbit*

Beak

Conical tooth

Fragment of mandible

SKULL

This fragmented skull of a young dinosaur was found by amateur fossil hunters in 1985 near Charmouth on England's southern coast. Identified as belonging to a *Scelidosaurus*, it has teeth in its front upper jaw, a characteristic feature in the skulls of primitive ornithischians.

■ LIFESTYLE ■

Scelidosaurus ambled slowly on all fours through a leafy landscape, stopping frequently to shear off low-growing soft-leaved plants or juicy fruits with its narrow beak. With less complex teeth and jaws than later ornithischians, it would have chewed with simple up-and-down jaw movements. Young individuals perhaps added extra protein to their diet by eating insects. Some *Scelidosaurus* fossil bones are preserved in marine sediments, prompting one authority to think that *Scelidosaurus* was amphibious. More probably, these creatures lived on riverbanks, and sometimes drowned, perhaps when the river overflowed. The corpses might then have been carried out to sea, to be buried and preserved.

SKIN

Scelidosaurus skin impressions show that between rows of bony studs, the skin bore a mosaic of little, rounded scales like those of *Heloderma*, the North American venomous lizard commonly known as the Gila monster.

BONY PLATES

Scelidosaurus was protected by individual bony plates, known as scutes. Their shape and size depended on their location on the neck, body, or tail.

Stiffened tail for balance

■ STANCE AND GAIT ■

Scelidosaurus may sometimes have reared to browse on the leafy twigs of trees but it would seem that its normal mode of locomotion was on all fours. Certainly the body-shape strongly suggests this: the hips are the highest point, but not so high as to make the hind limbs a sort of fulcrum on top of which the stiffened tail and the short neck and head might pivot. Moreover, the hands on the forelimbs appear designed for weight-bearing, and were as broad as the feet on the hind limbs. Cornered, it would have crouched, exposing only its tough, armoured, upper hide to a theropod's fangs and claws. Even its head and neck bore bony reinforcements that were thick and hard enough to break off the teeth of most attackers.

End of tibia

Metatarsals

End of fibula

Phalanges

Tarsals

Hoof-like claw bone

FOOT BONES

A detailed view of the bones of this *Scelidosaurus* foot reveal that it was long and quite broad. There were four toes: three long and one short. The long toes helped to spread the body's weight. Fleshy pads possibly cushioned the toes.

SCUTELLOSAURUS

Like *Scelidosaurus*, *Scutellosaurus* was a primitive ornithischian close to the ancestry of ankylosaurs and stegosaurs. A lightly armoured herbivore, this Early Jurassic dinosaur from Arizona was evidently descended from small, bipedal ancestors. *Scutellosaurus* could walk or run on its long hind limbs, balanced by its elongated tail. It is possible that the weight of the lengthy body and bony scutes made the animal front-heavy. This would cause it to go down on all fours, supporting the forepart of its body on its relatively long forelimbs and large hands.

SCUTES
Hundreds of scutes shielded *Scutellosaurus* from attack by theropods. The largest scutes ran down the back, possibly in one, but probably in two rows.

SKELETON
This partial skeleton of a *Scelidosaurus* (above) was discovered in the nineteenth century in a Lower Lias limestone block that still helps to hold the bones together. Preparators used acid baths to dissolve away some of the rock and thus reveal additional bones.

Skull

Cervical vertebra

Fibula

Caudal vertebrae

Tibia

Phalanges

Femur

Dorsal scute

Limpet-like scute

Narrow beak

Naris

Heavily armoured head

Thorny scute

Neck scute

Short neck

Muscular hind limb

Ankle

Scaly skin

Knee

Elbow

Forelimb

EXTERNAL VIEW
This restoration emphasizes the rows of sharp-edged bones, probably sheathed in horn, that protected the creature's neck, back, flanks, and tail. Rows of low, small plates guarded the back and neck, and clusters of thorny scutes helped protect the head.

Strong hind foot

Broad, strong hand (forefoot)

Hoof-like claw

STEGOSAURUS

S TEGOSAURUS ("ROOF LIZARD") gets its name from big bony plates that jutted upwards from the neck, back, and upper tail. A bony plate probably guarded each hip, and two pairs of spikes stuck out sideways from the end of the tail. As heavy as a big rhinoceros and about the length of a bus, *Stegosaurus* was the largest known plated dinosaur. It stood more than room-high at the hips and walked on elephantine limbs. Its small head was held low and ended in a toothless, horn-covered beak. Behind the beak were numerous teeth. It is not known if the tail drooped or was held aloft.

SEARCHING FOR FOOD
A strolling Stegosaurus *(above) had to be prepared to wield its spiky tail against aggressive carnivores. The greatest dangers probably came from* Allosaurus *and* Ceratosaurus, *but packs of smaller theropods may also have preyed on the great beast.*

▪ LIFESTYLE ▪

Fossil evidence suggests that *Stegosaurus* roamed wooded plains, browsing on low vegetation. A rival theory suggests that it was a high-level feeder, browsing at heights up to 3.5m (about 12ft), and that it was actually built to rear up. Some evidence lies in the fact that the hind limbs were longer than the forelimbs. *Stegosaurus*'s tall vertebral spines could have provided enough leverage for the back muscles to be able to lift the weight of the forepart of the body. The supple tail was better suited to being pressed against the ground than the rigid tails of most ornithischians. In this way, tail and hind limbs could have formed a tripod when a *Stegosaurus* reared up. Most dinosaurologists are, however, unconvinced by this theory. Ideas about *Stegosaurus*'s diet, too, have changed over the years. At first, it was thought that the animal had weak teeth and that it used to feed only on soft foods; today, however, this assumption is in some doubt. On the other hand, the narrow snout may indicate that *Stegosaurus* was a selective feeder and it may have picked out choice items such as seed fern "fruits" and the fleshy "flowers" of cycadeoids. *Stegosaurus*'s spectacular back plates probably helped soak up and shed heat, and rival males may also have used them in harmless threat displays. There were no plates covering the flanks, but a *Stegosaurus* would have been able to fend off enemies by swishing its tail, or backing into them like a porcupine. A discovery in 1992 revealed disc-shaped plates protecting the hips, and a pattern of disc-shaped bony studs that shielded the throat.

Caudal plate

Caudal vertebra

Caudal spike used in defence

Spiked tail could be swung from side to side

Chevron

Neural spine

Ischium

Pubis

Femur

Knee joint

Broad foot providing a stable base

RECONSTRUCTED SKELETON

This reconstruction, with an added outline of the beast's body, reveals the robust, bony framework of this large, heavy-bodied, plated dinosaur. Until 1992, scientists were unsure how its plates had been arranged upon the neck, back, and tail. Some believed they had been paired. Others thought they alternated. A third group put them in one row, with big plates overlapping. In 1992, a newly discovered skeleton, found in Colorado, proved the plates had formed two staggered rows.

ELONGATED SKULL

The skull of *Stegosaurus* (right) was narrow, elongated, and very low. Unlike a typical dinosaur skull, it lacked an antorbital fenestra (hole between the orbit and naris). A different *Stegosaurus* species might have had a shorter, blunter skull, although some experts have assigned that species to the genus *Diracodon*.

CHEEK TOOTH

The asymmetrical fossil cheek tooth (below) has been attributed to *Stegosaurus*. Ridges corrugate the top and one side of the crown. Such ridges would have helped the ornithischian to chew up plant foods. Most stegosaurs' teeth would have had fewer ridges.

Braincase

Orbit

Naris

Narrow, toothless beak

Jaw joint

Mandible

Complex ridges

Small, weak, leaf-shaped crown

Wear facet

Root

Ilium

Prepubic process

Dorsal plate

Hip joint

Dorsal vertebra

Cervical plate

Small, shallow skull

Weak, lower jaw

Scapula

Shoulder joint

Sturdy hind limb, much longer than a forelimb

Elbow joint

Short forelimb

Fibula

Humerus

Wrist joint

Tibia

Ulna

Short toe

Ankle joint

Broad, short forefoot

115

OVERHEAD VIEW

Stegosaurus's tail spikes can be clearly seen in the restoration (above). There are no shoulder spikes – although some stegosaurs had these. *Stegosaurus stenops* is also known to have had large, disc-shaped plates on its hips.

HEAT REGULATION

A rich blood supply to the skin covering the plates helped to regulate body temperature. If *Stegosaurus* stood sideways to the morning sun, the blood coursing around its sun-warmed plates grew hotter and quickly energized its body. If the animal stood with its back to the fiery, midday sun, the sun's rays did not strike the flat surface of the plates, which thus shed more heat than they gained. The asymmetrical arrangement of the plates would also have helped them lose heat to the air whatever the wind direction.

Caudal spike

Caudal plate

Dorsal plate

Caudal spike

FRONT VIEW

This angle emphasizes the tallest plates, some 76cm (2ft 6in) high, sticking up from the back. The plates probably served several purposes. They must have acted as signals for individuals to notice others of their kind. A male standing broadside to a smaller rival might have frightened him by a superior display of plates.

LIMBS The hind limbs were much longer than the forelimbs. Each of the hind feet had three short, broad toes supported by a large, broad pad. Each forefoot had a rather smaller pad, and five short, broad, weight-bearing digits. Some digits on both the hind limbs and the forelimbs bore hoof-like nails.

Large, broad foot

PLATES

The thin, erect, bony plates on the neck, back, and tail were graduated in size: the biggest above the back, the smallest over the neck and tail. The largest of all plates come from *Stegosaurus stenops*, which some scientists believe is a separate genus called *Diracodon*.

■ FACT FILE ■

STEGOSAURUS

A large quadruped, *Stegosaurus* had two rows of bony plates from neck to tail.

THE MESOZOIC ERA

MYA			
248	208	144	65

TRIASSIC   JURASSIC   CRETACEOUS

LOCATION
USA Colorado, Utah, Wyoming

TIME
150MYA

SIZE
Length 9m (29ft 6in)
Weight 2 tonnes (2 tons)

CLASSIFICATION
Family Stegosauridae
Infraorder Stegosauria
Suborder Thyreophora
Order Ornithischia

DIET
Low-growing plants

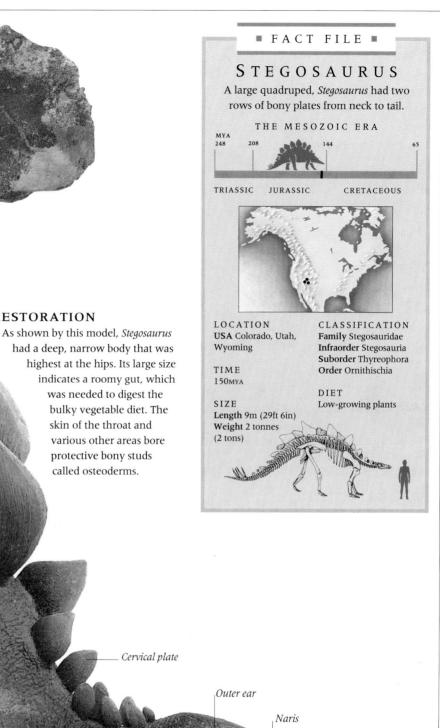

RESTORATION

As shown by this model, *Stegosaurus* had a deep, narrow body that was highest at the hips. Its large size indicates a roomy gut, which was needed to digest the bulky vegetable diet. The skin of the throat and various other areas bore protective bony studs called osteoderms.

Dorsal plate

Cervical plate

Outer ear

Naris

Long, narrow snout

Long hind limb

Short forelimb

HEAD This was small and low, with an elongated narrow snout, a toothless beak, cheeks, many small, serrated, leaf-like cheek teeth, and relatively weak jaws. The vegetable matter they ate might have been mashed up by swallowed gizzard stones.

KENTROSAURUS

I N THE EARLY 1900s, scores of bones unearthed in what is now Tanzania made *Kentrosaurus* ("spiky lizard") Africa's best-known plated dinosaur. *Kentrosaurus* resembled a smaller, narrower-spined version of the Chinese stegosaur *Tuojiangosaurus*. Six pairs of small, bony plates stuck up from its neck and shoulders. Behind these, three pairs of flat spines sprouted from its back; and five pairs of very long, sharp, narrow spines guarded its tail. *Kentrosaurus* might also have had a pair of plate-like hip or shoulder spines. As in other stegosaurs, there were no bony tendons to stiffen the tail or back.

RESTORATION
This illustration is based on an interpretation in which there are seven pairs of plates on the neck and back (others assume six), and a total of seven pairs of spines (instead of eight). A shoulder spine is also shown.

IN EAST AFRICA
Expedition leader Werner Janensch and his assistant Salim Tombali examine dinosaur bones unearthed between 1909 and 1911 in what is now Tanzania.

■ LIFESTYLE ■

Scientists found fossils of *Kentrosaurus* where a prehistoric river had wound its way almost to the ocean. The air was always warm there, and rainy periods alternated with droughts. Even when dry weather killed shallow-rooted plants, *Kentrosaurus* could always find vegetation growing in the moist soil near the river. As this dinosaur moved around on all fours and had short forelimbs and a short neck, it is likely that it ate low-growing ferns and shrubby vegetation. However, it might also have reared up on its long, strong hind limbs and – partly propped up by its tail – reached leafy twigs. Even so, *Kentrosaurus* scarcely competed for food with the immense and much taller, long-necked sauropods, such as *Dicraeosaurus*.

TRANSPORTING THE BONES
Porters carried thousands of loads of Kentrosaurus *and other dinosaur bones from Tendaguru Hill, Mtwara, to the Indian Ocean for shipment to Germany.*

■ SELF-DEFENCE ■

Such placid animals as the sauropods posed no threat to *Kentrosaurus*. Its principal enemies were the big, predatory theropods, such as *Allosaurus* and *Ceratosaurus*. If one of these tried to approach from behind, *Kentrosaurus* would be able to defend itself by backing sharply into the predator. An attack from the flank could be parried by lashing movements of the spiky tail.

TAIL BONES
In most stegosaurs, the caudal neural spines (high, narrow "tops" of tail vertebrae) slope back. *Kentrosaurus* was unusual, for beyond tail bone 18, neural spines lean forward. Other skeletal peculiarities were the protective chevrons shaped rather like ploughshares.

Caudal spike

Backward-leaning neural spine

Forward-leaning neural spine

Caudal vertebra

"Ploughshare-shaped" chevron

"Second brain"

Brain

BRAIN CASTS

The small cast (right) filled the cavity occupied by *Kentrosaurus*'s brain. The much larger cast (above) filled a big hollow in two sacral vertebrae. This led to a belief that stegosaurs had two brains: one in the head and a larger one in the hips. In fact, the "second brain" was simply a nerve relay station serving the hind limbs and tail.

■ FACT FILE ■

KENTROSAURUS

Kentrosaurus was a quadrupedal plant-eater with a low head, rows of protective plates along its neck and shoulders, and spikes along its back and tail.

THE MESOZOIC ERA

MYA 248	208	144	65
TRIASSIC	JURASSIC		CRETACEOUS

SIZE
Length 4.9m (16ft)
Weight 1 tonne (1 ton)

TIME
156–150MYA

LOCATION
Tanzania Mtwara

DIET
Low-growing plants

CLASSIFICATION
Family Stegosauridae
Infraorder Stegosauria
Suborder Thyreophora
Order Ornithischia

COMPOSITE SKELETON

This is one of two composite skeletons reconstructed in German museums from bones found in East Africa and brought to Europe in the early 1900s. The collection included hundreds of scattered parts of dismembered *Kentrosaurus* skeletons. There were more than 70 thigh bones alone. Much of the material once kept in Berlin's Humboldt Museum was, unfortunately, destroyed in the Second World War. This reconstruction suggests that *Kentrosaurus* was more akin to *Tuojiangosaurus* than to *Stegosaurus*.

Dorsal plate

Dorsal vertebra

Ilium

Ischium

Femur

Pubis

Rib

Elbow joint

Cervical vertebra

Cervical plate

Braincase

Knee joint

Ankle joint

Fibula

Tibia

Metacarpal

Scapula

Orbit

Humerus

Mandible

Phalanx

Ulna

Metatarsal

Radius

Phalanx

TUOJIANGOSAURUS

T UOJIANGOSAURUS ("Tuo River lizard") is the best-known plated dinosaur from southern China, where stegosaurs may have evolved before spreading to other continents. It was longer but lighter than today's heaviest rhinoceros, and stood taller than a human at the hips. It had a typical stegosaur's small, low head with a toothless beak and small cheek teeth, an arched back, bulky body, and pillar-like limbs. Neck, back, and tail supported up to 15 pairs of pointed, vertical plates; rounded plates on the neck gave way to tall ones along the back. Two pairs of spikes stuck out from the tail-tip, and each shoulder may have borne a plate-like spine.

LIFE RESTORATION
This lifelike restoration of the Chinese stegosaur Tuojiangosaurus *was based on the remains of two fossilized specimens.*

■ LIFESTYLE ■

Tuojiangosaurus plodded along river banks, browsing on the ferns and cycads that sprouted thickly in the rich river-valley soil. Head slung low, the dinosaur cropped mouthfuls of leaves with its horny beak, stuffed them in its cheeks, chewed them between its small, ridged cheek teeth, and swallowed the pulp for digestion in its roomy gut. *Tuojiangosaurus* would have spent most of its waking life just eating, swallowing, and digesting leaves.

■ COMMUNITIES ■

Life was usually placid for this and other herbivores whose fossils now lie in the Shangshaximiao Formation of southern China: *Mamenchisaurus* and *Omeisaurus* (these were vast, long-necked sauropods), the small, primitive ornithischian *Gongbusaurus,* and two more plated dinosaurs – *Chialingosaurus* and *Chungkingosaurus.* When several species of stegosaurs lived close together, distinctive plates or spines most probably served as recognition signals. Occasionally, a *Tuojiangosaurus* male squared up to a rival or met a large, aggressive theropod. Only its spikes, plates, and hide could save this slow-moving quadruped from the fangs and claws of predatory dinosaurs.

CAUDAL SPIKES

Four tall, slim, cone-shaped caudal (tail) spikes stuck up and outwards from the end of the creature's tail. Paired tail defences also figured in other well-preserved stegosaurs, including *Huayangosaurus, Kentrosaurus,* and *Stegosaurus.* Tail spikes evidently formed key defensive weapons for all members of the stegosaur group.

Ilium

Caudal vertebra

Caudal plate

Ischium

Pubis

Femur

Caudal spike

Chevron

Tibia

Fibula

TUOJIANGOSAURUS

Tuojiangosaurus was a quadrupedal plant-eater with a low head, two rows of protective plates from neck to tail, and spikes at the tip of the tail.

THE MESOZOIC ERA

MYA
248   208   144   65

TRIASSIC   JURASSIC   CRETACEOUS

SIZE
Length 23ft (7m)
Weight 1tonne (1 ton)

TIME
156MYA

LOCATION
China Sichuan

DIET
Low-growing plants

CLASSIFICATION
Family Stegosauridae
Infraorder Stegosauria
Suborder Thyreophora
Order Ornithischia

COMPARING TEETH

Tuojiangosaurus's cheek teeth (above) resembled those of *Stegosaurus* (top) in being small and ridged, well suited to a diet of leaves.

Dorsal vertebra

Dorsal plate

Scapula

Rib

Humerus

Ulna

FRONT VIEW

The front view (right) shows a skeleton mounted with each humerus (upper arm bone) angled out so that its lower end slants away from the body. Both elbows jut sideways, so the forelimbs are bent somewhat like a lizard's or a crocodile's. However, some scientists think stegosaurs walked with their forelimbs more erect, holding the front of the body higher.

Cervical plate

Cervical vertebra

Skull

Mandible

Dorsal vertebra

Dorsal plate

Ilium

Rib

Shoulder joint

Scapula

Humerus

Elbow joint

SKELETAL RECONSTRUCTION

Jutting bony plates and spikes dramatize the curvature of *Tuojiangosaurus*'s profile (left). The first almost complete dinosaur skeleton to be unearthed in China, *Tuojiangosaurus* became a prominent exhibit at the Zigong Dinosaur Museum in Sichuan. It was displayed with other dinosaurs found in the same Late Jurassic rock formation.

121

EDMONTONIA

E DMONTONIA ("OF EDMONTON") was one of the largest and latest of the nodosaurids – armoured dinosaurs without the broad "horns", contorted nasal passages, and bony tail club of their relatives the ankylosaurids. *Edmontonia* was a barrel-bodied quadruped that had evolved tyrannosaur-resistant armour. A jigsaw puzzle of interlocking bony plates reinforced the pear-shaped skull. Three rows of large bony plates guarded the neck and shoulders and a pavement of small, ridged plates covered the back, hips, and tail. Long, bony, forward-angled spikes stuck out from the sides, defending the flanks and shoulders.

▪ LIFESTYLE ▪

This heavy-bodied browser ambled slowly on pillar-like limbs through western North America's lowland glades and across meadows of herbaceous plants. Like today's Black Rhinoceros, *Edmontonia* was a relatively narrow-mouthed herbivore, which suggests that it was a selective feeder capable of cropping the juiciest low-growing plants. Sometimes, *Edmontonia* might have had to make do with tough-leaved shrubs: growth rings found in fossil trees suggest that although there were periods with good rainy seasons, these alternated with drier times in which tender-leaved, short-rooted plants would have withered.

▪ SELF-DEFENCE ▪

It used to be thought that when an *Edmontonia* was threatened, it would simply lie down with its legs beneath its body, turning itself into a living bomb shelter until the predator got tired and went away. It is more likely, however, that this well-armed nodosaurid wheeled around to face its enemy, then lunged forwards so that its long shoulder spines inflicted crippling wounds to the carnosaur's feet or shins. Flank and shoulder spines helped protect *Edmontonia* from an attack from the side, and wide hips formed a broad base that would have made the animal difficult to overturn. When two *Edmontonia* males met, they may have fought to win females or territory. Alternatively, the winner may simply have been the dinosaur with larger shoulder spines, scaring off the loser by a frontal threat display.

Orbit

Naris

Braincase

Beak

Mandible

SHEEP-LIKE SKULL
Seen from one side, the long, narrow skull of *Edmontonia* resembled that of a sheep. Its bones were thick and the rows of teeth were deeply in-curved, leaving room for large cheek pouches in which to store food.

Dorsal scute (protective plate)

COLLAR PLATES
These two bony plates (left) are from the largest and hindmost of the three rows of armour that protected the top of *Edmontonia*'s neck and the area between its shoulders. The plates shielded an area that would otherwise have been vulnerable to tyrannosaurid fangs. In life, a horn sheath would have covered the plates.

Crosswise row of armour plates

Armoured head

Shoulder spike capable of inflicting fearsome wounds

Large cheek

Relatively narrow mouth

Large, heavy foot

VIEWS OF A TOOTH

The cheek teeth of *Edmontonia* had a ridged, leaf-shaped crown, flattened from side to side and enamelled on both sides to resist wear. They were more primitive than most ornithischian teeth and did not interlock with one another. Although 4cm (1.6in) long including the elongated root, they were small for a nodosaurid. Even so, all nodosaurids had relatively larger teeth than ankylosaurids.

Ridged, leaf-shaped crown

Crown enamelled on both sides

Elongated root

■ FACT FILE ■

EDMONTONIA

Edmontonia was a quadrupedal plant-eater with an armour of bony plates.

THE MESOZOIC ERA

MYA				
248	208	144		65

TRIASSIC   JURASSIC   CRETACEOUS

LOCATION
Canada Alberta
USA Montana, Texas

TIME
74–72MYA

SIZE
Length 7m (23ft)
Weight 4 tonnes
(3.9 tons)

CLASSIFICATION
Family Nodosauridae
Infraorder Ankylosauria
Suborder Thyreophora
Order Ornithischia

DIET
Low-growing plants

EXTERNAL FEATURES

This restoration shows *Edmontonia*'s rock-like head, plated neck, and avenues of ridged plates covering the back and tail. Double-pointed shoulder spines posed a more serious wounding hazard to any predator. Even a tyrannosaurid would hesitate before it chanced its teeth on this heavy, armoured herbivore.

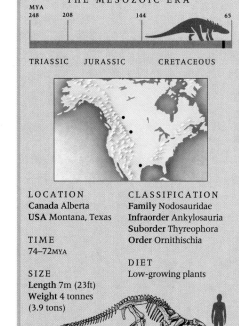

Tough, scaly skin

Small, ridged plates covering the tail

Flank spike providing protection against attack from behind

Powerful hind limb

Sturdy forelimb

Narrow snout

Splayed toes on large foot

DISCOVERY

Several skulls and skeletons of *Edmontonia* are known. Two, complete with their armour, may have dried out after the animals died and before they were covered in silt by flood waters.

Interlocking small plates

Braincase plate

THE SKULL ROOF

Viewed from above, the narrow snout gave the skull a pear-shaped appearance. Bony plates, fused to the underlying skull, thickened and reinforced its roof. The largest plate protected the braincase. Around the edges of this plate, a series of smaller plates interlocked like pieces in a rigid jigsaw puzzle.

SAUROPELTA

S AUROPELTA ("SHIELDED LIZARD") was the earliest and most primitive member of the nodosaurid family known to have lived in what is now North America. Advanced nodosaurids like *Edmontonia* had big, bony shoulder plates, but *Sauropelta*'s shoulders, back, and tail were covered with horn-sheathed, bony cones interspersed with rows of smaller bony studs. Other primitive features were premaxillary teeth (teeth in the top half of the beak); lack of a secondary palate (a device aiding simultaneous breathing and eating); and unfused neck bones nearest the skull. Like all nodosaurids, *Sauropelta* had a tapering tail with no tail club.

UNDER ATTACK
A Sauropelta *faces a pack of hungry* Deinonychus. *Its tough hide, protective cones and studs, and long shoulder spikes frustrated such small theropods. The armour-backed beast could defy even bigger enemies by crouching.*

■ LIFESTYLE ■

Like other ankylosaurs, as well as their relatives the stegosaurs, *Sauropelta* was an inoffensive, bulky-bodied herbivore that cropped low-growing plants with its beak and chewed them between its small, weak-looking cheek teeth. It lived in western North America in the late Early Cretaceous period, about 100 million years ago. Other herbivores of this period varied greatly in size and included relatively small bipedal hypsilophodontids and huge sauropods. Predators known to have lived at that time ranged from the turkey-sized *Microvenator* to *Deinonychus* and ostrich dinosaurs related to *Struthiomimus*. Big theropods, still undiscovered today, might have been the main enemies of *Sauropelta*. This cumbersome quadruped usually moved no faster than walking pace, although it probably had the ability to trot. Even so, its pillar-like legs could hardly have raised a gallop and it would not have had the speed to escape from a pack of long-legged, hungry dromaeosaurids. Confronted by their lethal, hooked talons, the nodosaurid would have been forced to stand its ground and rely on its armour for protection.

■ PRIMITIVE ARMOUR ■

Sauropelta's armour, primitive compared to that of its advanced relative *Edmontonia*, consisted of a flexible, "chain-mail" body covering, with spines on both sides of the neck. Spines probably also guarded the flanks, protecting the nodosaurid from an attack from the side. If ringed by enemies, *Sauropelta* may have lain down to protect the least well-guarded part of its body: its underbelly. The structure of the forelimb bones hints at this possibility, suggesting that the animal had strong shoulder muscles. These might have enabled *Sauropelta* to bend its arms with more flexibility than other ankylosaurs.

EXTERNAL FEATURES

Based on partial finds of several specimens, this recreated *Sauropelta* has spikes along the sides of the neck, bony plates on the upper neck, triangular plates along the flanks, and crosswise, bony cones on the back in a sea of smaller bony studs.

Armoured tail

BONY CONES

These three fossil cones from the back or tail of a *Sauropelta* must have protected their owner from attack by savage theropods. The cones were arranged in rows, rather like the bands of armour on a modern giant armadillo.

FOSSILIZED SPECIMEN

These two photographs show the external (top) and internal (bottom) aspects of an embedded *Sauropelta* fossil displayed in the American Museum of Natural History, New York. The top view shows *Sauropelta*'s flexible armour. Some of the massive limb bones can be seen in the lower view. This is the most complete skeleton of a North American nodosaurid ankylosaur. The skull, neck, parts of limbs, and end of tail are missing. Most of the tail vertebrae have been reconstructed.

Bony stud

Bony cone

Caudal vertebra

Dorsal vertebra

Femur

Rib

SAUROPELTA

Sauropelta was a quadrupedal plant-eater protected by bony shields.

THE MESOZOIC ERA

MYA 248	208		144		65

TRIASSIC   JURASSIC   CRETACEOUS

LOCATION
USA Montana, Wyoming

SIZE
Length 7.6m (25ft)
Weight 2.7 tonnes (2.7 tons)

TIME
114–97MYA

CLASSIFICATION
Family Nodosauridae
Infraorder Ankylosauria
Suborder Thyreophora
Order Ornithischia

DIET
Low-growing plants

Bony cone

Triangular flank plate

Bony stud

Neck spike

Upper neck plate

Vulnerable underside

Pillar-like leg

Blunt claw

Broad, flat snout

MINMI

MINMI WAS THE FIRST armoured ornithischian to be found in the southern hemisphere. It is named after Minmi Crossing, a place near the site in Queensland, Australia where the first skeleton was found. This herbivore has two unusual features: bony rods grew backwards from unique, flat bony plates beside the neural spines of the dorsal vertebrae; and a mosaic of small scutes (bony plates) protected the belly. *Minmi*'s classification is still uncertain. First placed in the nodosaurid family, it might prove to be a primitive ankylosaurid, or even part of a new, third family of armoured dinosaurs.

▪ LIFESTYLE ▪

Minmi was a four-legged, armoured herbivore that stomped around on all four sturdy limbs, cutting off leafy fronds with its beak and chewing them between its small, leaf-shaped cheek teeth. Its body was thickly covered with armour that would have discouraged attack. Even a theropod that succeeded in overturning a *Minmi* risked snapping off its teeth against the belly armour. The whole underside appears to have been covered with small, rounded scutes (bony plates) slightly over 5mm (about ¼ in) in diameter. It is possible that *Minmi* may have preferred running to passive resistance. This may have been facilitated by *Minmi*'s most remarkable feature, which was not found in any other known ankylosaur. Beside each dorsal (back) vertebra there was a bony plate, known as a paravertebra, some 2cm (¾ in) long by 4cm (1½ in) wide. Attached to this was a rod of bone, which was similar to the bony tendons found in ornithopods. The rods might have reinforced the spine and eased the strain on it when the lumbering animal pounded the ground as it ran.

▪ FOSSILIZATION ▪

Two fossil skeletons have been discovered, both in Australia. The animals seem to have lived in open woodland, and both specimens seem to have been washed out to sea by rivers when they died, settling upside down on the seabed. Clay filled the body cavities, and then hard marine sediments encased the carcasses. Later still, the sea retreated to expose the rocks in which the fossils lay entombed.

MINMI UNDER ATTACK
A theropod assaults a young Minmi *as older animals move in to drive it off. Predators like* Kakuru *preyed on the young, despite the protective armour that even covered their bellies.*

NEW INFORMATION

The discovery of a second skeleton in 1990 shed new light on *Minmi*'s armour. Low, flat, sharp plates jutted from the hips. Triangular plates like giant thorns guarded the tail, and bony scutes protected the shins. The front of the thigh shown in this restoration was more probably incorporated within the body wall.

Triangular plates protect the tail

NEAR MINMI CROSSING
The first Minmi *was found on level grassland in Australia. In landscapes like this erosion is so slow that rocks yield fossils at a miserly rate, and good discoveries are rare.*

FOSSIL AND FINDER
Ian Ievers kneels beside the first Minmi, *which he discovered in 1964. Acetic acid was later used to free its bones from the blocks of hard calcareous concretions in which they were embedded.*

FOSSIL SKELETON

Features shown in this partial skeleton include an armoured skull tapering to a narrow beak, neck plates, and shoulder scutes (bony plates). Rows of scutes, each lying between two ribs, are also visible running down the wide body. Traces of the shelf-like ilia (hip bones) remain, as do fragments of the limbs and tail.

Tail fragments

Rib

Neck plate

Narrow beak

Armoured, box-shaped skull

Hind limb fragments

Shelf-like ilium

Scute lying between two ribs

Shoulder scute

Low, flat, sharp plates protect the hips

Rows of scutes protect the back and upper flanks

High-ridged scute protects the shoulder

Larger plates protect the back of the neck

Turtle-shaped head

Scutes protect back of the shin

Belly covered with armour made of very small scutes

Sturdy forelimb

FACT FILE

MINMI

Minmi was a small, quadrupedal plant-eater with an armour of bony plates.

THE MESOZOIC ERA

MYA 248	208	144	65
TRIASSIC	JURASSIC		CRETACEOUS

CLASSIFICATION
Family Unknown
Infraorder Ankylosauria
Suborder Thyreophora
Order Ornithischia

DIET
Low-growing plants

LOCATION
Australia Queensland

TIME
119–113MYA

SIZE
Length 3m (10ft)

RESTORATION

Minmi had a low, somewhat box-shaped skull. Seen from the side, the head probably looked like a turtle's. Pairs of relatively large, flat plates guarded the back of the neck. High-ridged scutes rose from the shoulders, and rows of smaller scutes ran down the length of its back and upper flanks. Since its forelimbs were almost as long as its hind limbs, *Minmi* stood with an almost level back.

EUOPLOCEPHALUS

W ITH ITS TAIL CLUB, short, broad skull, and complex nasal passages, *Euoplocephalus* ("well armoured head") was typical of the ankylosaurid family. Slabs of bony armour, like glued-on crazy paving, protected almost all of its skull. Bony eyelids drooped like steely shutters to protect the vulnerable eyes, and four short horns protected the back of the head. The neck, body, and base of the tail were strengthened by bands of bony studs, spikes, and large, ridged horny plates, while the stiffened tail ended in a heavy, bony club. For all the armour, in time of danger (perhaps alerted by its sense of smell) *Euoplocephalus* was fairly lithe, and could lumber along at some speed.

COUNTERATTACK
Agile for its size, Euoplocephalus *could have sidestepped a big theropod's flank attack and felled its formidable enemy with a bone-snapping tail blow to shin or ankle.*

LOCOMOTION
Euoplocephalus *could run faster than a sauropod, slower than a ceratopsian.*

■ LIFESTYLE ■

Isolated finds of more than 40 fossil specimens suggest that *Euoplocephalus* led a solitary life. Around 70 million years ago, however, it was the most abundant kind of armoured dinosaur in western North America. This broad-beaked dinosaur ambled through forests, browsing on the undergrowth. It ate almost any low herbaceous plants, chewing the plant material between its small, ridged teeth. The crushed vegetation was then ground to a pulp inside a muscular enlargement of the intestine. The greatest danger for *Euoplocephalus* was that a carnosaur would turn it over to attack its relatively soft underbelly, which was less heavily armoured than the rest of its body.

Scapula

Dorsal vertebra

Rib

Lung

Gizzard

Small intestine

Ilium

Coracoid

Humerus

Radius

Wrist joint

Ventral antebrachial muscle

Ulna

Elbow joint

Heart

Liver

Large intestine

Toothless beak

Iliotibial muscle

Femur

Digital extensor muscle

Fibula

EUOPLOCEPHALUS

Euoplocephalus was a quadrupedal plant-eater with extensive armour, in the form of bony horns, plates, and studs, on its head and back.

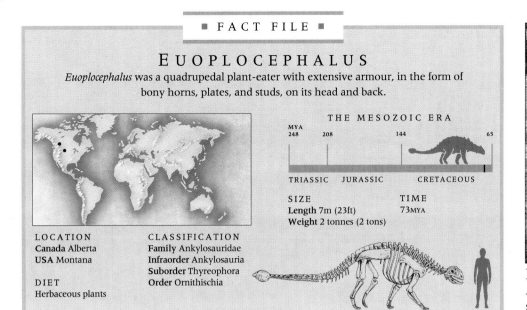

THE MESOZOIC ERA

MYA
248   208   144   65

TRIASSIC   JURASSIC   CRETACEOUS

SIZE
Length 7m (23ft)
Weight 2 tonnes (2 tons)

TIME
73 MYA

LOCATION
Canada Alberta
USA Montana

DIET
Herbaceous plants

CLASSIFICATION
Family Ankylosauridae
Infraorder Ankylosauria
Suborder Thyreophora
Order Ornithischia

FOSSILIZED SKIN

A close-up view of part of *Euoplocephalus*'s hide shows the bony mosaic that formed a flexible armour combining protection with mobility.

INTERNAL ANATOMY

Deep, curved ribs enclosed the heart and other internal organs, including the long, convoluted gut where plant food was broken down. Each massive scapula (shoulder blade) and strongly ridged humerus (upper arm bone) anchored forelimb muscles. In the hip region, fused spines arising from the vertebrae and broad, shelf-shaped ilia (hip bones) braced the muscles that moved the hind limbs and swung the tail club.

FOSSIL: TOP VIEW

Plates of tough skin, set with small, bony studs, lay across *Euoplocephalus*'s back. The animal was also protected by two lengthways rows of larger, blunt spikes. The head end faces right, although the skull is missing.

FOSSIL: BOTTOM VIEW

The same fossil appears here, from the underside and facing left. Clearly visible are the spinal column and the basket-like hip formation in which ribs grew out from the spine, fusing with a shelf-like ilium on either side.

Plate of tough, studded skin

Larger spike

Head end

Tail end

Head end

Tail end

Hip "ribs"

Spinal column

Shelf-like ilium

Caudal vertebra

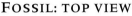

Lateral caudal musculature

Tail club

Ureter

Chevron

Ischium

FOSSILIZED TAIL CLUB

An ankylosaurid tail club comprised two large side plates and two small end plates fused with each other and attached to the tail-tip vertebrae. The bony tendons that stiffened the vertebrae anchored the powerful muscles responsible for swinging the tail.

Tail-tip vertebra

End plate

Side plate

ORNITHOPODS

O RNITHOPODS, OR "BIRD FEET", comprised a suborder of bipedal and bipedal/quadrupedal plant-eating ornithischian dinosaurs with feet rather like a bird's, a horny beak, leaf-shaped cheek teeth, a backward-angled pubic bone, a ridged ischium, and bony tendons that stiffened the tail. From dog-sized early ornithischians like *Lesothosaurus* (commonly believed too primitive to be counted as a true ornithopod), the group evolved uniquely effective teeth and jaws for chewing vegetation, and gave rise to Late Cretaceous giants like *Edmontosaurus*. The eight known ornithopod families belonged to one of the longest-lived and largest of all the groups of ornithischians.

✳ PRIMITIVE ✳ ORNITHISCHIANS

LESOTHOSAURUS was a bipedal, Early Jurassic, ornithischian plant-eater, 1m (3ft 3in) long, from southern Africa. It lacked the roomy cheeks of more developed ornithischians, yet it was once placed in the fabrosaurids, a supposed ornithopod family thought to be ancestral to all ornithischians. Fabrosaurids later proved to be a rag-bag of unrelated genera, and scientists found that *Lesothosaurus* lacked some key features that identified true ornithopods. However, it did exhibit some ornithopod features.

✳ "SMALL" ✳ ORNITHOPODS

HETERODONTOSAURIDAE were agile, dog-sized, Early Jurassic ornithopods. Unlike other ornithopods they had three types of teeth, including tusk-like canines, and cheek teeth with high, chisel-shaped crowns with serrated edges. Five named genera are known from southern Africa, and a sixth genus comes from China. Scientists think that heterodontosaurids were more primitive than the other ornithopods. Like pachycephalosaurs, they had a gap between the front upper teeth and those behind. Other shared traits led the palaeontologist Paul Sereno to the conclusion that ornithopods and marginocephalians sprang from a common ancestor and formed an ornithischian "supergroup" which he named the Cerapoda.

HYPSILOPHODONTIDAE had tiny, five-fingered hands, elongated shins, and four-toed feet. At least some had teeth in their upper beaks, a primitive ornithischian feature. There were perhaps 18 genera, from 90cm to 3.4m (3ft to 11ft) long, or more. The longest-lived ornithopod family, the hypsilophodontids lived from Middle

ORNITHOPODS IN AUSTRALIA

A group of Leaellynasaura *roams the edge of a flood plain in Early Cretaceous southeast Australia. These and other hypsilophodontid ornithopods became the most successful small, plant-eating dinosaurs.*

Jurassic to Late Cretaceous times and occurred as far apart as North America, Europe, Asia, Australia, and Antarctica. DRYOSAURIDAE looked as if they were smaller versions of the iguanodonts (see below). Unlike *Hypsilophodon*, *Dryosaurus* had three-toed feet and a toothless beak. The fewer than half a dozen genera were 2.7m to 6.5m (9ft to 21ft) long, and lived in North America, Europe, Africa, and New Zealand.

✳ IGUANODONTS ✳

CAMPTOSAURIDAE were named after *Camptosaurus*, with its long, low head, close-packed cheek teeth, and four-toed feet with hoof-like claws. There are at least four genera of these bulky ornithopods 3.5m to 7m (11ft 6in to 23ft) long which lived from the Middle Jurassic to the Late Jurassic. Their fossils have been found in North America, Europe, and Australia (if *Muttaburrasaurus* was indeed a camptosaurid and not, as some would say, an iguanodontid). IGUANODONTIDAE were big, bulky, bipedal/quadrupedal ornithopods with long heads, powerful legs with three-toed feet, hoof-like toe and finger nails, and spiky thumbs. There may have been about ten genera ranging from 4m to 9m (about 13ft to 29ft 6in) long. Despite

ORNITHOPODS LARGE AND SMALL

Iguanodon, *9m (29ft 6in) long, is shown towering over* Hypsilophodon. *Ornithopods ranged from dog-sized hypsilophodontids to 15m (49ft) long duckbilled hadrosaurs.*

CORYTHOSAURUS SKULL

EDMONTOSAURUS SKULL

HETERODONTOSAURUS SKULL

THREE ORNITHOPOD SKULLS
Corythosaurus *and* Edmontosaurus *had toothless beaks, mobile upper jaws, and batteries of up to 1,000 cheek teeth for cropping and chewing leaves. The more primitive* Heterodontosaurus *had three kinds of teeth but a simpler jaw design.*

similarities between these genera, some scientists believe that not all belonged to one family. Indeed, they consider *Iguanodon* and *Ouranosaurus* to be the only undoubted genera of Iguanodontidae. Iguanodontids in the broader sense lived from the Early to the Late Cretaceous in North (and perhaps also South) America, Africa, Europe, and Asia.

▪ HADROSAURS ▪

HADROSAURIDAE evolved from ancestors like *Iguanodon*. Also known as "duckbills", these dinosaurs were ornithischians with wide, toothless beaks, pavements of self-sharpening cheek teeth, and flat skulls or skulls with bony bumps. Their hands had

ORNITHOPOD FAMILY TREE

This diagram shows relationships between ornithopod families (the names ending in -idae), each of which is known to have contained several genera. All the members of the Ornithopoda had a premaxillary (upper front) tooth row below the level of the maxillary tooth row situated behind it, and a depressed jaw joint. *Lesothosaurus* was once called an ornithopod but lacked these typical features, and was probably closely related to the ancestral ornithischian that gave rise to both ornithopods and marginocephalians. Heterodontosaurids had more kinds of teeth than other ornithopods. The Euornithopoda ("true ornithopods") were a subgroup with a long prepubic process and other distinctive features. Small kinds like *Hypsilophodon* gave rise to huge hadrosaurid and lambeosaurid hadrosaurs ("duckbills") with toothless beaks and self-sharpening cheek teeth. These huge hadrosaurs were among the most common of the large, plant-eating dinosaurs of Late Cretaceous North America.

ORNITHOPODA

Euornithopoda

four fingers, and the palms may have formed a fleshy pad. There are more than two dozen known genera ranging from 3.7m to 15m (12ft to 49ft) long. They have been found in Late Cretaceous North and South America, Europe, and Asia. LAMBEOSAURIDAE had characteristic tall, hollow, bony head crests, but in other respects closely resembled hadrosaurids. Lambeosaurids are as a result often considered to be a subfamily of the Hadrosauridae. Both groups of these advanced ornithopods had keen senses, lived in herds, bred in colonies, and evidently tended their young. The fewer than a dozen lambeosaurid genera lived in Late Cretaceous North America and Asia.

HYPSILOPHODON HIP BONES
The long prepubis anchored a muscle which pulled the leg up and forward. The backward angled pubis left room below the hips for a bulky gut. This placed the bipedal ornithopod's centre of gravity conveniently below the hips.

Prepubis

Ilium

Ischium

Pubis

Lesothosaurus

Heterodontosauridae

Hypsilophodontidae

Dryosauridae

Camptosauridae

Iguanodontidae

Hadrosauridae

Lambeosauridae

KEY

Suborder

Infraorder

Relationship uncertain

LESOTHOSAURUS

N O LONGER THAN a large dog, *Lesothosaurus* had a small head, perhaps with small, fleshy cheeks, ridged cheek teeth, and a horny lower beak. Apart from a probably roomy belly, the little herbivore was lightly built, with a slim neck, hollow limb bones, long legs with elongated shins and upper toe bones, and short arms with five-fingered grasping hands (the fifth finger was smaller than the rest). Bony tendons stiffened its tail, counterbalancing the body at the hips. Such small ornithischians evolved the body plan for later two-legged, plant-eating dinosaurs.

■ LIFESTYLE ■

Lesothosaurus lived in the same kind of sandy semi-desert as the small, early ornithopod *Heterodontosaurus*. Like that dinosaur, "Lesotho lizard" could have foraged on all fours, cropping leaves and tender shoots from low, shrubby plants. But its jaws seem to have been less efficient than those of *Heterodontosaurus*, using a vertical motion rather than rotating the teeth to grind. As it ate, *Lesothosaurus* would have raised its head from time to time, gazing nervously around for enemies, always poised to race away if a large flesh-eater suddenly appeared. Long toe and shin bones show that *Lesothosaurus* was capable of running extremely fast. In many ways, the creature resembled a modern gazelle – a defenceless plant-eater on the alert at all times for danger because the only means of escaping an attacker is instant flight at high speed. The toe and shin bones are particularly like those of a gazelle.

■ IDENTITY OF FABROSAURUS ■

It is possible that the fossil bones named *Lesothosaurus* in 1978 are actually the same as those of *Fabrosaurus* ("Fabre's lizard"), named in 1964 from a worn piece of lower jaw. Although there is very little fossil evidence to allow an accurate comparison between the *Fabrosaurus* find and the later one, there are many authorities who are reasonably satisfied that the two creatures are the same animal. If the two sets of fossil bones named *Lesothosaurus* and *Fabrosaurus* do indeed turn out to be from one and the same dinosaur, then the creature will be called *Fabrosaurus* – the first name attributed to it. (In the event of duplicate identification, the name first given to an animal or plant always takes priority over any names it acquires later.)

SKULL
This had big cavities for the eye and jaw muscles, an opening in front of the eye, a short, pointed snout, and a lower jaw that may have ended in a horny beak. Teeth slightly set in from the outside of the skull and mandible suggest there were small cheeks.

Orbit

Braincase

Infratemporal fenestra

Naris

Beak

Slim neck

Shoulder

Short, strong forelimb

Femoral head

Five-fingered hand

Fourth trochanter

Long, slender, agile leg

FEMUR
A *Lesothosaurus* femur (thigh bone) shares features with the femurs of all dinosaurs, but details distinguish it from other kinds. Among these are the in-turned femoral head without a neck; greater and lesser trochanters (where leg muscles were attached) and a "hanging" fourth trochanter, all of distinctive sizes, shapes, and positions; and a larger lateral than medial condyle (at the end of the femur that articulated with the knee).

Medial condyle

Lateral condyle

Second toe

Hallux (first toe)

Claw

FRONT VIEW

Seen from the front, *Lesothosaurus* might have resembled a very large lizard walking on its hind limbs. While a few lizards can briefly lift their bodies off the ground and run on hind limbs only, none can stand or pace along with upright limbs, as shown here. Holding its head high enabled *Lesothosaurus* to scan the surroundings for low-growing plants and spot hungry theropods before they crept close enough to launch a dangerous attack.

LESOTHOSAURUS HERD
This diminutive plant-eating dinosaur might have roamed southern Africa in herds, like the small, swift gazelles of today.

Hip

Stiffened tail acts as a counterbalance

TAIL The length was gauged from an incomplete set of caudal bones.

SIDE VIEW

Lesothosaurus was a small, primitive, lightly built plant-eater with some – but not all – of the features found in ornithopods rather than other ornithischians. Like a small ornithopod, it had short arms and hands but long legs and feet. As in most sprinting creatures, the lower parts of the hind limb were the longest. *Lesothosaurus*'s shins were 25 per cent longer than its thighs, and its three-toed feet were as long as its shins.

Short thigh

Elongated shin

Long "sprinter's foot"

■ FACT FILE ■

LESOTHOSAURUS

Lesothosaurus was a bipedal herbivore. Diminutive and agile, it had a small head, strong legs, and a lengthy tail.

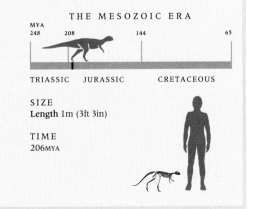

THE MESOZOIC ERA

MYA 248	208	144	65
TRIASSIC	JURASSIC	CRETACEOUS	

SIZE
Length 1m (3ft 3in)

TIME
206MYA

LOCATION
Lesotho Mafeteng
Venezuela

CLASSIFICATION
Family Unknown
Suborder Unknown
Order Ornithischia

DIET
Low-growing plants

HETERODONTOSAURUS

M ANY REPTILES POSSESS only one type of tooth. *Heterodontosaurus* ("different-teeth lizard") had three kinds: sharp upper front teeth that bit against a toothless, horny beak; long canine tusks that fitted into grooves in the top and bottom jaws; and high-crowned cheek teeth. This turkey-sized plant-eater was one of the earliest and smallest ornithopods ("bird feet") – dinosaurs with three long, forward-facing toes on each foot. Other bird-like features included its fused lower-leg, ankle, and upper-foot bones. The arms were muscular and each grasping hand bore three long, blunt-clawed digits and a small fourth and fifth finger.

■ LIFESTYLE ■

Heterodontosaurus seems to have rambled over southern African semi-deserts, searching for tasty plants to eat. Standing and browsing on all fours, *Heterodontosaurus* probably nipped off leaves and stems one by one with its narrow beak, before stuffing them into its roomy cheek pouches, and then chewing them with a rotating action of its jaws. Each time its high-crowned top and bottom teeth met, the downstroke of the upper jaw would have forced the two sides of the lower jaw slightly inwards. Unusual features of its shoulder, wrist, and hand joints could mean that *Heterodontosaurus* scrabbled in the sand for juicy roots and succulent tubers, or tore open termites' nests to feast upon the insects hidden within. Competing adult males doubtless threatened and even bit each other with their pointed, canine fangs. Females and young males probably did not have these long, sharp teeth. *Heterodontosaurus*'s enemies included theropods, flesh-eating, mammal-like reptiles, and quick-footed crocodilians living on dry land. The agile, small ornithopod would have run from these enemies at speed. Some experts claim that it galloped on all fours, but most scientists believe that it rose up and sprinted on its hind limbs only, lengthening its stride to accelerate. As it ran, its tail would have waggled furiously rather than sticking out rigidly behind like the stiffened tails of later ornithopods, such as *Hypsilophodon*.

DISCOVERY

Heterodontosaurus was named in 1962 by Alfred Crompton and Alan Charig. This small ornithopod was discovered by a team of fossil hunters led by experts from the University of London and from South Africa.

Palpebral bone

Orbit

Canine-like tooth

Cheek tooth

Radius

Ulna

Wrist joint

Phalanx

Metacarpal

Humerus

RESTORATION

A *Heterodontosaurus* pauses to lick a hand perhaps dirtied by digging up tubers or opening a termite mound.

ESCAPING AT SPEED
Surprised at a watering hole, seven small Heterodontosaurus *sprint off, pursued by two crested ceratosaurs. The ornithopods' tusks were no match for the theropods' teeth and claws.*

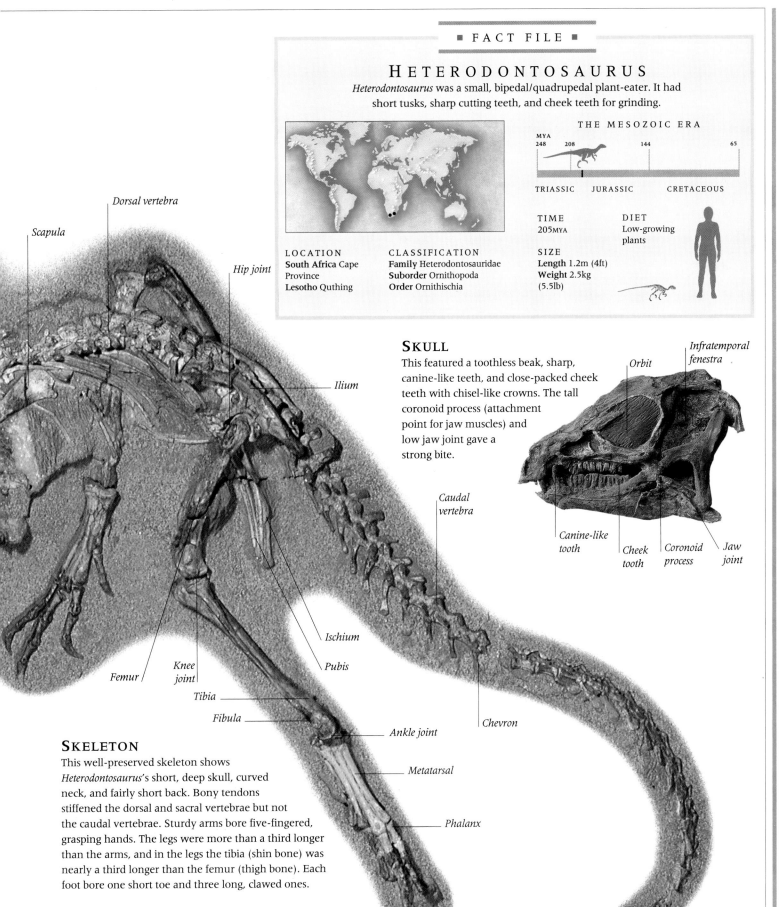

■ FACT FILE ■

HETERODONTOSAURUS

Heterodontosaurus was a small, bipedal/quadrupedal plant-eater. It had short tusks, sharp cutting teeth, and cheek teeth for grinding.

THE MESOZOIC ERA

MYA 248	208	144	65

TRIASSIC   JURASSIC   CRETACEOUS

LOCATION
South Africa Cape Province
Lesotho Quthing

CLASSIFICATION
Family Heterodontosauridae
Suborder Ornithopoda
Order Ornithischia

SIZE
Length 1.2m (4ft)
Weight 2.5kg (5.5lb)

TIME
205MYA

DIET
Low-growing plants

Scapula

Dorsal vertebra

Hip joint

Ilium

SKULL

This featured a toothless beak, sharp, canine-like teeth, and close-packed cheek teeth with chisel-like crowns. The tall coronoid process (attachment point for jaw muscles) and low jaw joint gave a strong bite.

Orbit

Infratemporal fenestra

Canine-like tooth

Cheek tooth

Coronoid process

Jaw joint

Caudal vertebra

Ischium

Pubis

Knee joint

Femur

Tibia

Fibula

Ankle joint

Chevron

Metatarsal

Phalanx

SKELETON

This well-preserved skeleton shows *Heterodontosaurus*'s short, deep skull, curved neck, and fairly short back. Bony tendons stiffened the dorsal and sacral vertebrae but not the caudal vertebrae. Sturdy arms bore five-fingered, grasping hands. The legs were more than a third longer than the arms, and in the legs the tibia (shin bone) was nearly a third longer than the femur (thigh bone). Each foot bore one short toe and three long, clawed ones.

HYPSILOPHODON

A N ORNITHOPOD little longer than the height of a human, *Hypsilophodon* ("high ridge tooth") was a gazelle-like dinosaur, engineered for both browsing and escaping danger. In its small head were large, keen eyes and a complex feeding mechanism: a horny beak with upper teeth; self-sharpening top and bottom cheek teeth that formed a cutting edge; strong, mobile jaws; and cheek pouches for storing food. *Hypsilophodon*'s short arms ended in five stubby digits tipped with strong claws. Its sprinter's hind limbs featured elongated shins and tall upper foot bones supported by three forward-facing, sharp-clawed toes.

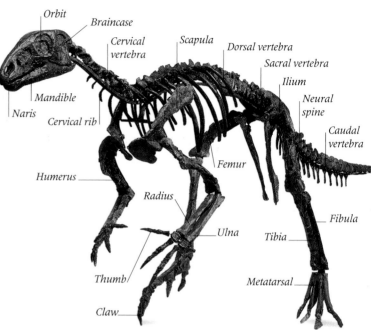

Orbit
Braincase
Cervical vertebra
Scapula
Dorsal vertebra
Sacral vertebra
Ilium
Neural spine
Caudal vertebra
Mandible
Naris
Cervical rib
Humerus
Femur
Radius
Fibula
Ulna
Tibia
Thumb
Metatarsal
Claw

■ LIFESTYLE ■

Hypsilophodon nibbled low-growing plants among the lush fern and horsetail meadows that lay between the rivers, lakes, and swamps of the coastal floodplain that covered much of southern England 120 million years ago. This best-known member of the hypsilophodontid family nipped off fronds with its beak, stuffed them in roomy cheek pouches, and then pulped them with a powerful chewing action. Each time it closed its jaws, the upper jaws splayed out but the lower jaws moved in so that, as the jaws met, the top and bottom teeth obliquely sheared past one another. Chewing leaves eventually wore down even *Hypsilophodon*'s high-crowned cheek teeth, but new teeth grew to take their place. Timid *Hypsilophodon*'s survival probably depended on group living. Since 1849 the remains of about 24 *Hypsilophodon* have been discovered in the Isle of Wight. Some individuals lay close together, perhaps part of a herd trapped in prehistoric coastal quicksands. Just as in a herd of modern antelopes, while most members of the herd were eating with their heads down, a few individuals would have been scanning the countryside for danger. Running away was the defenceless creatures' only option when attacked by hungry carnosaurs. *Hypsilophodon* was one of the fastest dinosaurs of all. At top speed it could also dodge from side to side to evade a pursuer. Its long, tendon-stiffened tail helped it keep its balance when running and manoeuvring at speed. Without a few seconds' warning, however, even *Hypsilophodon* could not escape the big fast-running theropods whose bones are also found on the Isle of Wight.

THOMAS HENRY
HUXLEY
In 1869 he named
Hypsilophodon.

SKELETON

Detailed study of its skeleton discloses that *Hypsilophodon* was a browsing sprinter, with an advanced jaw mechanism and longer shins than thighs. Unlike those more advanced ornithopods the four-fingered, three-toed hadrosaurs, this ornithopod had five-fingered hands and four forward-facing toes. But the fifth finger was tiny and the fourth toe was normally too short to reach the ground, much like the vestigial digits of many animals today.

A HYPSILOPHODON HERD

Eight timid *Hypsilophodon* keep close together as they hurry along, turning their heads watchfully from side to side. Each individual is safer from big theropods than if it roamed about independently.

Beak

Lung
Gizzard
Small intestine
Kidney
Femoral muscle
Ureter
Caudal vertebra

Cervical musculature

Neural spine

Scapula

Heart

Cloaca
Chevron
Tail

Caudal musculature

Liver
Large intestine
Pubis
Ischium
Hind limb

Anterior crural muscle
Gastrocnemius muscle
Hallux (first toe)

Claw
Foot

Metatarsal
Toe

INTERNAL ANATOMY

Based on up-to-date studies, this model shows a short, deep head and small hands. The pubis slants back against the ischium, letting the food-laden intestine extend farther back than in sauropods. Thus the centre of gravity lies under the hips.
Bipedal *Hypsilophodon* was not front-heavy like most saurischian herbivores.

HIND LIMB

A model of a *Hypsilophodon* hind limb reveals this dinosaur's muscles and the elongated bones that they operated. One scientist has likened *Hypsilophodon*'s leg to a long pendulum designed to swing very quickly back and forth.

Iliofemoral muscle

Short caudofemoral muscle

Iliofibular muscle

Tibial flexor muscle

Gastrocnemius muscle

Common digital extensor muscle

Tibia

Fibula

Tarsal

Metatarsal

Toe

Hoof-like claw

TAIL

The hind limbs acted as a sort of fulcrum over which the head and neck and the tail seesawed in near-equilibrium. The long, tapered tail was stiffened with rows of bony tendons. It was unlikely to touch the ground except when the animal was relaxing or asleep.

■ FACT FILE ■

HYPSILOPHODON

Hypsilophodon was a swift, bipedal plant-eater. Small and agile, it had sharp eyesight, a horny beak, and cheek pouches for storing food.

THE MESOZOIC ERA

MYA			
248	208	144	65

TRIASSIC   JURASSIC   CRETACEOUS

DIET
Low-growing plants

TIME
120MYA

SIZE
Length 2.3m
(7ft 6in)

LOCATION
England East Sussex, Isle of Wight
Spain Teruel
USA South Dakota

CLASSIFICATION
Family Hypsilophodontidae
Suborder Ornithopoda
Order Ornithischia

DISCOVERY

Experts thought the first-known *Hypsilophodon* (found in 1849) was an *Iguanodon*. Later finds with distinctive teeth convinced Thomas Huxley that this was a "new" dinosaur genus.

IGUANODON

I GUANODON ("IGUANA TOOTH") was a large, heavy ornithopod that flourished in large numbers. It owes its name to its tall, ridged cheek teeth, similar to those of a modern iguana lizard, though larger. *Iguanodon* cropped vegetation with its horny beak and chewed with its cheek teeth, with an unusual sliding action of the jaws. It had five-fingered hands that were unique and highly specialized. Each had a spiked thumb, three middle fingers with hoof-like claws, and a grasping fifth finger.

IGUANODON'S DISCOVERER Iguanodon *was discovered by Dr Gideon Mantell, who named the dinosaur in 1825.*

Tall, unworn tooth

Short tooth worn down by chewing vegetation

LOWER CHEEK TEETH

Two *Iguanodon* teeth (above) show variations in the extent of wear. The tall tooth has an unworn edge. The short tooth was worn down by chewing tough vegetation but was kept sharp by sliding against the upper teeth.

Dorsal vertebrae

Sacral vertebrae

Cervical vertebrae

Prepubic process

Ilium

Rib

Pubis

Humerus

Femur

Ulna

Tibia

Fibula

Metatarsal

◾ LIFESTYLE ◾

Iguanodon was probably a peaceful herbivore capable of standing and walking either on its hind limbs or on all fours. Young animals, with their relatively short arms, were probably usually two-legged. However, adults had longer, stronger arms and could have lowered the forward part of the body to rest on the three weight-bearing middle fingers of each hand, for example to drink or to browse on low-growing horsetails. A few trackways suggest that adults sometimes walked on all fours too. Yet most fossil tracks attributed to *Iguanodon* show only prints left by its big, three-toed feet. *Iguanodon* could stand on its long, muscular hind legs to reach tree leaves. When walking on its hind limbs, it would have thrust its head forwards, holding its back and tail stiff and nearly horizontal. *Iguanodon* could have escaped from large predators such as *Baryonyx* by running on two legs. If cornered, however, the ornithischian would have defended itself by jabbing out with its spiked thumbs. It is unlikely that any carnosaur would have dared tackle a whole group of *Iguanodon*, and quite likely this dinosaur did roam the land in herds. One clue is a group of fossil carcasses found close together at a site in Germany. Scientists suspect that a large herd was engulfed and drowned in a flash flood before it had a chance to escape.

VERSATILE HANDS

The hoofed fingers formed a "foot" for walking. When the hand was raised, the wrist could rotate and bring the fifth finger in towards the palm. The spiked thumb was unable to bend.

BONY TENDONS

Criss-crossed bony tendons overlaid these vertebrae (spinal bones) from the upper part of *Iguanodon*'s tail (left), as well as vertebrae above the hips and in the back. The tendons strengthened key regions of the spinal column and stiffened the tail.

Bony tendon

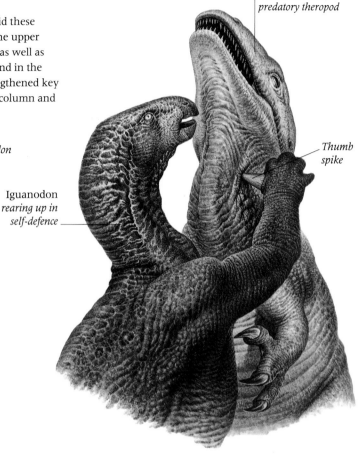

Carnosaur, a big predatory theropod

Thumb spike

Iguanodon rearing up in self-defence

MODERN SKELETAL RECONSTRUCTION

This modern reassembly of an *Iguanodon* skeleton (main illustration, below) reflects a new understanding about the stiffness of the spinal vertebrae and the angle at which each tail bone met its neighbours. As a result of this new understanding, it is now known that *Iguanodon* had a horizontal back, and that its head was forward-pointing and held relatively low, counterbalanced by the long, stiff, heavy tail.

HIP The arrangement of the ilium, ischium, and pubis (bones that form the main part of the pelvic girdle) shows that *Iguanodon* was an ornithischian ("bird-hipped") dinosaur.

Caudal vertebrae

Ischium

Chevron

Neural spine

SPIKED THUMB

If attacked by a large, sharp-toothed, sharp-clawed theropod, *Iguanodon* might have reared up on its hind limbs and counterattacked with its spiked thumb. Strong, bony, and stiletto-like, this thumb could have penetrated the attacker's scaly hide or inflicted wounds on the throat, eyes, or belly.

OLD SKELETAL RECONSTRUCTION

Iguanodon skeletons used to be reconstructed in an upright, kangaroo-like posture (left). However, in the 1970s experts realized that such a posture was impossible, because it would have meant breaking the stiffened tail to enable it to bend where it reached the ground.

FOOT The three-toed foot was strongly built to support *Iguanodon*'s weight. The upper bones of the foot were relatively long, which indicates that this dinosaur walked on its toes.

BREEDING BEHAVIOUR

A model depicts a mother *Iguanodon* tending her nest and eggs. No known *Iguanodon* nests and eggs have ever been discovered, but most palaeontologists are confident in assuming that this dinosaur constructed an earthen nest and cared for eggs and young in the same way as alligators do.

Tail balancing the body

Earth nest shaped with the hands

DISCOVERY

In 1825, *Iguanodon* became only the second dinosaur to gain a scientific name. An *Iguanodon* shin bone had been found in 1809, but not recognized; it was subsequently forgotten, until it was identified in the 1970s.

Naris

Large head

Toothless beak

MUTTABURRASAURUS

A 7m (23ft) Australian relative of *Iguanodon*, *Muttaburrasaurus* had a hollow arch above its snout, as in some hadrosaurs. Its toothless beak was similar to *Iguanodon*'s, but its cheek teeth were adapted for shearing (cutting), unlike the grinding cheek teeth of *Iguanodon*.

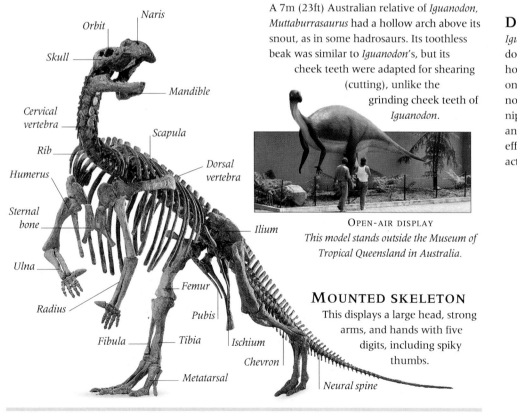

Orbit

Naris

Skull

Mandible

Cervical vertebra

Scapula

Rib

Dorsal vertebra

Humerus

Sternal bone

Ilium

Ulna

Femur

Radius

Pubis

Fibula *Tibia* *Ischium*

Chevron

Metatarsal

Neural spine

OPEN-AIR DISPLAY
This model stands outside the Museum of Tropical Queensland in Australia.

MOUNTED SKELETON

This displays a large head, strong arms, and hands with five digits, including spiky thumbs.

DIET

Iguanodon probably browsed low down, feeding on the ferns and horsetails that formed savannas on the marshy delta lands of northwest Europe. *Iguanodon* nipped off mouthfuls of foliage and then chewed it with an effective, sideways swinging action of the jaws.

Spike-like thumb

Hand with five digits

IGUANODON

Iguanodon was a large bipedal/quadrupedal plant-eater with cheek teeth for grinding, hoof-like claws, and spiky thumbs used for defence.

THE MESOZOIC ERA

MYA
248   208   144   65

TRIASSIC   JURASSIC   CRETACEOUS

SIZE
Length 9m (29ft 6in)
Weight 4.5 tonnes
(4.4 tons)

TIME
140–110 MYA

LOCATION
Belgium Hainaut
England Southeast
Germany Nordrhein-
Westfalen
Spain Castellón, Cuenca,
Teruel
USA South Dakota

CLASSIFICATION
Family Iguanodontidae
Suborder Ornithopoda
Order Ornithischia

DIET
Horsetails, ferns,
possibly flowering plants

HIND LIMB ANATOMY

A restoration of the internal anatomy of an *Iguanodon* hind limb reveals its supporting structure of femur, tibia, fibula, and tarsal and metatarsal bones. Muscles joined to limb and pelvic bones worked in pairs to pull the whole leg back and forth. Other pairs of muscles contracted alternately to bend or straighten the lower leg at the knee.

Short caudo-femoral muscle
Ilium
Iliofemoral muscle
Iliotibial muscle
Ambiens muscle
External pubo-ischio-femoral muscle
Tibial flexor muscle
Iliofibular muscle
Femur
Common digital extensor muscle
Anterior tibial muscle
Gastrocnemius muscle
Tibia
Fibula
Tarsal
Metatarsal
Toe
Hoof-like claw

BONES OF THE HAND

The specialized function of each finger is reflected in its structure. A spiky bone formed the thumb. Long and short phalanges ending in blunt, little "hooves" constituted the three weight-bearing middle fingers. Short, jointed bones made the tapering "little finger" flexible.

Blunt claw bone like a hoof
Phalanx
Long phalanx
Phalanx
Short phalanx
Tapering "little finger"
Thumb-claw
Metacarpal
Wrist joint
Carpal
Ulna
Radius

Thigh

Knee
Hind limb
Ankle
Foot
Hoof-like nail

Heavy, stiff tail

LOCOMOTION

Evidence for giving this model *Iguanodon* a bipedal pose includes fossil tracks left by big three-toed feet in the same rock layers as *Iguanodon* skeletons. Only a few of the tracks include small imprints produced by the hands, so the creature's weight was for the most part only on the hind limbs.

OURANOSAURUS

A BLEND OF the familiar and the unusual, *Ouranosaurus* ("brave monitor lizard") had certain characteristics in common with its well-known relative, *Iguanodon*. These included hind limbs that were longer and stronger than the forelimbs, hoof-like claws on the toes and fingers, spiked thumbs, and teeth with high-ridged crowns. It also had distinctive features: low bumps over the eyes, a hadrosaur-like beak, and bony, sail-bearing blades jutting from the backbone.

SAHARA EXPEDITION
Palaeontologists examine a find of Ouranosaurus *bones in 1971.*

MARSH DWELLERS
The sail-backed ornithopod Ouranosaurus *shared lush African riversides with reptiles including* Sarcosuchus, *a crocodile up to 15m (49ft) long.*

■ LIFESTYLE ■

In behaviour, *Ouranosaurus* was probably much like *Iguanodon*. The structure of its hands suggests that it rested and ambled on all fours. Its hands were smaller than *Iguanodon*'s but its wrist bones were very strong. Although each hand's three middle fingers were hoofed and could not grasp things, they could either stretch out or bend back to form a weight-bearing "foot" when *Ouranosaurus* went down on all fours. To run, however, adults must have reared on their pillar-like hind limbs. The young would have walked on their two back legs all the time because their forelimbs were proportionally shorter. *Ouranosaurus* had a duck-like beak and powerful jaws with which it cropped and chewed vegetation such as low-growing cycadeoids and early flowering plants of the river floodplain. The purpose of the skin sail stretched across the high spines rising from its backbone is still not known. If males had taller sails than females, they might have served as visual signals to attract a mate or to scare a rival. The sail might also have served as a heat regulator. Like several other sail-backed dinosaurs and large prehistoric reptiles, *Ouranosaurus* lived in a hot, dry climate where there was a constant danger of overheating. During the hot afternoons, *Ouranosaurus* might have kept cool by standing with its sail edge-on to the sun, allowing heat to escape from the sail's skin. On chilly mornings it might have warmed up by standing broadside to the sun to let its heat warm the blood inside the sail.

SKELETON EXPOSED
A Tuareg tribesman gazes at the articulated skeleton of an Ouranosaurus. *The sand that covered it had simply blown away.*

Neural spine

Chevron

Caudal vertebra

FLAT-TOPPED SKULL

Seen from the side (left) and above (right) the skull was flat-topped, with a forehead bump. The snout was lower than *Iguanodon*'s, the mandible shallower. A tall coronoid process (attachment point for jaw muscles) denotes a strong bite. Both dinosaurs had ridged, leaf-shaped teeth. A hinge let the two sides of the upper jaw slide outwards as the lower jaw moved up to chew.

Braincase
Orbit
Forehead bump
Paroccipital process
Coronoid process
Mandible
Ridged, leaf-shaped tooth

Jugal bone
Naris
Duck-like beak
Orbit
Maxilla

Braincase
Cervical vertebra
Premaxilla
Mandible
Predentary bone
Humerus
Thumb spike

SKELETON

This specimen is on display in a museum in Venice. Tall, blade-shaped neural spines rise from the dorsal and caudal vertebrae (back and tail bones). These supported a skin sail. Spines this tall were unique among ornithischians. The forelimb bones are much shorter and slimmer than the hind-limb bones, perhaps especially in juveniles. The digits, including thumb spikes, were smaller than those of *Iguanodon*. The femur is longer than the tibia, suggesting that the legs provided firm support rather than speed.

Sternal bone
Scapula
Radius
Ulna
Phalanx
Dorsal vertebra
Rib
Ilium
Prepubic process
Hip joint
Femur
Sacral vertebra
Knee joint
Tibia
Ankle joint
Nail

■ FACT FILE ■

OURANOSAURUS

Ouranosaurus was a large, bipedal/quadrupedal herbivore. It had an elongated head, a toothless beak, and a skin sail along its back and tail.

THE MESOZOIC ERA

MYA
248   208   144   65

TRIASSIC   JURASSIC   CRETACEOUS

TIME
115MYA

DIET
Leafy vegetation

SIZE
Length 7m (23ft)

LOCATION
Niger Agadez

CLASSIFICATION
Family Iguanodontidae
Suborder Ornithopoda
Order Ornithischia

EDMONTOSAURUS

Teeth arranged in small groups

Dentary bone (jawbone)

L ONGER THAN the baseline of a tennis court and as heavy as an elephant, "Edmonton lizard" (of Edmonton, Alberta, Canada) was one of the biggest duckbilled dinosaurs. With its powerful jaws, bulky body, small forelimbs, strong hind limbs, and deep tail, it resembled an unusually large *Iguanodon*. But it had a flatter, more duck-like beak, hundreds of close-packed cheek teeth, and inflatable skin flaps over large nasal cavities. Also, the backbone curved down sharply at the shoulders, and each hand bore only four digits embedded in a fleshy pad.

■ LIFESTYLE ■

Duckbills were once thought to have been aquatic animals, gobbling soft waterplants, and swimming by thrusting water back with their webbed hands and by waggling their rudder-like tails. In fact their fingers were not webbed (they were partly enclosed in a mitten-like web), their tails seem too inflexible for sculling, and their teeth appear designed for chewing tough-leaved land plants. Scientists now think *Edmontosaurus* lived on land. It could have stood or ambled on all fours, but would have reared to hurry, striding on its great hind limbs with back held level and the tail balancing the body. The big duckbill seems to have been capable of sprinting at up to 50 km/h (30 mph) and it could probably have loped along for miles at almost half that speed. Without sharp teeth or claws to protect it, *Edmontosaurus* would have had to flee from *Tyrannosaurus* or other carnosaurs that haunted western North America in the last days of the dinosaurs. Usually, *Edmontosaurus* wandered in slow-moving herds, perhaps made noisy by bellowing calls. Such calls, which caused the nasal skin flaps to inflate, might have been made to entice mates, to threaten rivals, or to summon straying young. The herds cropped herbaceous undergrowth and tree leaves in forests near the western shores of the great inland sea. Remains of undigested seeds, fruits, twigs, and pine-tree needles lay inside the carcass of one mummified *Edmontosaurus*; perhaps they formed the last meal that this animal ate before it died.

TEETH OF LOWER JAW
Teeth were arranged in batteries on upper and lower jaws. Each battery consisted of up to 60 closely-packed groups of three to five teeth. When chewing, the upper batteries slid sideways over the lower ones.

INFLATABLE NASAL SAC
Flaps of skin lay across the front of *Edmontosaurus*'s face. Normally these lay flat and wrinkly (above). When the animal uttered its call (left) the skin flaps inflated and amplified the sound.

Caudal vertebra

Tibia

Metatarsal

Phalanges of foot

Part of broken femur

FOSSILIZED SKIN
Clustered bumps feature among the mass of smaller scales on Edmontosaurus's *skin. Maybe these bumps formed brightly coloured patches.*

MOUNTED SKELETON

Hadrosaur features included a unique skull form, three teeth or more in each position, no thumb, a reduced pubic shaft, and from eight to ten sacral vertebrae.

Orbit

Braincase

Cervical vertebra

Naris

Dorsal vertebra

Ilium

Cervical rib

Mandible

Sacral vertebra

Neural spine

Scapula

Caudal vertebra

Humerus

Prepubic process

Rib

Femur

Ulna

Radius

Pubic shaft

Tibia

Ischium

Chevron

Fibula

Metatarsal

FOSSILIZED SKELETON

This fossilized *Edmontosaurus* skeleton was found embedded in a rock with most bones from head to tail in their original positions. Discoveries of such near-complete remains are far rarer than finds of scattered bones or single teeth.

Ossified tendon

Rib

Humerus

Scapula

Maxilla

Orbit

Femur

Phalanges of hand

Metacarpals

Mandible

Predentary bone

Naris

HADROSAURID GROUPS

Edmontosaurus belonged to one of four hadrosaurid duckbill groups: edmontosaurs, saurolophs, brachylophosaurs, and gryposaurs. Both edmontosaurs and saurolophs blew up facial balloons that could produce sounds. Brachylophosaurs and gryposaurs had arched snouts, possibly for butting.

145

MAIASAURA

WITH ITS BROAD, duck-like beak, powerful jaws, and batteries of self-sharpening cheek teeth, *Maiasaura* ("good mother lizard") is a typical example of the "duckbilled" dinosaurs. It is placed in the family Hadrosauridae on account of its lack of a hollow head crest, and in the subdivision known as the brachylophosaurs because of the solid, horn-like crest above its eyes and the triangular projections on its cheek bones. *Maiasaura* was first discovered in 1978, since when thousands of specimens have been found.

MAIASAURA HATCHLING
This baby Maiasaura *has broken its eggshell and is about to emerge.*

VULNERABLE YOUNG

Museum skeletons depict a young ornithopod falling prey to a hungry *Troodon*. Agile, lightweight theropods might have invaded a *Maiasaura* colony to seize defenceless infants.

■ LIFESTYLE ■

Immense herds of *Maiasaura* ranged along the upper level of the coastal plane between North America's Rocky Mountains and the prehistoric interior sea. Fossil finds suggest some were tens of thousands strong. Scientists believe these herds migrated north and south with the seasons in search of food, stamping broad trackways along the upper coastal plain. While they stayed close together in their herd, sheer strength of numbers would have kept these bulky creatures reasonably safe from attack by tyrannosaurids. Prowling tyrannosaurids would also explain why *Maiasaura* bred in colonies. Each year many females trekked back to the same nesting site, scooping out mud nests 2m (about 6ft) across, and laying up to 20 elongated, oval eggs. Heat from a covering layer of rotting vegetation then helped the eggs to hatch.

Meanwhile, the mothers stayed nearby to protect them. Like most birds, the mothers also brought their babies food. The worn teeth and unformed limb bones of some fossil *Maiasaura* babies show that they had been eating solid food before they had grown strong enough to forage on their own.

Sacral vertebrae

Caudal vertebrae

Ilium

Pubis

Ischium

Femur

Chevron

Tibia

Neural spine

Fibula

JUVENILE SKELETON

Apart from its diminutive size, the skeleton of this juvenile *Maiasaura* differed from an adult's skeleton in several ways. The short snout and big eyes probably evoked a maternal response, as such features do in living mammals. In hatchlings, cartilage, not bone, formed the limb bones' undeveloped ends.

Ankle joint

Phalange

Metatarsal

MAIASAURA NEST
Maiasaura *hatchlings crouch in the protection of their mud-mound nest, among still unhatched eggs. Babies evidently stayed so long in their nests that, as they grew, they trampled on and crushed the shells of eggs that did not hatch.*

Dorsal vertebrae

Infratemporal fenestra

Orbit

Cervical vertebrae

Skull roof

Prepubis

Naris

Mandible

Predentary bone

Tooth

Scapula

RESTORATION OF HEAD
A close-up view shows a *Maiasaura*'s long, rather horse-like head and a ridge above the eye formed by a bony skull crest. Males might have butted one another with their crests.

Rib

Sternal bone

FORELIMBS *Maiasaura* is distinguished from the lambeosaurids by having only a small deltopectoral crest on the humerus (upper arm bone). In lambeosaurids, the crest was noticeably larger. Presumably *Maiasaura*'s crest anchored smaller, weaker muscles than those of the lambeosaurids.

Humerus

Elbow joint

Delto-pectoral crest

Ulna

Metacarpals

Radius

Phalanges

Wrist joint

147

CORYTHOSAURUS

TWO DOZEN OR SO identified skulls make *Corythosaurus* ("helmet lizard") one of the best-known of America's duckbilled dinosaurs. High, hollow, bony head crests that enclosed convoluted nasal passages are characteristic of the lambeosaurid hadrosaurs, to which this large ornithopod belonged. Confusingly, not every *Corythosaurus* had an identical head crest. Size and shape depended on sex and age. Before this was clarified, it was thought that there were seven species. Now just one is recognized.

COLLECTING CORYTHOSAURUS
In the early 1900s, flatboat-based fossil hunters found Corythosaurus *by the Red Deer River in Alberta, Canada.*

Caudal vertebra

Fossilized skin

FOSSILIZED SKIN

Impressions of *Corythosaurus* skin have survived with this length of fossilized caudal vertebrae. The skin's scales are pebbly, not overlapping, as in many reptiles.

Hip

◼ LIFESTYLE ◼

Corythosaurus lived on the coastal plain between North America's western mountains and a prehistoric inland sea. Herds would have trampled paths through the rich forest of cycadophytes, magnolias, ferns, palms, and cypress trees, browsing upon the leaves and fruits of low-growing trees, and cropping low-growing flowering plants. Sometimes a *Corythosaurus* herd must have crossed paths with a herd of another hadrosaurid – *Corythosaurus* fossils occur in a rock formation that also holds those of *Gryposaurus*, *Prosaurolophus*, *Lambeosaurus*, and *Parasaurolophus*. If herds of different duckbills intermingled, distinctive head crests and a keen sense of smell would have helped herd members to keep in touch with one another. Males' head crests must have been especially important in the breeding season, when the crest might have changed colour to attract a mate. During courtship or to dominate rivals, the males probably produced a loud, low trumpeting sound by forcing air from the windpipe up into a cavity in the crest, then through two side pockets, and out through the nostrils. This amplified the male's voice, making it resonate.

Tail

Thigh

Knee

HADROSAUR UNGUAL

This fossil bone is from the tip of one of the three large fingers of a hadrosaur hand. It supported a large, blunt claw.

Hind limb

Ankle

Foot

Toe

MOUNTED SKELETON

A distinctive head crest, somewhat like half a dinner plate on its edge, proclaims this hadrosaur to be a *Corythosaurus*. The hollow head crest, elongated spines rising from the vertebrae, robust limb bones, and ischium with an expanded, foot-like ending were features seen in other members of its family, the Lambeosauridae. Like all hadrosaurs, *Corythosaurus* had a "duck's bill", batteries of cheek teeth, a U-shaped neck, and ossified tendons stiffening the back and tail.

Caudal vertebra
Ilium
Femur
Dorsal vertebra
Bony crest
Orbit
Scapula
Mandible
Cervical vertebra
Chevron
Ischium
Fibula
Rib
Neural spine
Metatarsal
Ulna
Phalanx
Phalanx
Tibia
Radius
Metacarpal

HEAD CREST FUNCTIONS
Professor James Hopson of the University of Chicago debunked the notion that lambeosaurid crests were snorkels, and suggested their use in signalling.

Bony crest
Cheek pouch
Naris
Toothless beak

IDENTIFYING HEAD CRESTS

Only males possessed a crest as big and fully formed as this. Females and young had smaller crests. These differences emerged in 1975, when University of Pennsylvania comparative anatomist Peter Dodson published the results of careful measurements of many lambeosaurid skulls. *Corythosaurus* and *Hypacrosaurus* had fairly similar crests, but *Corythosaurus* had lower spines arising from its vertebrae. The unusual shape of *Corythosaurus*'s head crest earned it the popular name of "cocked-hat crest".

Neck
Shoulder
Wrist
Forelimb
Elbow
Hand
Finger
Claw

■ FACT FILE ■

CORYTHOSAURUS

Corythosaurus was a quadrupedal/bipedal plant-eater with a distinctive, helmet-shaped head crest.

THE MESOZOIC ERA

MYA
248   208   144   65

TRIASSIC   JURASSIC   CRETACEOUS

TIME
75MYA

DIET
Plants

CLASSIFICATION
Family Lambeosauridae
Suborder Ornithopoda
Order Ornithischia

SIZE
Length 10m (33ft)
Weight 3.8 tonnes
(3.7 tons)

LOCATION
Canada Alberta
USA Montana

149

LAMBEOSAURUS

L AMBEOSAURUS ("LAMBE'S LIZARD") was a large, robust, duckbilled dinosaur with a head crest that has often been compared in shape to a hatchet. The crest was hollow: the cavity inside was an extension of the nasal passage, and most probably amplified the sound of the animal's calls. The crest may have supported a frill of skin that ran down the neck, back, and tail. Three species of *Lambeosaurus* are known, each with a differently shaped crest. The hadrosaurs or "duckbills" were a group comprising two families: lambeosaurids such as *Lambeosaurus* and *Corythosaurus*, with hollow crests and short lower jaws, and hadrosaurids such as *Edmontosaurus*.

■ LIFESTYLE ■

Finds of skeletons as far apart as Canada and Mexico suggest that *Lambeosaurus* ranged a long way north and south, west of North America's Late Cretaceous inland sea. Herds probably migrated after a food supply that fluctuated with the seasons. As each *Lambeosaurus* slowly browsed its way across the countryside, its narrow beak could have snipped off the twigs and fronds of favourite species of plants. Hadrosaurid duckbills, with broader beaks, were probably less choosy eaters. Horned dinosaurs, with their parrot-like beaks, perhaps munched plants that neither group of duckbills was equipped to tackle. The varied feeding habits of the different duckbills and all the other ornithischians that shared the same habitat helped to prevent overcropping of the vegetation. The same sharing of food resources happens today among herbivores of the African savannas.

■ SIGNALS ■

Members of a *Lambeosaurus* herd could recognize each other visually by variations in their crests. If an animal lost sight of its herd, however, it would have been able to regain contact by sound. The tubes inside a *Lambeosaurus*'s crest acted as a sound box, amplifying the voice and producing low, resonant cries. It is possible that the various lambeosaurid dinosaurs could all be recognized by their voices: *Lambeosaurus*'s crest would have made a different sound from that created by *Corythosaurus*'s helmet-shaped crest. *Prosaurolophus* lacked a crest but was equipped with nasal "balloons". These would have inflated when the animal was about to call, perhaps to produce a loud bellow like that of an elephant seal today.

Orbit
Braincase
Bony crest
Naris
Premaxilla
Infratemporal fenestra
Sclerotic ring
Mandible
Tooth
Braincase
Orbit
Infratemporal fenestra
Mandible

SKULLS COMPARED

The small *Lambeosaurus* skull (top) is probably from a juvenile. It is tempting to assume that a skull with a large crest (above) was that of a male, while females had smaller crests. However, there is not yet enough good evidence for this.

Strong, flexible neck
Hatchet-shaped crest
Spur of crest
Cheek pouch
Short lower jaw
Palm of hand was a fleshy pad

Forward-bulging crest
Long crest with a tubular hollow

HEAD SHAPES

One species, *Lambeosaurus magnicristatus* (left), had a forward-bulging crest. The lambeosaurid *Parasaurolophus* (right), had a longer, backswept, bony crest. *Kritosaurus* (far right), a hadrosaurid, had a hump before the eyes, probably covered in thick skin, but no crest.

Dorsal vertebra

Ilium

Hip joint

Caudal vertebra

DRINKING POSTURE

This restoration, in which the flesh is superimposed on a mounted skeleton, shows a *Lambeosaurus* down on all fours to drink at a pool. Hadrosaur hands ended in fleshy pads like the feet of a camel: this is known both from fossil handprints and from fossil finger bones that are still encased in a sheath of preserved skin.

Neural spine

Chevron

Long, thick tail

CANADIAN FIND

The restoration seen on these pages represents a species known as *Lambeosaurus lambei*, which was found in Alberta, Canada. It was named in 1923 by William A. Parks, an authority on Canadian dinosaurs.

Ischium

Femur

Braincase

Orbit

Naris

Mandible

Scapula

Tibia

Femur

Ischium

BABY HADROSAUR

Like any newborn human baby, a hatchling hadrosaur had a head that seemed disproportionately large in relation to the lengths of spine and limb bones. These would catch up with the head as the body grew.

Fibula

Tibia

Ankle joint

Metatarsals

Phalanges

■ FACT FILE ■

LAMBEOSAURUS

Lambeosaurus was a quadrupedal/bipedal plant-eater with a large body, long legs, and a prominent head crest.

Low hump covered in thick skin

THE MESOZOIC ERA

MYA 248	208	144	65

TRIASSIC JURASSIC CRETACEOUS

SIZE
Length 15m (49ft)

TIME
75MYA

LOCATION
Canada Alberta
USA Montana
Mexico Baja California

CLASSIFICATION
Family Lambeosauridae
Suborder Ornithopoda
Order Ornithischia

DIET
Flowering plants

MARGINOCEPHALIANS

M ARGINOCEPHALIA ("margined heads") were a suborder of bipedal/quadrupedal plant-eating ornithischians with a narrow shelf or deep bony frill at the back of the skull; broad hips; no obturator process (a projection on the ischium); and no symphysis (cartilaginous union of bones) between the pubic bones. These dinosaurs probably shared an ancestor with the ornithopods. The first known marginocephalians were small, Late Jurassic bipeds with a tiny skull ridge. Late Cretaceous forms included huge, horned quadrupeds with bony skull frills, cutting beaks, self-sharpening cheek teeth, and powerful jaws. They were among the most abundant large, plant-eating dinosaurs of Late Cretaceous western North America. They are divided into two infraorders: Pachycephalosauria and Ceratopsia. Two closely related Ceratopsian families form the subgroup Neoceratopsia.

BREEDING HAZARDS
Two adults of the protoceratopsid Protoceratops *guard young from an oviraptorid dinosaur.*

■ PACHYCEPHALOSAURIA ■

"Thick-headed lizards" were very small to moderately large, bipedal herbivores which evolved broad, stocky bodies and immensely thick skulls decorated with knobs and sometimes spikes (most are only known from skullcap fragments). Rows of bony tendons stiffened the middle section of the tail. Primitive ornithischian features included teeth in the front of the jaw, and small, leaf-shaped cheek teeth. The group seemingly evolved in East Asia by Late Jurassic times, but most known genera lived during the Late Cretaceous, when one of the three families evidently spread to North America, and another family apparently reached Europe.
CHAOYANGOSAURIDAE formed the earliest known family, with cheek projections a bit like those

of *Psittacosaurus*, lobed upper front teeth, and sharp canine-like teeth. The two Late Jurassic genera came from China.
PACHYCEPHALOSAURIDAE were the dome-headed pachycephalosaurs with a thick, high-domed cranium that evidently shielded the brain when rival males banged heads forcibly together. Pachycephalosaurids ranged from 90cm to 4.6m (3ft to 15ft) long. All the known types lived in Late Cretaceous times. Of the eight known genera, one was discovered in Madagascar, five in North America, and two in East Asia.
HOMALOCEPHALIDAE were flat-headed pachycephalosaurs. These

resembed the pachycephalosaurids but their thick cranium was flat, not domed, and rival males probably engaged in head-to-head pushing contests. Homalocephalids ranged from 50cm to 3m (20in to 10ft). Three genera lived in Late Cretaceous East Asia, and one apparently in Europe.

■ CERATOPSIA ■

"Horned faces" were bipedal and quadrupedal ornithischians whose special features included flared cheekbones and a rostral bone that formed the top tip of a deep, narrow, parrot-like beak. The Psittacosauridae were apparently more primitive than either the Protoceratopsidae or the Ceratopsidae. In 1986, palaeontologist Paul Sereno put these last two under the collective heading of Neoceratopsia ("new horned faces").
PSITTACOSAURIDAE or "parrot lizards" were basically bipedal herbivores around 2m (6ft 6in) long. Key features included an "old-fashioned" ornithischian body and a highly evolved skull. The snout was relatively shorter than any other ornithischian's and formed a deep,

TWO MARGINOCEPHALIANS
These models of a huge, horned, quadrupedal ceratopsid, Styracosaurus, *and a small bipedal pachycephalosaurid,* Stegoceras, *stress the contrasts in size and form found among marginocephalians.*

PSITTACOSAURUS SKULL

STEGOCERAS SKULL

TRICERATOPS SKULL

MARGINOCEPHALIAN SKULLS

Three photographs (not to scale) contrast the skull of the thick-skulled pachycephalosaurid Stegoceras *(middle) with the skulls of two ceratopsians: the small, parrot-like psittacosaurid* Psittacosaurus *(top) and the immense ceratopsid* Triceratops *with long brow horns and neck frill (bottom).*

MARGINOCEPHALIAN FAMILY TREE

This diagram shows relationships between the marginocephalian families (the names ending in -idae). Scientists long disagreed about where pachycephalosaurs belonged within the Ornithischia, and variously grouped them with stegosaurs, ankylosaurs, and ornithopods. The idea that the Pachycephalosauria were a sister group to the Ceratopsia was confirmed in the mid-1980s, when it was recognized that both groups shared features derived from a common ancestor. In the Late Cretaceous, pachycephalosaurids and protoceratopsids seemingly migrated, by a land bridge, to North America, where protoceratopsids probably gave rise to ceratopsids.

Ilium

Prepubis

Ischium

Pubis

HOMALOCEPHALE HIP BONES

The front end of the ilium formed a shelf above a prepubis far longer than the pubis. In ceratopsids the whole top of the ilium formed a shelf and the prepubis was a long, flared blade.

Pachycephalosauridae

Pachycephalosauria

Homalocephalidae

Chaoyangosauridae

MARGINOCEPHALIA

Psittacosauridae

Ceratopsia

Protoceratopsidae

Neoceratopsia

Ceratopsidae

KEY

- Suborder
- Infraorder
- Subordinate group

narrow beak with high nostril holes. The half dozen or so known species belonged to the genus *Psittacosaurus*, which lived in late Early Cretaceous Central, East, and Southeast Asia. (A species found in Thailand suggests that Indochina had joined with Asia before the Late Cretaceous).
PROTOCERATOPSIDAE or "first horned faces" included about eight genera of quadrupedal and bipedal/quadrupedal herbivores 1m to 3 m (3ft 3in to 10ft) long or more. All had a bony frill at the back of the skull, and some also had bumps above the brow and nose. Self-sharpening cheek teeth, only enamelled on one side, were designed to shear and crush, and may have evolved to cope with the flowering plants arising in Late Cretaceous times. Protoceratopsids occurred in Central and East Asia, and spread to western North America.

CERATOPSIDAE or "horned faces" included some 18 named genera of quadrupedal, rhinoceros-like herbivores up to 9m (29ft 6in) long. Deep, shelf-like, bony skull frills and brow and nose horns adorned their huge heads. There were two subfamilies: Centrosaurinae had short, deep faces, relatively short frills, and longer nose horns than brow horns; Chasmosaurinae had long, shallow faces, and relatively long frills and brow horns. Both of these Late Cretaceous groups lived in western North America.

153

PACHYCEPHALOSAURUS

T HE LARGEST of the bone-headed dinosaurs, *Pachycephalosaurus* is known from only one skull and a few immensely thick skull roofs. "Thick-headed lizard" cushioned its brain inside a domed braincase up to 25cm (10in) thick. Bony knobs edged the dome's rear rim, and short spikes projected upwards from the snout. The teeth were tiny. From what is known of other dinosaurs in the same family, it is surmised that *Pachycephalosaurus* was the length of a large car, with a fairly short, thick neck, short arms, a bulky body, long legs, and a heavy tail that was held rigid by a basketwork of hard, bony tendons.

CLASH OF THE BONEHEADS
Prenocephale *males collide at full tilt.* Prenocephale *was smaller than its North American relative* Pachycephalosaurus, *and lived at an earlier time, in Mongolia.*

■ LIFESTYLE ■

Scientists suspect that *Pachycephalosaurus* and its dome-headed relatives had been the bipedal dinosaurian equivalents of today's bighorn sheep. In the mating season, big males evidently ran at one another, clashing heads together to decide which would dominate and mate with a whole herd of females. Scientists have conjectured that the thickness and height of the dome on *Pachycephalosaurus*'s head varied with age. Besides crash-helmet skulls, evidence that such beasts used their heads as battering rams lies in ridge-and-groove extensions of the spinal vertebrae. These enabled the vertebrae to interlock, so that they could hold the back and tail rigid. When two males banged heads, the shock of the impact would have travelled through the skull and along the backbone to the legs without damaging the brain. When faced with predators, however, even head-butting may not have been a sufficient defence. Self-preservation probably depended on an effective early-warning system and a quick get-away. Large olfactory lobes in the brain imply a keen sense of smell. Large eye sockets that faced somewhat forwards suggest that the animal had sharp eyes capable of binocular vision. While feeding, a *Pachycephalosaurus* herd would have been keenly aware of how close they could safely allow a tyrannosaur to approach before they ran away.

■ DIET ■

What the bone-headed dinosaurs ate is uncertain. Their small, ridged teeth could not have chewed up tough, fibrous plants as effectively as the teeth of the duckbills and horned dinosaurs, both of which lived at the same time as the thick-heads. Perhaps *Pachycephalosaurus* lived on a mixed diet of leaves, seeds, fruits, and insects.

Thickened dome of skull roof

Bony spike

Bony nodule

Maxilla

Orbit

SKULL

A thick, knobbly, high-domed skull guarded the tiny brain, which was set deep in a mass of solid bone.

Heavy tail held rigid for most of its length

EXTERNAL FEATURES

This model's head is based on a superbly preserved skull found in Montana in 1940. Because remains other than those of skulls are unknown, the body proportions and size had to be estimated from the known skeletons of other pachycephalosaurs, especially *Stegoceras*. Comparisons between skulls suggest that *Pachycephalosaurus* grew to 4.6m (15ft), in other words to about twice the length of *Stegoceras*.

OTHER BONEHEADS

Prenocephale (far left) and *Stygimoloch* (left), like *Pachycephalosaurus,* were in the Pachycephalosauridae, a family of high-domed, bone-headed dinosaurs that clashed heads together. *Homalocephale* (below) is placed within the Homalocephalidae, a family of flat-headed boneheads, in which the males probably tussled head to head in non-violent shoving contests.

PRENOCEPHALE

STYGIMOLOCH

HOMALOCEPHALE

Scaly skin

Bony nodule

Skull shelf

Domed head

Stout neck

Bony spikes projecting up from the snout

Short arm

Long leg – strong but perhaps not capable of running fast

SKULL SHELF

The small rim of bony nodules jutting from the back of the head is evidence that, despite their bipedal stance, *Pachycephalosaurus* and its kin were not ornithopods but relatives of the psittacosaurids and ceratopsids.

STEGOCERAS

Stegoceras ("horny roof") was a goat-sized pachycephalosaurid, known from one partial skeleton and dozens of mostly partial skulls. The skulls evidently became thicker and higher with age, especially in males. A male's dome overgrew the bony skull shelf. *Stegoceras* was about 2.4m (8ft) long, and lived in Alberta (Canada) and Montana (USA) in the Late Cretaceous. This dinosaur was named by Lawrence Lambe in 1902.

STANCE

Stegoceras typically held its back level, balancing the weight of its head and body with a heavy, stiffened tail.

SKELETON

In *Stegoceras* and other pachycephalosaurs, the femur (thigh bone) is longer than the tibia (shin bone). This pattern might suggest that they could not run very fast.

Femur

Rib

Scapula

Tibia

Phalanges

■ FACT FILE ■

PACHYCEPHALOSAURUS

Pachycephalosaurus was a bipedal plant-eater. The largest of the bone-headed dinosaurs, it had a distinctive, thick, dome-shaped skull.

THE MESOZOIC ERA

MYA 248	208	144	65

TRIASSIC   JURASSIC   CRETACEOUS

LOCATION
USA Montana, South Dakota, Wyoming

DIET
Plants

CLASSIFICATION
Family Pachycephalosauridae
Infraorder Pachycephalosauria
Suborder Marginocephalia
Order Ornithischia

TIME
68–65MYA

SIZE
Length 4.6m
(15ft)

155

PSITTACOSAURUS

P SITTACOSAURUS ("PARROT LIZARD") was a two-legged herbivore about 2m (6ft 6in) long. It resembled the ornithopod *Hypsilophodon*, but had a deeper, longer body, a shorter tail, longer arms, and four-fingered, grasping hands. The fourth finger and the first of the four toes were very short. But *Psittacosaurus*'s oddest feature was its short, deep head with a parrot-like beak, formed partly by the rostral bone unique to ceratopsians. Other ceratopsian features included pointed cheek bones, cutting cheek teeth, and a tiny ridge foreshadowing the horned dinosaurs' huge neck frills. There were at least four species of *Psittacosaurus*, the only known genus in the family Psittacosauridae.

■ LIFESTYLE ■

Psittacosaurus's cutting beak and self-sharpening cheek teeth suggest that it ate vegetation too tough for most other herbivores to tackle. Perhaps this ceratopsian dinosaur had evolved a way of getting nourishment from old-established kinds of plants. Yet it seems more than just coincidence that the ceratopsians appeared at about the same time as flowering plants came on the scene. Maybe *Psittacosaurus* gnawed the juicy but fibrous trunks of young palm trees. But whatever it ate evidently demanded more than being simply ground up into short pieces in the mouth. *Psittacosaurus* used additional digestive measures: polished pebbles found with one skeleton had served as gastroliths or "stomach millstones", grinding food inside a bird-like crop. Scientists believe that farther back inside the gut, bacteria and enzymes had probably completed the digestion process in special fermentation chambers. *Psittacosaurus* usually walked and ran on its hind limbs. While standing upright, it could have used its hands, which had stubby, short claws, to pull down branches to its mouth. Sometimes, however, it might have gone down on all fours, supported by its long, strong arms, while its jaws scissored through tough, low-growing leaves. Like the hands, the toes of *Psittacosaurus* also bore short, stubby claws. Without the sharp horns and bony neck frills of the later ceratopsians to deter carnosaurs, a threatened *Psittacosaurus* would have had either to flee or to try to hide from its predators. *Psittacosaurus* babies are known from two fossils, which show them to have been only about the size of modern songbirds.

Sacral vertebrae

Caudal vertebrae

Chevron

Neural spine

Ilium

Ischium

Femur

Fibula

Tibia

Ankle joint

Metatarsals

Phalanges

MOUNTED SKELETON

This reveals a rather ornithopod-like, bipedal dinosaur with a fairly long body balanced by the tail, robust arms, four-fingered, broad-clawed hands, hind limbs with slightly longer shins than thighs, and four-toed, broad-clawed feet. Unlike any ornithopod, it had a short, deep snout with a "parrot's beak".

Small horn on the cheek

Finger

Forelimb

Elbow

Toe

Ankle

Tail

Claw

Knee

Thigh

Hind limb

RESTORATION

Psittacosaurus fossils have been found lying in this death pose. But quite healthy individuals probably also lay down on all fours to sleep, and an active *Psittacosaurus* might have used its sturdy arms as props when it lowered its head to drink or feed at ground level.

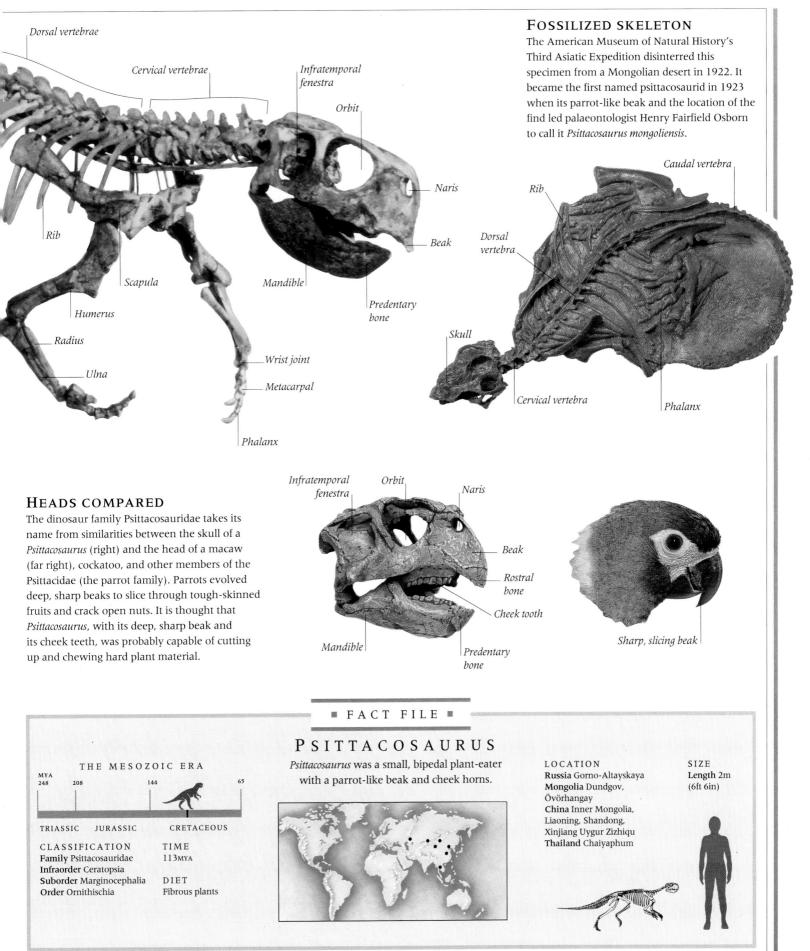

Dorsal vertebrae

Cervical vertebrae

Infratemporal fenestra

Orbit

Naris

Beak

Rib

Scapula

Humerus

Radius

Ulna

Mandible

Predentary bone

Wrist joint

Metacarpal

Phalanx

FOSSILIZED SKELETON

The American Museum of Natural History's Third Asiatic Expedition disinterred this specimen from a Mongolian desert in 1922. It became the first named psittacosaurid in 1923 when its parrot-like beak and the location of the find led palaeontologist Henry Fairfield Osborn to call it *Psittacosaurus mongoliensis*.

Caudal vertebra

Rib

Dorsal vertebra

Skull

Cervical vertebra

Phalanx

HEADS COMPARED

The dinosaur family Psittacosauridae takes its name from similarities between the skull of a *Psittacosaurus* (right) and the head of a macaw (far right), cockatoo, and other members of the Psittacidae (the parrot family). Parrots evolved deep, sharp beaks to slice through tough-skinned fruits and crack open nuts. It is thought that *Psittacosaurus*, with its deep, sharp beak and its cheek teeth, was probably capable of cutting up and chewing hard plant material.

Infratemporal fenestra

Orbit

Naris

Beak

Rostral bone

Cheek tooth

Mandible

Predentary bone

Sharp, slicing beak

■ FACT FILE ■

PSITTACOSAURUS

Psittacosaurus was a small, bipedal plant-eater with a parrot-like beak and cheek horns.

THE MESOZOIC ERA

MYA
248   208   144   65

TRIASSIC   JURASSIC   CRETACEOUS

CLASSIFICATION
Family Psittacosauridae
Infraorder Ceratopsia
Suborder Marginocephalia
Order Ornithischia

TIME
113MYA

DIET
Fibrous plants

LOCATION
Russia Gorno-Altayskaya
Mongolia Dundgov,
Övörhangay
China Inner Mongolia,
Liaoning, Shandong,
Xinjiang Uygur Zizhiqu
Thailand Chaiyaphum

SIZE
Length 2m
(6ft 6in)

PROTOCERATOPS

P ROTOCERATOPS ("first horned face") was discovered by an American expedition to Mongolia in the early 1920s. The numerous skeletons belonged to four-legged plant-eaters with outsize heads, bony neck frills, sharp, shearing cheek teeth, and parrot-like beaks. Some of these features identified *Protoceratops* as an early Asian model for the huge, horned dinosaurs of North America, the ceratopsids. *Protoceratops* gave its name to the protoceratopsids, a whole new family of dinosaurs. Finds of nests, eggs, and young gave the first clear indications of family life in a dinosaur community.

EGG DISCOVERY
Roy Chapman Andrews inspecting his great find of Protoceratops *eggs.*

■ LIFESTYLE ■

Protoceratops inhabited a hostile region of hot, dry, windswept sand dunes. The climate comprised a rainy season, during which water filled lakes and streams, and a dry season, during which the rains stopped and most of the surface water evaporated. Drought-resistant plants were able to thrive in this harsh environment, and it seems likely that *Protoceratops*'s massive jaws, sharp beak, and shearing teeth evolved to slice up the tough-leaved vegetation. This solidly built protoceratopsid probably lived in herds that wandered over a fairly small home range and came back to the same breeding grounds year after year.

■ BREEDING COLONIES ■

Evidence for such breeding grounds includes concentrated fossil finds of individuals of all ages near groups of nests, some of which were made on top of older ones. At mating time, males probably courted females by displaying their own relatively larger neck frills and nasal bumps. After mating, each female dug a shallow hole in the sand and filled it with a clutch of elongated, hard-shelled eggs laid in a spiral pattern. She then covered her eggs with sand and let the sun's heat hatch them. Meanwhile the mother guarded her nest against plundering theropods. *Oviraptor* and *Velociraptor* bones have been unearthed in *Protoceratops* nesting colonies. *Oviraptor*'s strong, toothless beak could have crushed up eggshells, while the more formidably armed *Velociraptor* could have preyed upon young and even adult protoceratopsids. One *Velociraptor* evidently died in combat with a *Protoceratops*, which also perished in the struggle.

EXTERNAL APPEARANCE
Protoceratops could run with reasonable speed but was a solidly built quadruped that was heavier, but not longer, than a tall human.

SKULL AND NECK FRILL
The skull and jaws of *Protoceratops* appear almost absurdly overgrown. Like its later, larger relatives, *Protoceratops* had a deep beak, a ridge above the nose, and a large, bony frill that stuck out over the neck. As individuals matured, the bony frill grew bigger, for display, and the nose ridge taller, either for show or for use in butting contests.

Bony frill

Naris

Beak

Infratemporal fenestra

Rostral bone

Jugal bone

Predentary bone

Mandible

Dentary bone

NEST AND EGGS
This fossil clutch of Protoceratops *eggs was found just as it had been laid more than 80 million years ago.*

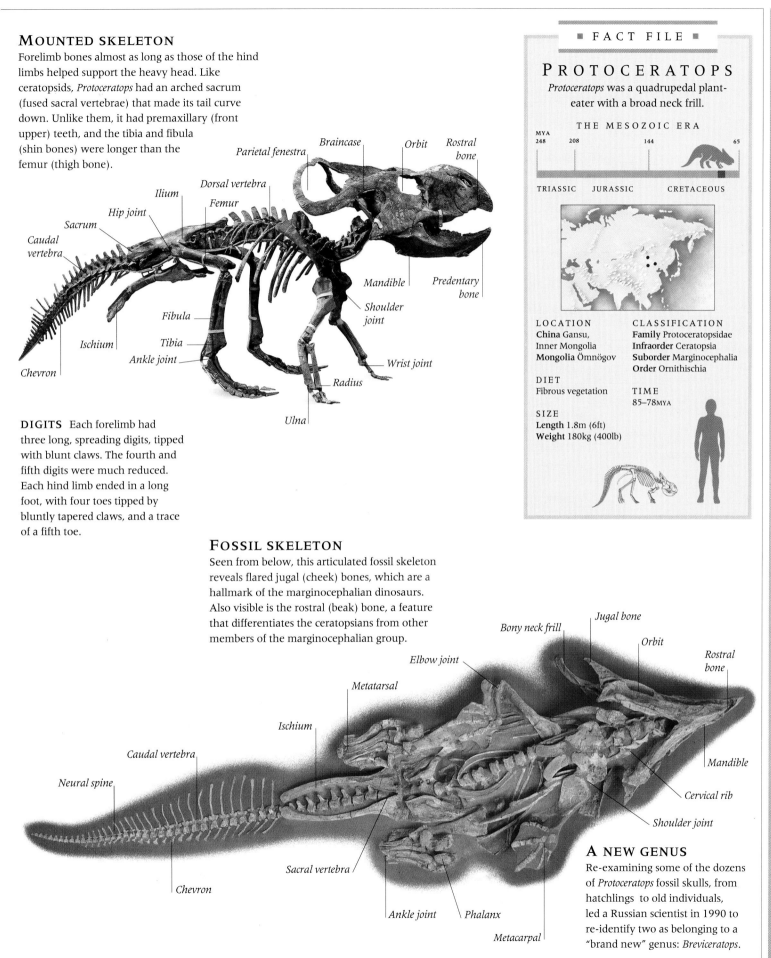

MOUNTED SKELETON

Forelimb bones almost as long as those of the hind limbs helped support the heavy head. Like ceratopsids, *Protoceratops* had an arched sacrum (fused sacral vertebrae) that made its tail curve down. Unlike them, it had premaxillary (front upper) teeth, and the tibia and fibula (shin bones) were longer than the femur (thigh bone).

Parietal fenestra

Braincase   *Orbit*   *Rostral bone*

Dorsal vertebra

Ilium

Hip joint

Femur

Sacrum

Caudal vertebra

Mandible

Predentary bone

Shoulder joint

Fibula

Ischium

Tibia

Ankle joint

Wrist joint

Chevron

Radius

Ulna

DIGITS Each forelimb had three long, spreading digits, tipped with blunt claws. The fourth and fifth digits were much reduced. Each hind limb ended in a long foot, with four toes tipped by bluntly tapered claws, and a trace of a fifth toe.

FOSSIL SKELETON

Seen from below, this articulated fossil skeleton reveals flared jugal (cheek) bones, which are a hallmark of the marginocephalian dinosaurs. Also visible is the rostral (beak) bone, a feature that differentiates the ceratopsians from other members of the marginocephalian group.

Jugal bone

Bony neck frill

Orbit

Rostral bone

Elbow joint

Metatarsal

Ischium

Mandible

Caudal vertebra

Cervical rib

Neural spine

Shoulder joint

Sacral vertebra

Chevron

Ankle joint

Phalanx

Metacarpal

A NEW GENUS

Re-examining some of the dozens of *Protoceratops* fossil skulls, from hatchlings to old individuals, led a Russian scientist in 1990 to re-identify two as belonging to a "brand new" genus: *Breviceratops*.

CENTROSAURUS

SKULL AND HEAD
A profile view of the skull (above) shows the long nasal horn and short, rounded neck frill pierced by fenestrae (openings). Two bony hooks overhung the frill from the back. Although they are shown in the profiled head (left), they might have been concealed by skin and muscle.

Labels (skull): Bony hook, Parietal fenestra, Braincase, Neck frill, Orbit, Infratemporal fenestra, Nasal horn core, Neck frill, Naris, Mandible, Rostral bone, Predentary bone

Labels (head): Bony hook, Rudimentary brow horn, Nose horn, Predentary bone

HIPS, LEGS, AND TAIL Hip anatomy featured a shelf-like ilium (upper hip bone), a long prepubis, and a downcurved ischium. In the legs, the femur was longer than the tibia. *Centrosaurus* had hoofed, four-toed feet. An arched sacrum (lower back bone) made the base of the unstiffened tail slope down.

Labels: Ambiens muscle, Ilium, Prepubis, Femur, Ilio-tibial muscle, Neural spine, Sacrum, Ischium, Lateral caudal musculature, Chevron, Knee joint, Tibia, Gastrocnemius muscle, Four-toed foot

T HE HORNED DINOSAUR *Centrosaurus* ("well-horned lizard") resembled a large rhinoceros. Like the rhinoceros, it had a heavy head, strong shoulders, pillar-like legs, broad-hoofed toes, a small tail, and a long, pointed nasal horn. In *Centrosaurus*, the massive head also had two small brow horns above the eyes. From the back of its rounded neck frill, two long, bony hooks curved forward and down, and two shorter hooks curled back and inwards. *Centrosaurus* grew to two-thirds the length of the largest horned dinosaur. It belonged to the centrosaurines: a ceratopsid subfamily whose members had short, deep faces, and a nose horn longer than the horns on their brows.

■ LIFESTYLE ■

As in *Triceratops* and other ceratopsids, the jaws of *Centrosaurus* were designed for munching tough vegetation. Large muscles, some anchored to the neck frill, slammed shut these huge jaws to deliver an immensely powerful bite. Cheek teeth with long cutting blades scissored each mouthful of tough stems into small pieces. These pieces might then have been mashed by swallowed stomach stones, ready for digestion. *Centrosaurus* lived among the meandering rivers and swampy forests of what is now Alberta, Canada. It shared this habitat with other big plant-eaters: horned, duck-billed, bone-headed, and armoured ornithischians, and with predatory dinosaurs of all sizes, from small elmisaurids and ferocious dromaeosaurids to the terrible tyrannosaurid *Albertosaurus*. Apart from dinosaurs, there were various small mammals, birds, crocodiles, turtles, salamanders, frogs, and freshwater fishes. Relatives of some of these creatures are still alive today.

■ MIGRATION ■

From Alberta's forests, *Centrosaurus* herds, thousands strong, probably migrated far north where plants grew quickly in the Arctic's mild, daylit summer months. These creatures could have rambled distances as great as 110 km (about 70 miles) a day. Even if a flooded river blocked their path, instinct would have urged the densely crowded herd to plunge in and try to swim across. Sometimes, if the current proved too strong, hundreds would have drowned, their bodies eventually drifting to shore or foundering on a sand bar. The mountain of rotting meat would have then provided a feast for carnosaurs living in the surrounding area.

CENTROSAURUS

Centrosaurus was a quadrupedal plant-eater. Characteristic features included a long, curved horn on its snout and a bony neck frill.

THE MESOZOIC ERA

MYA 248	208	144	65
TRIASSIC	JURASSIC	CRETACEOUS	

SIZE
Length 6.1m (20ft)
Weight 2.7 tonnes
(2.6 tons)

TIME
75MYA

LOCATION
Canada Alberta

DIET
Fibrous plants

CLASSIFICATION
Family Ceratopsidae
Infraorder Ceratopsia
Suborder Marginocephalia
Order Ornithischia

SKELETON AND MUSCLES

Strong bones and ligaments anchored the sheets and bundles of muscles that operated the jaws, held up the heavy head and neck, underpinned the belly, and powered the limbs and tail. A deep ribcage supported the massive shoulder girdle (the bones to which the forelimbs were attached).

Scapular muscle

Shoulder musculature

Rounded neck frill

Parietal strut

Brow horn

Nose horn core

Naris

Ventral cervical musculature

Anterior brachial muscle

Jaw adductor muscle

Rostral bone

Predentary bone

Abdominal muscle

Anterior antebrachial muscle

Wrist joint

Posterior antebrachial muscle

THREATENED CENTROSAURS

Scared by the sudden arrival of a hungry *Albertosaurus*, three female *Centrosaurus* and a juvenile hurry away. Two males defiantly remain, swinging their horned heads.

FORELIMB POSTURE

Differing views are held by experts on the posture of the front limbs of *Centrosaurus* and all other ceratopsians. One view is that the forelimbs were upright, as shown below and elsewhere on this page. The other is that they were splayed like those of a lizard, with the elbows sticking out.

STYRACOSAURUS

T HE HORNED dinosaur *Styracosaurus* ("spiked lizard") was so named because of the six long, bony spikes that fanned out from the back of its neck frill. These spikes were outgrowths of the small knobs, known as epoccipital bones, that gave a scalloped effect to the rim of the neck frill. The neck frill was a feature common to most ceratopsid dinosaurs, but the spikes were not. When *Styracosaurus* was alive, each of the four longest spikes of its neck frill, as well as its imposing nose horn, were probably about as long as a man's arm.

▪ LIFESTYLE ▪

Styracosaurus's spiky head and neck frill would have shielded its neck and shoulders from attack by large predators such as *Tyrannosaurus*. Rival males probably also brandished their nasal horns and frill spikes at each other in competition for mates. Two males might have edged sideways until their frill spikes interlocked, and then begun a shoving contest rather like the head-to-toe thrusting of two antlered red deer stags competing for a herd of hinds. *Styracosaurus*'s powerful shoulders would have been extremely useful in this sort of fight. Pushing contests may not always have injured the contestants badly, but several ceratopsian skeletons do show that injuries did occur. The fights may not have been rare.

▪ CLASSIFICATION ▪

Although the frill spikes and other skull features of *Styracosaurus* might seem to be very distinctive, some scientists think *Styracosaurus*, *Centrosaurus*, and some supposed specimens of *Monoclonius* all formed a single genus. It is possible that such features as the size and number of horns or spikes varied with age, sex, and perhaps species. To complicate this notion, a drawing published in 1990 suggested there may have been a species of *Styracosaurus* with only two frill spikes and a remarkable nasal horn that overhung the beak. Then in 1992 came news of a "missing link" between *Styracosaurus* and *Pachyrhinosaurus*. Such finds will shed new light on ceratopsid identities and evolution.

SKULL AND HEAD

Frill spike
Parietal fenestra (frill opening)
Supraorbital ridge
Neck frill
Nose horn core
Braincase
Orbit
Naris
Mandible

Features of *Styracosaurus*'s skull included a neck frill with six long spikes and large fenestrae (openings). In living animals, tough skin would have covered the frill openings (left).

Relatively short tail

SKELETON

Styracosaurus's skeleton featured a ceratopsid's typically deep beak, massive skull, sturdy shoulder and hip girdles, robust limb bones, roomy ribcage, and short tail. The short neck frill characterizes the subfamily Centrosaurinae. *Styracosaurus*'s long neck frill spikes are usually thought to be unique to this genus.

Epoccipital bone
Braincase
Nose horn core
Orbit
Naris
Mandible
Predentary bone
Rostral bone
Ulna
Radius
Phalanx
Metacarpal

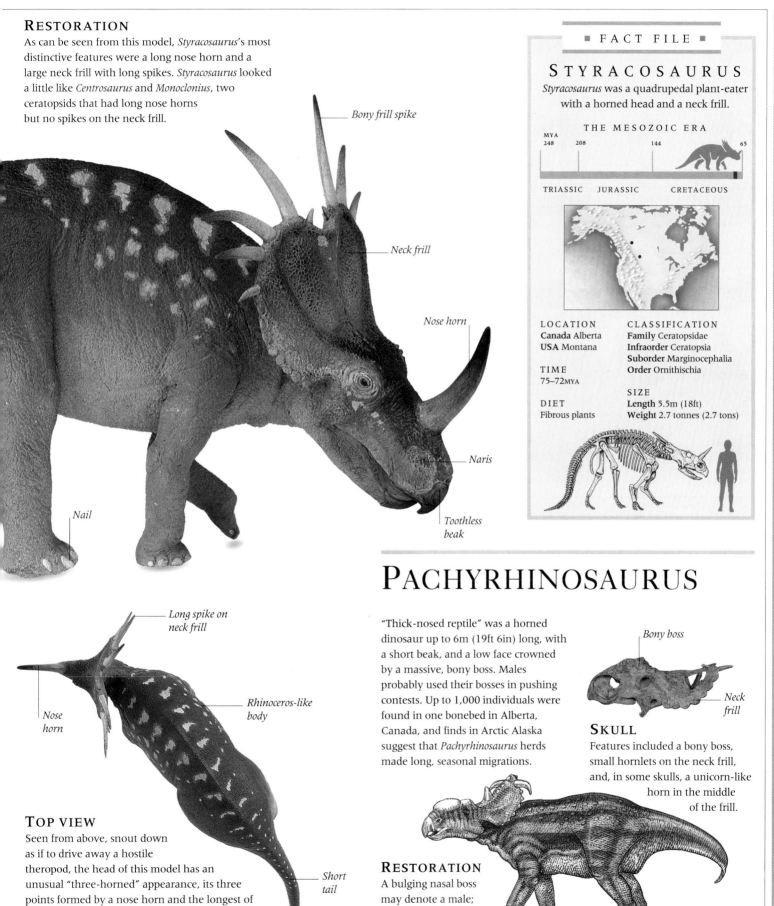

RESTORATION

As can be seen from this model, *Styracosaurus*'s most distinctive features were a long nose horn and a large neck frill with long spikes. *Styracosaurus* looked a little like *Centrosaurus* and *Monoclonius*, two ceratopsids that had long nose horns but no spikes on the neck frill.

Bony frill spike

Neck frill

Nose horn

Naris

Toothless beak

Nail

STYRACOSAURUS

Styracosaurus was a quadrupedal plant-eater with a horned head and a neck frill.

THE MESOZOIC ERA

MYA 248	208	144	65
TRIASSIC	JURASSIC	CRETACEOUS	

LOCATION
Canada Alberta
USA Montana

TIME
75–72MYA

DIET
Fibrous plants

CLASSIFICATION
Family Ceratopsidae
Infraorder Ceratopsia
Suborder Marginocephalia
Order Ornithischia

SIZE
Length 5.5m (18ft)
Weight 2.7 tonnes (2.7 tons)

TOP VIEW

Seen from above, snout down as if to drive away a hostile theropod, the head of this model has an unusual "three-horned" appearance, its three points formed by a nose horn and the longest of the neck-frill spikes. Otherwise the bulky body resembles that of a present-day rhinoceros.

Long spike on neck frill

Nose horn

Rhinoceros-like body

Short tail

PACHYRHINOSAURUS

"Thick-nosed reptile" was a horned dinosaur up to 6m (19ft 6in) long, with a short beak, and a low face crowned by a massive, bony boss. Males probably used their bosses in pushing contests. Up to 1,000 individuals were found in one bonebed in Alberta, Canada, and finds in Arctic Alaska suggest that *Pachyrhinosaurus* herds made long, seasonal migrations.

Bony boss

Neck frill

SKULL

Features included a bony boss, small hornlets on the neck frill, and, in some skulls, a unicorn-like horn in the middle of the frill.

RESTORATION

A bulging nasal boss may denote a male; females probably had cup-shaped bosses.

163

TRICERATOPS

I N THE 1880s, the high plains to the east of the Rocky Mountains yielded a strange pair of fossil brow horn cores. Further finds revealed they had come from a huge, horned, plant-eating ornithischian. "Three-horned face" proved to be the largest known ceratopsid – heavy as an elephant, with a massive body, and a head as long as the height of a human. A broad, bony frill stuck out from the back of its deep-beaked skull, and two long, hollow-based brow horns jutted above its eyes. The nose horn was short. *Triceratops* is placed within the chasmosaurine subfamily, most of whose members have long neck frills.

ADULT AND YOUNG

An old engraving shows a mother Triceratops *standing protectively over her baby. If a* Tyrannosaurus *menaced a* Triceratops *herd, the adults might have formed an outward-facing ring around their young.*

HATCHER'S SPRING

This discovery site in eastern Wyoming takes its name from the pioneer collector of horned dinosaurs, John Bell Hatcher.

■ LIFESTYLE ■

One of the last and most numerous of all the horned dinosaurs, *Triceratops* roamed in herds through the rather modern-looking forests that thrived in the cool, dry climate to the west of North America's shrinking interior sea. Their heavy heads held low, the great creatures munched herbaceous plants. Perhaps they also used their long brow horns to press down low, leafy branches in order to chop off mouthfuls of twigs and leaves with the sharp sides of their beaks, and to slice them up between batteries of shearing cheek teeth. The neck frill's rich blood supply probably served as a heat exchanger, shedding surplus heat when in the shade, and warming the body when in the sun. Sometimes a trial of strength decided which animal should dominate the herd: two males would meet head-to-head, lock horns, and twist until the weaker animal gave way. A hollow high in the skull functioned as a shock-absorber, cushioning the brain. Evidence of old, healed wounds in the cheek and frill bones of some *Triceratops* skulls suggests injuries caused by horns when rival males fiercely fought each other. It is likely, however, that a male more commonly asserted his authority by a harmless display of threatening behaviour: lowering his head to show off his frill, and then brandishing the frill from side to side to deter his rival and cause him to withdraw.

Hip joint

Ilium

Prepubis

Ischium

Caudal vertebra

Chevron

Tibia

Fibula

Neural spine

Ankle joint

Metatarsals

Phalanges

Scapula

Femur

Rib

Knee joint

Elbow joint

Ulna

Radius

BRAIN CAST

This cast of a *Triceratops* brain was produced by using the brain cavity of a skull (far right) as a mould, and filling it with a liquid that took the space the brain once occupied. When the substance solidified it was peeled away and measured, giving clues to brain shape, size, and areas of most and least development.

SKULL SECTION

The brain cavity used to make the cast (left) can be seen in the longitudinal section through a *Triceratops* skull (right). By studying cavity and cast, experts have deduced that big ceratopsians like this were faster and more agile than the stegosaurs, but slower than the ornithopods and theropods, and that they had less keen senses.

Brow horn core

Brain cavity

Braincase

Dorsal vertebra

Neck frill (enlarged parietal and squamosal skull bones)

Shoulder joint

MOUNTED SKELETON

A mounted skeleton stresses the immense size of *Triceratops*'s skull, more than one-third the length of the entire animal. Other features include the short neck covered by the neck frill, the short tail, and powerful, heavily built limbs. *Triceratops* walked on its toes.

Brow horn core

Skull roof

Cervical rib

Orbit

Nose horn core

SKULL

Like all the long-frilled ceratopsids, *Triceratops* had a long, low face with a long snout, and the brow horns were longer than the nose horn. *Triceratops*'s neck frill might look impressive, but there were other chasmosaurine ceratopsids whose frills were proportionally even longer.

Naris

Rostral bone

Coracoid

Sternal bone

Humerus

Wrist joint

Leaf-shaped crown

Tooth

Mandible

Predentary bone

Metacarpals

Phalanges

Root

SELF-SHARPENING TEETH

One side of the crown was hardened by enamel, but the other was not. As the dinosaur chewed its food, the softer side wore down faster than the hard side, always leaving a sharp cutting edge.

CHANGES IN CLASSIFICATION

Variations in the skulls of different *Triceratops* specimens once persuaded scientists that there had been 16 different species. A subsequent re-examination of the evidence led to the conclusion that there was only one. Since then there has been a fresh re-examination, which has caused some scientists to believe that there were probably two or three species.

WORK IN PROGRESS

A museum craftsman examines the brow horn core of a Triceratops *skull, suspended from a hoist during reconstruction work.*

LANDSCAPE

Triceratops *inhabited a countryside of open woodland with flowering plants and conifers, many of which resembled species growing today.*

CHASMOSAURUS

This medium-sized chasmosaurine ceratopsid grew up to 4.9m (16ft) long and weighed about 2.2 tonnes (2.2 tons). Skulls of many individuals have been discovered in western North America, where *Chasmosaurus* pre-dated its close relative *Triceratops* by several million years. One scientist has claimed to be able to tell males from females. He has also identified at least three *Chasmosaurus* species from what is now Alberta, Canada, and a fourth from Texas.

SKULL AND NECK FRILL

A front view of *Chasmosaurus*'s skull reveals narrow, bony struts: scaffolding to support the frill and reduce its weight. In life, skin covered the fenestrae (openings). From the back of the skull, the neck frill projected quite a way over the neck and shoulders.

Parietal fenestra

Epoccipital bone

Nose horn core

Neck frill

Brow horn core

Naris

FRONT VIEW OF HEAD AND FRILL

This view of *Chasmosaurus*'s head reveals that the ceratopsid had a small nose horn and two long brow horns rather like those of a cow.

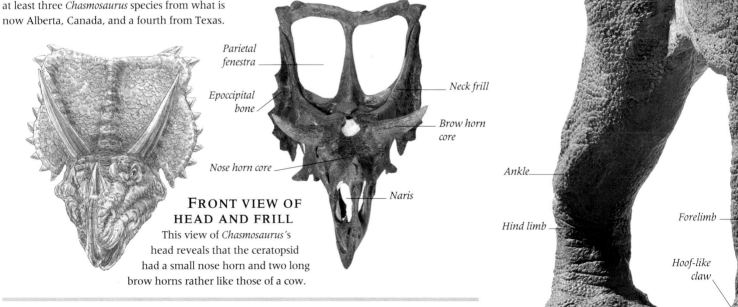

Thick, scaly skin

Thigh

Ankle

Hind limb

Forelimb

Hoof-like claw

EXTERNAL APPEARANCE

Triceratops rather resembled an immense rhinoceros. Like a rhinoceros, its heavy body depended for support on sturdy limbs, and short, broad feet with weight-supporting pads beneath the toes. But unlike any rhinoceros, this dinosaur had a bony neck frill, two long brow horns, and only one short nose horn. Largest of all horned dinosaurs, the monster is known from 50 complete and partial skulls. No complete *Triceratops* skeleton has yet been found.

RECONSTRUCTED HORN

Horn ended in a sharp point

The bony horn cores that sprout from fossil skulls were sheathed with horn in life. This model depicts a *Triceratops* horn as it would have appeared before its owner died. The result is a longer, sharper, and even more formidable weapon than fossil horn cores lead us to think. Fossil hunter Othniel Marsh initially mistook cores like this for prehistoric bisons' horns.

Epoccipital bone

Neck frill protecting neck and shoulders

Long brow horn

Short nose horn

Naris

Toothless beak

Broad, blunt ending

FOSSILIZED HOOF BONE (UNGUAL)

In a *Triceratops* skeleton, three fingers on each "hand" and all four toes ended in a broad, rounded bone known as an ungual. This picture shows a fossilized ungual. When *Triceratops* was alive, each ungual was protected by an outer layer of horn, equivalent to the claws of other animals. Thus *Triceratops*'s hands each had a set of three small hooves, while each of its feet had four.

Hoof-like shape

A TO Z OF DINOSAURS

 THIS SECTION is a dictionary of all the names of dinosaur genera that had appeared in print up to the time this book went to press. A total of 638 names are listed, 170 of which have proved (or appear to be) simply duplications of one kind or another. Several new dinosaur genera are identified with each year that passes, and there might be thousands more still awaiting discovery.

A TO Z OF DINOSAURS

This section comprises a comprehensive list of currently known dinosaur genera. Each scientifically valid genus name is followed by a pronunciation guide. If a genus is covered in the **Dinosaur Profiles** (pp. 36–167), only a page reference is given. If a genus is not profiled, the **A to Z of Dinosaurs** also gives a derivation of the name, some notes about the animal, and a page reference that allows you to look up a dinosaur in the same family. Where no relative is profiled, details of the dinosaur's classification are listed. The letters *n.d.* (*nomen dubium* – "doubtful name") indicate that the genus is little known, or that it is invalid. Where a genus is listed with an equals sign (=), the second name is the scientifically valid name; if the second name has a question mark, this indicates that it is possibly the valid name. Informal or unofficial names appear in quotation marks.

A **Abelisaurus** (ah-BEEL-i-SORE-rus: "Abel's lizard") A bipedal carnivore 9m (29ft 6in) long: a ceratosaur related to *Carnotaurus* (p. 48). Lived in the Late Cretaceous. Found in Argentina.

Abrictosaurus (a-BRIK-toh-SORE-us: "awake lizard") A bipedal herbivore similar to *Heterodontosaurus* (p. 134). Found in South Africa.

Acanthopholis (ae-KAN-tho-FOLE-is: "spine bearer") A quadrupedal, armoured herbivore 5.5m (18ft) long: an ankylosaur related to *Edmontonia* (p. 122). Lived in the Early and Late Cretaceous. Found in England. (*n.d.*)

Acrocanthosaurus (a-kroh-kan-thoh-SORE-us: "top-spined lizard") A sail-backed, bipedal carnivore up to 12m (39ft) long: a theropod related to *Allosaurus* (p. 52). Lived in the Early Cretaceous. Found in Oklahoma and Texas, USA.

Adasaurus (ah-DAH-SORE-us: "Ada lizard") A bipedal carnivore 2m (6ft 6in) long: a theropod related to *Deinonychus* (p. 70). Lived in the Late Cretaceous. Found in Mongolia.

Aegyptosaurus (ee-jip-toh-SORE-us: "Egyptian lizard") A quadrupedal herbivore 16m (53ft) long: a sauropod related to *Saltasaurus* (p. 106). Lived in the Late Cretaceous. Found in Egypt and Niger.

Aeolosaurus (ee-OH-LOH-SORE-us: "wind lizard") A quadrupedal herbivore 16m (53ft) long: a sauropod related to *Saltasaurus* (p. 106). Lived in the Late Cretaceous. Found in Argentina.

Aepisaurus (ee-pi-SORE-us: "elephant lizard") A quadrupedal herbivore about 15m (49ft) long: a sauropod of unknown family. Lived in the Early Cretaceous. Found in France. (*n.d.*)

Aetonyx = *Massospondylus* (p. 88).

Agathaumas (aga-THOW-mas: "much wonder") A quadrupedal, horned herbivore; possibly *Triceratops* (p. 164). Lived in the Late Cretaceous. Found in Wyoming, USA. (*n.d.*)

Agilisaurus (a-jil-i-SORE-us: "agile lizard") A small, bipedal herbivore: an ornithopod related to *Hypsilophodon* (p. 136). Lived in the Middle Jurassic. Found in China. Named in 1990.

Agrosaurus (ag-roh-SORE-us: "field lizard") A bipedal/quadrupedal herbivore: a prosauropod of unknown family and doubtful date (possibly Early Jurassic). Found in Australia. (*n.d.*)

Alamosaurus (AL-a-moh-SORE-us: "Alamo lizard") A quadrupedal herbivore up to 21m (69ft) long: a sauropod related to *Saltasaurus* (p. 106). Lived in the Late Cretaceous. Found in Utah and New Mexico, USA.

Albertosaurus (al-BERT-oh-SORE-rus: "Alberta lizard") A bipedal carnivore up to 8m (26ft) long. Similar to *Tyrannosaurus* (p. 54). Lived in the Late Cretaceous. Found in western North America.

Albisaurus (al-bi-SORE-us: "white lizard") A dinosaur (or probable dinosaur) known only from sparse Late Cretaceous remains. Identity uncertain. Found in the Czech Republic. (*n.d.*)

Alectrosaurus (a-LEK-troh-sore-us: "eagle lizard") A bipedal carnivore 5m (16ft 6in) long. Related to *Tyrannosaurus* (p. 54). Lived in the Late Cretaceous. Found in China and Mongolia.

Algoasaurus (AL-goh-a-sore-us: "Algoa lizard") A quadrupedal herbivore 9m (29ft 6in) long: a sauropod known only from sparse remains. Lived in the Early Cretaceous. Found in South Africa. (*n.d.*)

Alioramus (ay-lee-oh-RAY-mus: "different branch") A bipedal carnivore 6m (19ft 6in) long with a low head. Related to *Tyrannosaurus* (p. 54). Lived in the Late Cretaceous. Found in Mongolia.

Aliwalia (ah-lee-WAL-ee-a: "Aliwal") An early, large, bipedal carnivore up to 11m (36ft) long. Related to *Herrerasaurus* (p. 40). Lived in the Late Triassic. Found in South Africa. (*n.d.*)

Allosaurus (al-oh-SORE-us) See p. 52.

Alocodon (ay-LOH-koh-don: "wing tooth") A small, bipedal herbivore: an ornithischian known only from teeth. Lived in the Late Jurassic. Found in Portugal. Classification uncertain.

Altispinax (al-ti-SPINE-ax: "high spines") A large, bipedal carnivore: a theropod known only from a tooth. Lived in the Early Cretaceous. Found in Germany. Classification uncertain. (*n.d.*)

Alvarezsaurus (AL-va-rez-SORE-us: "Alvarez lizard") A bipedal carnivore like *Struthiomimus* (p. 64), but unrelated. Lived in the Late Cretaceous. Found in Argentina. Named in 1991. Classification: Alvarezsauridae, Ceratosauria, Theropoda, Saurischia.

Amargasaurus (a-MAR-ga-SORE-us "Amarga lizard") A sail-backed, quadrupedal herbivore 9m (29ft 6in) long: a sauropod. Lived in the Early Cretaceous. Found in Argentina. Described in 1991. Classification: Dicraeosauridae, Sauropoda, Sauropodomorpha, Saurischia.

Ammosaurus (a-moh-SORE-us: "sand lizard") A bipedal/quadrupedal herbivore 2.4m (8ft) long: a prosauropod related to *Plateosaurus* (p. 86). Lived in the Early Jurassic. Found in Connecticut and Arizona, USA.

Amphicoelias (am-fi-SEEL-yas: "with hollow-ended vertebrae") A large, quadrupedal herbivore: a sauropod related to *Diplodocus* (p. 100). Lived in the Late Jurassic. Found in Colorado, USA.

Amphisaurus = *Anchisaurus* (p. 84).

Amtosaurus (am-toh-SORE-us: "Amtgay lizard") A large, bipedal/quadrupedal herbivore: a hadrosaur known only from a partial skull. Lived in the Late Cretaceous. Found in Mongolia. (*n.d.*)

Amygdalodon (ay-mig-DAL-oh-don: "almond tooth") A large, quadrupedal herbivore: a sauropod related to *Cetiosaurus* (p. 92). Lived in the Middle Jurassic. Found in Argentina.

Anatosaurus = *Edmontosaurus* (p. 144) and *Anatotitan*.

Anatotitan (an-at-oh-TIE-tan: "giant duck") A bipedal/quadrupedal herbivore 12m (39ft) long: a hadrosaur related to *Edmontosaurus* (p. 144). Lived in the Late Cretaceous. Found in western North America. Named in 1990.

Anchiceratops (AN-ki-SERRA-tops: "close-horned face") A quadrupedal, horned dinosaur up to 5m (16ft 6in) long: a ceratopsian related to *Triceratops* (p. 164). Lived in the Late Cretaceous. Found in western North America.

Anchisaurus (AN-ki-SORE-us) See p. 84.

Andesaurus (AN-dee-SORE-us: "Andes lizard") A large, quadrupedal herbivore: a sauropod related to *Saltasaurus* (p. 106). Lived in the Late Cretaceous. Found in Argentina. Named in 1991.

Acrocanthosaurus   *Albertosaurus*   *Allosaurus*

Ankylosaurus (an-KIE-loh-SORE-us: "stiff lizard") An armoured dinosaur up to 10m (33ft) long, related to *Euoplocephalus* (p. 128). Lived in the Late Cretaceous. Found in western North America.

Anodontosaurus = *Dyoplosaurus.*

Anoplosaurus (an-oh-ploh-SORE-us: "unarmoured lizard") A poorly known herbivore, probably *Acanthopholis*. Lived in the Early Cretaceous. Found in England. (*n.d.*)

Anserimimus (an-ser-ih-MEEM-us: "goose mimic") A bipedal, bird-like carnivore or omnivore: a theropod related to *Gallimimus* (p. 62). Lived in the Late Cretaceous. Found in Mongolia.

Antarctosaurus (an-tark-toe-SORE-us: "southern lizard") A quadrupedal herbivore about 18m (59ft) long: a sauropod related to *Saltasaurus* (p. 106). Lived in the Late Cretaceous. Found in Argentina.

Anthodon = *Paranthodon.*

Antrodemus = *Allosaurus* (p. 52).

Apatodon = *Allosaurus?* (p. 52).

Apatosaurus (ah-PAT-oh-SORE-us) See p. 102.

Aragosaurus (a-ra-goh-SORE-us: "Aragon lizard") A large, quadrupedal herbivore: a sauropod related to *Camarasaurus* (p. 96). Lived in the Early Cretaceous. Found in Spain.

Aralosaurus (ar-al-oh-SORE-us: "Aral lizard") A bipedal herbivore: a hadrosaur related to *Maiasaura* (p. 146). Lived in the Late Cretaceous. Found in Kazakhstan.

Archaeopteryx (ark-ee-OP-ter-iks) See p. 74.

Archaeornis = *Archaeopteryx* (p. 74).

Archaeornithoides (ark-ee-or-nee-THOY-deez: "like ancient bird") A small, bird-like carnivore. Skull features are reminiscent of *Troodon* (p. 68) and *Baryonyx* (p. 58). Lived in the Late Cretaceous. Found in Mongolia. Named in 1992. Classification: Archaeornithoididae, Tetanurae, Theropoda, Saurischia.

Archaeornithomimus (ark-ee-or-nee-thoh-MEEM-us: "ancient bird mimic") A bipedal, bird-like carnivore or omnivore: an ostrich dinosaur related to *Gallimimus* (p. 62). Lived in the Late Cretaceous. Found in China.

Arctosaurus (ark-toe-SORE-us: "Arctic lizard") A possible theropod known from a Late Triassic vertebra, from Arctic Canada. (*n.d.*)

Argyrosaurus (ahr-guy-roe-SORE-us: "silver lizard") A quadrupedal herbivore 21m (69ft) long, with thigh bones more than 2m (6ft 6in) long: a sauropod related to *Saltasaurus* (p. 106). Lived in the Late Cretaceous. Found in Argentina and Uruguay.

Aristosaurus = *Massospondylus* (p. 88).

Aristosuchus = *Calamospondylus?*

"Arkansaurus" = *Archaeornithomimus?*

Arrhinoceratops (ay-rine-oh-SERRA-tops: "nose-horned face") A large, quadrupedal, horned herbivore: a ceratopsian related to *Triceratops* (p. 164). Lived in the Late Cretaceous. Found in Alberta, Canada.

Arstanosaurus (AHR-stan-oh-SORE-us: "Arstan lizard") Name for fossils of what proved to be a horned and a duckbilled dinosaur. Lived in the Late Cretaceous. Found in Kazakhstan. (*n.d.*)

Asiaceratops (AY-zya-SERRA-tops: "Asia horned face") A small, mainly bipedal, horned herbivore: a ceratopsian related to *Protoceratops* (p. 158). Lived in the Late Cretaceous. Found in Uzbekistan, Mongolia, and China. Named in 1989.

Asiatosaurus (AY-zya-toh-SORE-us: "Asian lizard") A large, quadrupedal herbivore; a sauropod perhaps related to *Camarasaurus* (p. 96) or *Mamenchisaurus* (p. 104). Lived in the Early Cretaceous. Found in Mongolia and China. (*n.d.*)

Astrodon (AS-troh-don: "star tooth") A quadrupedal herbivore perhaps more than 10m (33ft) long; a sauropod related to *Brachiosaurus* (p. 94). Lived in the Early Cretaceous. Remains found in eastern North America, and possibly England and South Africa. (*n.d.*)

Astrodonius = *Astrodon.*

Atlantosaurus (at-lan-toh-SORE-us: "Atlas lizard") A quadrupedal herbivore 23m (75ft) long. (*n.d.*)

Atlascopcosaurus (AT-las-kop-koh-SORE-us: "Atlas Copco lizard") A bipedal herbivore about 2.7m (9ft) long: an ornithopod related to *Hypsilophodon* (p. 136). Lived in the Early Cretaceous. Found in Australia.

Aublysodon (oh-BLIS-oh-don: "blunt tooth") A bipedal carnivore like *Tyrannosaurus* (p. 54), but smaller. Lived in the Late Cretaceous. Remains found in western North America and possibly China. Classification: Aublysodontidae, Tetanurae, Theropoda, Saurischia.

Austrosaurus (OS-troh-SORE-us: "southern lizard") A quadrupedal herbivore 15m (49ft) long: a sauropod perhaps related to *Cetiosaurus* (p. 92). Lived in the late Early and early Late Cretaceous. Found in Australia.

Avaceratops (AY-va-SERRA-tops: "Ava's horned face") A quadrupedal herbivore with a short nose horn: a ceratopsian related to *Centrosaurus* (p. 160). Lived in the Late Cretaceous. Found in Montana.

Avimimus (ay-vee-MEEM-us) See p. 76.

Avipes (AY-VEE-pace: "bird foot") A bipedal carnivore about 1m (3ft 3in) long: a theropod of doubtful identity. Lived in the Late Triassic. Found in Germany. (*n.d.*)

Azendohsaurus (ay-zen-doh-SORE-us: "Azendoh lizard") A bipedal herbivore 1.8m (6ft) long. Perhaps related to *Thecodontosaurus*. Lived in the early Late Triassic. Found in Morocco.

B **Bactrosaurus** (bak-troh-SORE-us: "Bactrian lizard") A bipedal/quadrupedal herbivore up to 6m (19ft 6in) long: a primitive hadrosaur related to *Lambeosaurus* (p. 150). Lived in the Late Cretaceous. Found in China.

Bagaceratops (bag-a-SERRA-tops: "small horned face") A horned herbivore 1m (3ft 3in) long: a ceratopsian related to *Protoceratops* (p. 158). Lived in the Late Cretaceous. Found in Mongolia.

Bahariasaurus (ba-ha-ree-a-SORE-us: "Bahariya lizard") A bipedal carnivore (or possibly omnivore): a theropod perhaps related to ostrich dinosaurs. Lived in the Late Cretaceous. Found in northern Africa.

Barapasaurus (bah-RAP-oh-SORE-us: "big leg lizard") A quadrupedal herbivore up to 18m (59ft) long: a primitive sauropod related to *Cetiosaurus* (p. 92) or in another family (Barapasauridae or Vulcanodontidae). Lived in the Early Jurassic. Found in India.

Barosaurus (bar-oh-SORE-us) See p. 98.

Barsboldia (barz-BOL-di-a: "Barsbold") A large, bipedal/quadrupedal herbivore: a hadrosaur related to *Lambeosaurus* (p. 150). Lived in the Late Cretaceous. Found in Mongolia.

Baryonyx (bar-ee-ON-iks: "heavy claw") See p. 58.

Becklespinax (bek-l-SPINE-ax: "Beckles' spines") A large, bipedal carnivore: a theropod with a skin and bone "sail" on its back. Named in 1991 from supposed *Altispinax* spinal bones. Lived in the Early Cretaceous. Found in England. Classification: Carnosauria, Tetanurae, Theropoda, Saurischia.

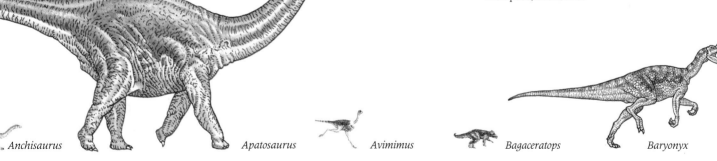

Anchisaurus   *Apatosaurus*   *Avimimus*   *Bagaceratops*   *Baryonyx*

Bellusaurus (bel-yoo-SORE-us) A quadrupedal herbivore at least 5m (16ft 6in) long: a sauropod related to *Cetiosaurus* (p. 92). Lived in the Middle Jurassic. Found in China.

Betasuchus (bee-ta-SYOO-kus: "B crocodile") A bipedal carnivore with slim thigh bones. Possibly related to *Carnotaurus* (p. 48). Lived in the Late Cretaceous. Found in the Netherlands.

Bihariosaurus (bi-HAR-i-oh-SORE-us: "Bihor lizard") A fairly large, bipedal/quadrupedal herbivore somewhat like *Iguanodon* (p. 138). Lived in the Late Cretaceous. Found in Romania. Named in 1989. Classification: Camptosauridae, Euornithopoda, Ornithopoda, Ornithischia.

Blikanasaurus (bli-KAHN-a-SORE-us: "Blikana lizard") A quadrupedal herbivore 5m (16ft 6in) long, with strong, stocky hind limbs. Lived in the Late Triassic. Found in South Africa. Classification: Blikanasauridae, Prosauropoda, Sauropodomorpha, Saurischia.

Borogovia (bo-roh-GOH-vee-a: "Borogove") A small, bipedal carnivore with a large, second toe-claw: a theropod related to *Troodon* (p. 68). Lived in the Late Cretaceous. Found in Mongolia.

Bothriospondylus (both-ree-oh-SPON-di-lus: "excavated vertebrae") A large, quadrupedal herbivore: a sauropod related to *Brachiosaurus* (p. 94). Lived in the Middle Jurassic–Early Cretaceous. Found in England, France, and Madagascar.

Brachiosaurus (brak-ee-oh-SORE-us) See p. 94.

Brachyceratops (brak-ee-SERRA-tops: "short horned face") A quadrupedal, horned herbivore up to 4m (13ft) long: a ceratopsian related to *Centrosaurus* (p. 160). Lived in the Late Cretaceous. Found in Alberta, Canada, and Montana, USA.

Brachylophosaurus (brak-ee-lohf-oh-SORE-us: "short-crested lizard") A bipedal/quadrupedal herbivore: a hadrosaur related to *Maiasaura* (p. 146). Lived in the Late Cretaceous. Found in Alberta, Canada, and Montana, USA.

Brachypodosaurus (brak-ee-pod-oh-SORE-us: "short-foot lizard") A quadrupedal, armoured, or plated herbivore known only from an upper arm bone. A nodosaurid ankylosaur or perhaps a stegosaur. Lived in the Late Cretaceous. Found in India. (*n.d.*)

Brachyrophus = *Camptosaurus.*

Bradycneme = *Elopteryx?*

Breviceratops (brev-ee-SERRA-tops: "short horned face") A small, quadrupedal, horned, dinosaur, perhaps an ancestor of *Protoceratops* (p. 158). Lived in the Late Cretaceous. Found in Mongolia. Named in 1990.

Brontosaurus = *Apatosaurus* (p. 102).

Bruhathkayosaurus (broo-hath-kay-oh-SORE-us: "huge body lizard") A huge, bipedal carnivore, perhaps a ceratosaur related to *Carnotaurus* (p. 48). Lived in the Late Cretaceous. Found in India. Named in 1987. (*n.d.*)

C **Caenagnathus** (seen-ag-NAYTH-us: "recent jaw") A small, bipedal carnivore, perhaps related to *Troodon* (p. 68). Lived in the Late Cretaceous. Found in western Canada. Classification: Caenagnathidae, Tetanurae, Theropoda, Saurischia.

Calamosaurus = *Calamospondylus.*

Calamospondylus (kal-a-moh-SPON-di-lus: "quill vertebrae") A small, bipedal carnivore: perhaps related to *Ornitholestes* (p. 78). Lived in the Early Cretaceous. Found in England.

Callovosaurus (kal-oh-voh-SORE-us: "Callovian lizard") A bipedal/quadrupedal herbivore 3.5m (11ft 6in) long: somewhat like *Iguanodon* (p. 138). Lived in the Middle Jurassic. Found in England. Classification: Camptosauridae, Euornithopoda, Ornithopoda, Ornithischia.

Camarasaurus (kam-are-ah-SORE-us) See p. 96.

Camelotia (kam-el-OH-ti-a: "of Camelot") A quadrupedal herbivore 9m (29ft 6in) long: a prosauropod similar to *Riojasaurus* (p. 90). Lived in the Late Triassic. Found in England.

Camptonotus = *Camptosaurus.*

Camptosaurus (kamp-toh-SORE-us: "bent lizard") A bipedal/quadrupedal herbivore up to 7m (23ft) long: somewhat like *Iguanodon* (p. 138). Lived in the Late Jurassic to Early Cretaceous. Found in western USA, England, and Portugal. Classification: Camptosauridae, Euornithopoda, Ornithopoda, Ornithischia.

Campylodon = *Campylodoniscus.*

Campylodoniscus (kamp-i-LOH-don-isk-us: "bent toothed") A large, quadrupedal herbivore: a sauropod perhaps related to *Saltasaurus* (p. 106). Lived in the Late Cretaceous. Found in Argentina. (*n.d.*)

Carcharodontosaurus (kar-kar-o-don-toh-SORE-us: "Carcharodon lizard") A bipedal carnivore 8m (26ft) long with features seen in *Allosaurus* (p. 52) and *Tyrannosaurus* (p. 54). Lived in the late Early and early Late Cretaceous. Found in North Africa.

Cardiodon = *Cetiosaurus?* (p. 92).

Carnotaurus (kar-noh-TORE-us) See p. 48.

Cathetosaurus (kath-e-toh-SORE-us: "upright lizard") A large, quadrupedal herbivore: a sauropod related to *Camarasaurus* (p. 96). Lived in the Late Jurassic. Found in Colorado, USA. (*n.d.*)

Caudocoelus = *Teinurosaurus.*

Caulodon = *Camarasaurus* (p. 96).

Centrosaurus (SEN-troh-SORE-us) See p. 160.

Ceratops (SERRA-tops: "horned face") A quadrupedal, horned herbivore: a ceratopsian related to *Triceratops* (p. 164). Lived in the Late Cretaceous. Found in Colorado and Montana, USA. (*n.d.*)

Ceratosaurus (seh-rat-oh-SORE-us) See p. 42.

Cetiosauriscus (see-tee-oh-SORE-is-kus: "like whale lizard") A quadrupedal herbivore 15m (49ft) long: a sauropod related to *Diplodocus* (p. 100). Lived in the Late Jurassic. Found in England, and perhaps in Switzerland.

Cetiosaurus (see-tee-oh-SORE-us) See p. 92.

Changdusaurus (jang-doo-SORE-us: "Changdu lizard") A large, quadrupedal, plated herbivore: a stegosaur related to *Tuojiangosaurus* (p. 120). Lived in the Jurassic. Found in Tibet. (*n.d.*)

Chaoyangosaurus (kow-yung-oh-SORE-US: "Chaoyang lizard") A small, bipedal herbivore with jutting cheeks: perhaps an ancestor of marginocephalians such as *Pachycephalosaurus* (p. 154) and *Psittacosaurus* (p. 156). Lived in the Late Jurassic. Found in China. Classification: Chaoyangosauridae, Pachycephalosauria, Marginocephalia, Ornithischia.

Chasmosaurus (kaz-moh-SORE-us) See p. 166.

Chassternbergia (chas-STERN-BERG-i-a: "Charles Sternberg") A large, quadrupedal, armoured herbivore: an ankylosaur resembling *Edmontonia* (p. 122). Lived in the Late Cretaceous. Found in Alberta, Canada, and Montana, USA. (*n.d.*)

Cheneosaurus = *Hypacrosaurus.*

Chialingosaurus (jya-ling-oh-SORE-us: "Chia-ling lizard") A quadrupedal, plated herbivore 4m (13ft) long: a stegosaur related to *Tuojiangosaurus* (p. 120). Lived in the Middle Jurassic. Found in China.

Chiayusaurus (jya-yoo-SORE-us: "Chia-yu lizard") A large, quadrupedal herbivore: a sauropod only known from teeth. Lived in the Late Cretaceous. Found in China. (*n.d.*)

Chilantaisaurus (ji-lan-tie-SORE-us: "Ch'i-lan-t'ai lizard") A large, bipedal carnivore related to *Allosaurus* (p. 52). Lived in the Late Cretaceous. Found in China.

Chindesaurus (chin-de-SORE-us: "ghost lizard") A bipedal carnivore up to 4m (13ft) long; similar to *Herrerasaurus* (p. 40). Lived in the early Late Triassic. Found in Arizona, USA. Classification: Staurikosauridae, Theropoda, Saurischia.

Brachylophosaurus   *Camptosaurus*   *Carnotaurus*

Chingkankousaurus (jing-kan-koo-SORE-us: "Ch'ing-kang-kou lizard") A large, bipedal carnivore: perhaps like *Tyrannosaurus* (p. 54). Lived in the Late Cretaceous. Found in China.

Chinshakiangosaurus (KIN-sha-KYANG-oh-SORE-us: "Kinsha-kiang lizard") A large, quadrupedal herbivore: a prosauropod related to *Riojasaurus* (p. 90). Lived in the Early Jurassic. Found in China.

Chirostenotes (kie-ros-ten-OH-teez: "slender hands") A bipedal carnivore 2m (6ft 6in) long, with long, narrow fingers and claws. Lived in the Late Cretaceous. Found in Alberta, Canada. Classification: Elmisauridae, Tetanurae, Theropoda, Saurischia.

Chondrosteosaurus (kon-dros-ti-oh-SORE-us: "bony cartilage lizard") A large, quadrupedal herbivore: a sauropod perhaps like *Camarasaurus* (p. 96). Lived in the Early Cretaceous. Found in England.

Chondrosteus = *Chondrosteosaurus*.

Chuandongocoelurus (jwan-dong-oh-sel-YEW-rus: "Chuandong hollow tail") A small, bipedal carnivore related to *Ornitholestes* (p. 78). Lived in the Middle Jurassic. Found in China.

Chubutisaurus (choo-boo-ti-SORE-us: "Chubut lizard") A quadrupedal herbivore up to 23m (75ft) long: a sauropod possibly similar to *Brachiosaurus* (p. 94). Lived in the Late Cretaceous. Found in Argentina.

Chungkingosaurus (JOONG-KING-oh-SORE-us: "Chungking lizard") A quadrupedal, plated herbivore: a small stegosaur related to *Tuojiangosaurus* (p. 120). Lived in the Late Jurassic. Found in China.

Cionodon (sigh-OH-NOH-don: "columnar tooth") A large, bipedal/quadrupedal herbivore: a poorly known hadrosaur. Lived in the Late Cretaceous. Found in Colorado, USA. Possibly *Edmontosaurus* (p. 144). (*n.d.*)

Claorhynchus = *Triceratops* (p. 164).

Claosaurus (klay-oh-SORE-us: "broken lizard") A bipedal/quadrupedal herbivore 3.7m (12ft) long: a primitive hadrosaur. Lived in the Late Cretaceous. Found in Kansas, USA.

Clasmodosaurus (klaz-mod-oh-SORE-us: "fragment tooth lizard") A large, quadrupedal herbivore: a sauropod perhaps related to *Saltasaurus* (p. 106). Lived in the Late Cretaceous. Found in Argentina. (*n.d.*)

Clevelanotyrannus = *Nanotyrannus*.

Coelophysis (SEEL-oh-FIE-sis) See p. 46.

Coelosaurus = *Ornithomimus*?

Coeluroides (SEEL-yew-ROY-deez: "Coelurid form") A bipedal carnivore 2m (6ft 6in) long: perhaps related to *Ornitholestes* (p. 78). Lived in the Late Cretaceous. Found in India. (*n.d.*)

Coelurus (seel-YEW-rus: "hollow tail") A bipedal carnivore 1.8m (6ft) long: perhaps related to *Ornitholestes* (p. 78). Lived in the Late Jurassic. Found in Wyoming, USA.

Coloradia = *Coloradisaurus*.

Coloradisaurus (kol-oh-rah-di-SORE-us: "Colorados lizard") A bipedal/quadrupedal herbivore: a prosauropod related to *Plateosaurus* (p. 86). Lived in the Late Triassic. Found in Argentina.

Compsognathus (komp-soh-NAY-thus) See p. 80.

Compsosuchus (komp-soh-SYOO-kus: "elegant crocodile") A large, bipedal carnivore: perhaps like *Allosaurus* (p. 52). Lived in the Late Cretaceous. Found in India.

Conchoraptor (KON-KOH-rap-tor: "conch thief") A small, bird-like, toothless carnivore related to *Oviraptor* (p. 66). Lived in the Late Cretaceous. Found in Mongolia.

Corythosaurus (koh-rith-oh-SORE-us) See p. 148.

Craspedodon (kras-PED-oh-don: "edge tooth") A large bipedal/quadrupedal herbivore: an ornithopod related to *Iguanodon* (p. 138). Lived in the Late Cretaceous. Found in Belgium.

Crataeomus (krat-ay-OH-mus: "great shoulder") A quadrupedal, armoured herbivore about 1.8m (6ft) long: named from bones perhaps of the ankylosaurs *Danubiosaurus* and *Struthiosaurus.* Lived in the Late Cretaceous. Found in Austria and Romania. (*n.d.*)

Craterosaurus (krate-er-oh-SORE-us: "bowl lizard") A quadrupedal, plated herbivore 4m (13ft) long: related to *Stegosaurus* (p. 114). Lived in the Early Cretaceous. Found in England.

Creosaurus = *Allosaurus* (p. 52).

Cryptodraco (krip-toh-DRAK-oh: "hidden dragon") A quadrupedal, armoured herbivore: an ankylosaur related to *Sauropelta* (p. 124). Lived in the Late Jurassic. Found in England.

Cryptosaurus = *Cryptodraco*.

Cumnoria = *Camptosaurus*.

D **Dacentrurus** (DAY-sen-TROO-rus: "pointed tail") A quadrupedal, plated herbivore 4.6m (15ft) long: a stegosaur similar to *Kentrosaurus* (p. 118). Lived in the Late Jurassic. Found in England, France, and Portugal.

Dachongosaurus (DA-JUNG-oh-SORE-us: "Dachong lizard") A large, quadrupedal herbivore: perhaps like *Cetiosaurus* (p. 92). Lived in the Jurassic. Found in China.

Dachungosaurus = *Dachongosaurus*.

Damalasaurus (DA-MAL-a-SORE-us: "Damala lizard") A huge, quadrupedal herbivore: a sauropod related to *Brachiosaurus* (p. 94). Lived in the Jurassic. Found in Tibet. (*n.d.*)

Dandakosaurus (dan-dak-oh-SORE-us: "Dandako lizard") A bipedal carnivore. Lived in the Early Jurassic. Found in India. Named in 1990. Classification uncertain. (*n.d.*)

Danubiosaurus (DAN-yoo-bee-oh-SORE-us: "Danube lizard") A small, quadrupedal, armoured herbivore: an ankylosaur related to *Sauropelta* (p. 124). Lived in the Late Cretaceous. Found in Austria.

Daptosaurus = *Deinonychus* (p. 70).

Daspletosaurus (das-PLEE-toh-SORE-us: "frightful lizard") A large, bipedal carnivore resembling *Tyrannosaurus* (p. 54). Lived in the Late Cretaceous. Found in Alberta, Canada.

Datousaurus (dah-too-SORE-us: "Datou lizard") A quadrupedal herbivore 15m (49ft) long: a sauropod related to *Cetiosaurus* (p. 92). Lived in the Middle Jurassic. Found in China.

Deinocheirus (DINE-oh-KEE-rus: "terrible hand") A large, bipedal carnivore or herbivore with forelimbs 2.4m (8ft) long: perhaps resembling a giant *Gallimimus* (p. 62). Lived in the Late Cretaceous. Found in Mongolia. Classification: Deinocheiridae, Tetanurae, Theropoda, Saurischia.

Deinodon = *Albertosaurus*?

Deinonychus (die-NON-i-kus) See p. 70.

Denversaurus (DEN-ver-SORE-us: "Denver lizard") A quadrupedal, armoured herbivore: an ankylosaur similar to *Edmontonia* (p. 122). Lived in the Late Cretaceous. Found in South Dakota, USA. (*n.d.*)

Dianchungosaurus (dyan-jong-oh-SORE-us: "Dianchung lizard") A small, bipedal herbivore: perhaps related to *Heterodontosaurus* (p. 134). Lived in the Early Jurassic. Found in China. (*n.d.*)

Diceratops (die-SERRA-tops: "two-horned face") A large, quadrupedal, horned dinosaur: a ceratopsian once believed to be *Triceratops* (p. 164). Lived in the Late Cretaceous. Found in Wyoming, USA.

Diclonius (die-KLONE-ee-us: "two stems") A large, bipedal/quadrupedal herbivore: a poorly known hadrosaur. Lived in the Late Cretaceous. Found in Montana, USA. (*n.d.*)

Dicraeosaurus (die-KRAY-oh-SORE-us: "forked lizard") A quadrupedal herbivore 20m (66ft) long: a sauropod with forked spines rising from its vertebrae. Lived in the Late Jurassic. Found in Tanzania. Classification: Dicraeosauridae, Sauropoda, Sauropodomorpha, Saurischia.

Chirostenotes   *Coelophysis*   *Coelurus*   *Deinocheirus*   *Deinonychus*

Didanodon = *Lambeosaurus* (p. 150).

Dilophosaurus (die-LOAF-oh-SORE-us)
See p. 44.

Dimodosaurus = *Plateosaurus* (p. 86).

Dinodocus = *Pelorosaurus*?

Dinosaurus = *Plateosaurus* (p. 86).

Diplodocus (di-PLOH-de-kus) See p. 100.

Diplotomodon (di-ploh-TOM-oh-don: "double cutting tooth") A large, bipedal carnivore known from a tooth, perhaps from *Dryptosaurus*. Lived in the Late Cretaceous. Found in New Jersey, USA. (*n.d.*)

Diracodon (die-RAK-oh-don: "double tooth") A large, quadrupedal, plated dinosaur: a stegosaur probably descended from *Stegosaurus* (p. 114). Lived in the Late Jurassic. Found in Wyoming, USA. (*n.d.*)

Dolichosuchus (DOL-i-koh-SYOO-kus: "long crocodile") A large, bipedal carnivore known from a limb bone, perhaps *Halticosaurus*. Lived in the Late Triassic. Found in Germany. (*n.d.*)

Doryphorosaurus = *Kentrosaurus* (p. 118).

Dracopelta (drak-oh-PEL-ta: "armoured dragon") A quadrupedal, armoured herbivore about 2m (6ft 6in) long: an ankylosaur related to *Sauropelta* (p. 124) Lived in the Late Jurassic. Found in Portugal.

Dravidosaurus (drav-id-oh-SORE-us: "Dravidanadu lizard") A quadrupedal, plated herbivore 3m (10ft) long: a stegosaur related to *Kentrosaurus* (p. 118). Lived in the Late Cretaceous. Found in India. (*n.d.*)

Drinker (DRIN-ker: "Drinker") A bipedal herbivore up to 2m (6ft 6in) long: an ornithopod perhaps related to *Hypsilophodon* (p. 136). Lived in the Late Jurassic. Found in Wyoming, USA. Named in 1990.

Dromaeosaurus (DROH-may-oh-SORE-us: "running lizard") A bipedal carnivore 1.8m (6ft) long: like *Deinonychus* (p. 70). Lived in the Late Cretaceous. Found in Alberta, Canada, and Montana, USA.

Dromiceiomimus (droh-MEE-see-oh-MEEM-us: "emu mimic") A bipedal, bird-like carnivore or omnivore: an ostrich dinosaur 3.5m (11ft 6in) long, related to *Struthiomimus* (p. 64). Lived in the Late Cretaceous. Found in Alberta, Canada.

Dromicosaurus = *Massospondylus* (p. 88).

Dryosaurus (dry-oh-SORE-us: "oak lizard") A bipedal herbivore 4m (13ft) long: an ornithopod similar to *Hypsilophodon* (p. 136), but maybe more closely related to *Iguanodon* (p. 138). Lived in the Middle–Late Jurassic. Found in western USA and Tanzania. Classification: Dryosauridae, Euornithopoda, Ornithopoda, Ornithischia.

Dryptosauroides (drip-toh-SORE-OY-deez: "Dryptosaurus form") A large, bipedal carnivore: perhaps related to *Dryptosaurus*. Lived in the Late Cretaceous. Found in India. (*n.d.*)

Dryptosaurus (drip-toh-SORE-us: "wounding lizard") A bipedal carnivore 6m (19ft 6in) long with slender legs. Lived in the Late Cretaceous. Found in New Jersey, USA. Classification: Dryptosauridae, Tetanurae, Theropoda, Saurischia.

Dynamosaurus = *Tyrannosaurus* (p. 54).

Dyoplosaurus (die-oh-ploh-SORE-us: "double-armed lizard") A large, quadrupedal, armoured herbivore: an ankylosaur like *Euoplocephalus* (p. 128). Lived in the Late Cretaceous. Found in Alberta, Canada.

Dysalotosaurus = *Dryosaurus*.

Dysganus (DISS-gah-nus: "rough lustre") A large, quadrupedal, horned herbivore known from teeth: a ceratopsian of doubtful identity. Lived in the Late Cretaceous. Found in Montana, USA. (*n.d.*)

Dyslocosaurus (diz-loh-koh-SORE-us: "bad place lizard") A large, quadrupedal herbivore: a sauropod like *Diplodocus* (p. 100) but with more (four or five) toe-claws per hind foot. Lived in the Late Jurassic or possibly Late Cretaceous. Found in Wyoming, USA. Named in 1992.

Dystrophaeus (dis-troh-FAY-us: "coarsely jointed") A large, quadrupedal herbivore: a poorly known sauropod: perhaps related to *Diplodocus* (p. 100). Lived in the Late Jurassic. Found in Utah, USA. (*n.d.*)

Dystylosaurus (DIS-TIL-oh-SORE-us: "two beam lizard") A huge, quadrupedal dinosaur: a sauropod related to *Brachiosaurus* (p. 94). Lived in the Late Jurassic. Found in Colorado, USA.

E **Echinodon** (EE-KIE-noh-don: "spiny tooth") A bipedal/quadrupedal herbivore 60cm (2ft) long: a primitive, possibly armoured, ornithischian: perhaps related to *Scelidosaurus* (p. 112) or *Heterodontosaurus* (p. 134). Lived in the Late Jurassic. Found in England.

Edmontonia (ed-mon-TONE-ee-ah) See p. 122.

Edmontosaurus (ed-MON-toh-SORE-us)
See p. 144.

Efraasia = *Sellosaurus*.

Elaphrosaurus (ee-LAF-roh-sore-us: "running lizard") A bipedal, bird-like carnivore or omnivore 3.5m (11ft 6in) long: an ostrich dinosaur more primitive than *Struthiomimus*. Lived in the Late Jurassic. Found in Tanzania and maybe Wyoming.

Elmisaurus (EL-mi-SORE-us: "foot lizard") A bipedal carnivore 3m (10ft) long with bird-like feet. Lived in the Late Cretaceous. Found in Mongolia and Alberta, Canada. Classification: Elmisauridae, Tetanurae, Theropoda, Saurischia.

Elopteryx (EE-LOP-ter-ix: "small wing") A small, bipedal carnivore: perhaps related to *Deinonychus* (p. 70). Lived in the Late Cretaceous. Found in Romania. (*n.d.*)

Elosaurus = *Apatosaurus* (p. 102).

Emausaurus (EE-mao-SORE-us ("EMAU lizard") An armoured, quadrupedal herbivore 2m (6ft 6in) long, somewhat like *Scelidosaurus* (p. 112). Lived in the Early Jurassic. Found in Germany. Named in 1990 from the initial letters of a German university.

Embasaurus (EM-BA-sore-us: "Emba lizard") A large, primitive, poorly known, bipedal carnivore named from two spinal bones. Lived in the Early Cretaceous. Found in Kazakhstan. (*n.d.*)

Enigmosaurus (en-ig-moh-SORE-us: "enigmatic lizard") A bipedal or quadrupedal carnivore or herbivore 7m (23ft) long: related to *Segnosaurus* (p. 108). Lived in the Late Cretaceous. Found in Mongolia.

Eoceratops (EE-oh-SERRA-tops: "early horned face") A large, quadrupedal, horned herbivore: perhaps *Chasmosaurus* (p. 166). (*n.d.*)

Eolosaurus = *Aeolosaurus*.

Eoraptor (EE-oh-RAP-tor: "early plunderer") A bipedal carnivore no bigger than a large dog: an early theropod more primitive than *Herrerasaurus* (p. 40). Thought to be close to the common ancestor of all dinosaurs. Lived in the Late Triassic. Found in Argentina. Described in 1993.

Epachthosaurus (e-PAK-thoh-SORE-us) A large, quadrupedal herbivore: a sauropod related to *Saltasaurus* (p. 106). Lived in the Late Cretaceous. Found in Argentina.

Epanterias = *Allosaurus*? (p. 52).

Erectopus (ee-REK-toh-pus: "upright foot") A bipedal carnivore related to *Carnotaurus* (p. 48). Lived in the Early Cretaceous. Found in France.

Erlikosaurus (AIR-lik-oh-SORE-us: "Erlik's lizard") A bipedal or quadrupedal carnivore or herbivore 5m (16ft 6in) long: related to *Segnosaurus* (p. 108). Lived in the Late Cretaceous. Found in Mongolia.

Euacanthus = *Polacanthus*.

Eucamerotus = *Chondrosteosaurus*.

Eucentrosaurus = *Centrosaurus* (p. 160).

Eucercosaurus (yoo-ser-koh-SORE-us: "well-tailed lizard") A poorly known, large herbivore: perhaps an ornithopod, related to *Iguanodon* (p. 138). Lived in the Early Cretaceous. Found in England.

Eucnemesaurus = *Euskelosaurus*.

Euhelopus (yoo-HEL-oh-pus: "good marsh foot") A quadrupedal herbivore 15m (49ft) long: a sauropod related to *Mamenchisaurus* (p. 104). Lived in the Late Jurassic. Found in China.

Euoplocephalus (you-op-loh-SEF-ah-lus)
See p. 128.

Eureodon = *Tenontosaurus*.

Dromaeosaurus   *Dromiceiomimus*   *Dryosaurus*   *Eustreptospondylus*

Euronychodon (YOO-roh-NIKE-oh-don: "European nail tooth") A bipedal carnivore known from teeth: perhaps like *Deinonychus* (p. 70). Lived in the Late Cretaceous. Found in Portugal. Named in 1991. (*n.d.*)

Euskelosaurus (yoo-SKEL-oh-SORE-us: "primitive leg lizard") A quadrupedal herbivore 10m (33ft) long: a prosauropod related to *Plateosaurus* (p. 86). Lived in the Late Triassic. Found in South Africa.

Eustreptospondylus (yoo-STREP-toh-SPON-die-lus) See p. 50.

F **Fabrosaurus** (FAB-roh-sore-us: "Fabre's lizard") A small, bipedal herbivore. Might possibly be *Lesothosaurus* (p. 132).

Fenestrosaurus = *Oviraptor* (p. 66).

Frenguellisaurus = *Herrerasaurus* (p. 40).

"Fukuisaurus" (foo-KOO-i-SORE-us: "Fukui lizard") Informal name of a large, bipedal/quadrupedal herbivore: perhaps like *Iguanodon* (p. 138). Lived in the Early Cretaceous. Found in Japan.

Fulengia (foo-LENG-ee-a: "Lufeng beast" – in anagram form) A bipedal/quadrupedal herbivore perhaps related to *Plateosaurus* (p. 86): a "lizard" redescribed as a baby prosauropod. Lived in the Early Jurassic. Found in Lufeng, China.

Fulgurotherium (FOOL-GOO-roh-THEE-ree-um: "lightning beast") A bipedal herbivore 2m (6ft 6in) long: like *Hypsilophodon* (p. 136). Lived in the Early Cretaceous. Found in Australia.

"Futabasaurus" (foo-tah-bah-SORE-us: "Futaba lizard") Informal name of a large, bipedal carnivore: perhaps like *Tyrannosaurus* (p. 54). Lived in the Late Cretaceous. Found in Japan.

G **"Gadolosaurus"** (gad-oh-loh-SORE-us: mistranslation of hadrosaur) A large, bipedal/quadrupedal herbivore: an ornithopod related to *Iguanodon* (p. 138). Lived in the Early Cretaceous. Found in Central Asia.

Gallimimus (gal-lee-MEEM-us) See p. 62.

Garudimimus (ga-roo-dee-MEEM-us: "Garuda mimic") A bird-like, bipedal carnivore or omnivore: an ostrich dinosaur related to *Gallimimus* (p. 62), but with short toes. Lived in the Late Cretaceous. Found in Mongolia.

Gasosaurus (gas-oh-SORE-us: "gas lizard") A bipedal carnivore 4m (13ft) long, perhaps *Kaijiangosaurus*. Lived in the Middle Jurassic. Found in China.

Genyodectes (GEN-yoh-DEK-teez: "biting jaw") A large, bipedal carnivore with long, curved fangs. Lived in the Late Cretaceous. Found in Argentina. Classification uncertain.

Geranosaurus (GER-AN-oh-SORE-us: "crane lizard") A small, bipedal plant-eater: an ornithopod like *Heterodontosaurus* (p. 134). Lived in the Early Jurassic. Found in South Africa. (*n.d.*)

Gigantosaurus = *Pelorosaurus* and *Barosaurus* (p. 98).

Gigantoscelus = *Euskelosaurus*.

Gilmoreosaurus (GIL-more-oh-SORE-us: "Gilmore's lizard") A bipedal herbivore: a rather small, primitive hadrosaur. Lived in the Late Cretaceous. Found in China.

Giraffatitan = *Brachiosaurus* (p. 94).

Gongbusaurus (GONG-boo-SORE-us: "Gongbu lizard") A bipedal herbivore about 1.5m (5ft) long: perhaps like *Hypsilophodon* (p. 136). Lived in the Late Jurassic. Found in China.

Gorgosaurus = *Albertosaurus?*

Goyocephale (GOY-oh-SEF-ah-lee: "decorated head") A bipedal herbivore 2m (6ft 6in) long: a bone-headed dinosaur with a flatter skull than *Pachycephalosaurus* (p. 154). Lived in the Late Cretaceous. Found in Mongolia. Classification: Homalocephalidae, Pachycephalosauria, Marginocephalia, Ornithischia.

Gravisaurus (GRAV-i-SORE-us: "heavy lizard") A large, quadrupedal herbivore: an ornithopod related to *Iguanodon* (p. 138). Lived in the Early Cretaceous. Found in Niger. Named in 1988.

Gravitholus (GRAV-i-THOH-lus: "heavy dome") A bipedal herbivore 3m (10ft) long: a bone-headed dinosaur related to *Pachycephalosaurus* (p. 154). Lived in the Late Cretaceous. Found in Alberta, Canada.

Gresslyosaurus = *Plateosaurus* (p. 86).

Griphornis = *Archaeopteryx* (p. 74).

Griphosaurus = *Archaeopteryx* (p. 74).

Gryponyx = *Massospondylus* (p. 88).

Gryposaurus (GRIPE-oh-SORE-us: "griffin lizard") A large, bipedal/quadrupedal herbivore: a hump-nosed hadrosaur related to *Maiasaura* (p. 146). Lived in the Late Cretaceous. Found in Alberta, Canada.

Gyposaurus = *Anchisaurus* (p. 84).

H **"Hadrosauravus"** = *Gryposaurus*.
Hadrosaurus (HAD-roh-SORE-us: "big lizard") A bipedal/quadrupedal herbivore up to 10m (33ft) long: a hook-nosed hadrosaur related to *Edmontosaurus* (p. 144). Lived in the Late Cretaceous. Found in New Jersey, USA.

Halticosaurus (HAL-ti-coh-SORE-us: "nimble lizard") A bipedal carnivore 5.5m (18ft) long: a primitive, predatory dinosaur. Lived in the Late Triassic. Found in Germany and perhaps France. Classification: Halticosauridae, Ceratosauria or Tetanurae, Theropoda, Saurischia.

Haplocanthosaurus (hap-loh-KANTH-oh-SORE-us: "single-spine lizard") A quadrupedal herbivore up to 22m (72ft) long: a sauropod related to *Cetiosaurus* (p. 92). Lived in the Late Jurassic. Found in Colorado and Wyoming, USA.

Haplocanthus = *Haplocanthosaurus*.

Harpymimus (HAR-pee-MEEM-us: "harpy mimic") A bipedal, bird-like carnivore or omnivore: an ostrich dinosaur related to *Gallimimus* (p. 62). Lived in the late Early Cretaceous. Found in Mongolia.

Hecatasaurus = *Telmatosaurus*.

Heishansaurus (hay-shan-SORE-us: "Mount Hei lizard") A poorly known quadrupedal or bipedal herbivore: perhaps an ankylosaur or pachycephalosaur. Lived in the Late Cretaceous. Found in China.

Helopus = *Euhelopus*.

Heptasteornis (HEP-tas-tee-OR-nis: "seven mountains bird") A small, bipedal carnivore: a troodontid or dromaeosaurid theropod. Perhaps *Elopteryx*. Lived in the Late Cretaceous. Found in Romania. (*n.d.*)

Herrerasaurus (eh-ray-rah-SORE-us) See p. 40.

Heterodontosaurus (HET-er-oh-DONT-oh-SORE-us) See p. 134.

Heterosaurus = *Iguanodon* (p. 138).

Hierosaurus = *Nodosaurus?*

Hikanodon = *Iguanodon* (p. 138).

"Hironosaurus" (hi-ron-oh-SORE-us: "Hirono-machi lizard") Informal name for a large, bipedal/quadrupedal herbivore: a hadrosaur. Lived in the Late Cretaceous. Found in Japan.

"Hisanohamasaurus" (his-an-oh-ham-ah-SORE-us: "Hisano-hama lizard") Informal name for a large, quadrupedal herbivore: a sauropod perhaps like *Diplodocus* (p. 100). Lived in the Late Cretaceous. Found in Japan.

Homalocephale (home-ah-loh-SEFF-ah-lee: "even head") A bipedal herbivore 3m (10ft) long: a bone-headed dinosaur with a flatter head than *Pachycephalosaurus* (p. 154). Lived in the Late Cretaceous. Found in Mongolia. Classification: Homalocephalidae, Pachycephalosauria, Marginocephalia, Ornithischia.

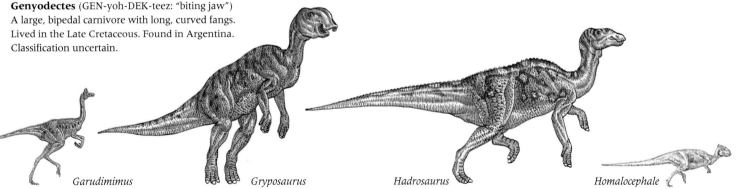

Garudimimus   *Gryposaurus*   *Hadrosaurus*   *Homalocephale*

Hoplitosaurus = *Polacanthus.*

Hoplosaurus = *Struthiosaurus.*

Hortalotarsus = *Massospondylus* (p. 88).

Huayangosaurus (hoy-YANG-oh-SORE-us: "Huayang lizard") A quadrupedal, plated herbivore 4.6m (15ft) long: a primitive stegosaur with front teeth. Lived in the Middle Jurassic. Found in China. Classification: Huayangosauridae, Stegosauria, Thyreophora, Ornithischia.

Hulsanpes (HUL-SAN-pes: "Khulsan foot") A small, bipedal carnivore related to *Deinonychus* (p. 70). Lived in the Late Cretaceous. Found in Mongolia.

Hylaeosaurus (HIGH-lee-oh-SORE-us: "woodland lizard") A quadrupedal, armoured herbivore 4m (13ft) long: an ankylosaur related to *Sauropelta* (p. 124). Lived in the Early Cretaceous. Found in England.

Hypacrosaurus (high-PAK-roh-SORE-us: "high-spined reptile") A bipedal/quadrupedal herbivore 9m (29ft 6in) long: a hadrosaur very similar to *Corythosaurus* (p. 148). Lived in the Late Cretaceous. Found in western North America.

Hypselosaurus (HIP-sel-oh-SORE-us: "high ridge lizard") A quadrupedal herbivore 12m (39ft) long: a sauropod related to *Saltasaurus* (p. 106). Lived in the Late Cretaceous. Found in France and Spain.

Hypsibema (HIP-si-BEE-ma: "high step") A name based on fossil hadrosaur scraps. Lived in the Late Cretaceous. Found in North Carolina, USA. (*n.d.*)

Hypsilophodon (hip-sih-LOH-foh-don) See p. 136.

Hypsirophus = *Stegosaurus* (p. 114).

I **Iguanodon** (ig-WHA-noh-don) See p. 138.

Iguanosaurus = *Iguanodon.*

Iliosuchus (eye-li-oh-SYOO-kus: "crocodile-hipped") A moderately sized, bipedal carnivore: perhaps related to *Megalosaurus*. Lived in the Middle Jurassic. Found in,England.

Indosaurus (in-doh-SORE-us: "Indian lizard") A moderately sized, bipedal carnivore, perhaps with a horned head, and related to *Carnotaurus* (p. 48). Lived in the Late Cretaceous. Found in India.

Indosuchus (in-doh-SYOO-kus: "Indian crocodile") A large, bipedal carnivore, perhaps related to *Abelisaurus*. Lived in the Late Cretaceous. Found in India.

Ingenia (in-GAY-nee-a: "Ingenia") A small, bird-like, bipedal, toothless carnivore or omnivore related to *Oviraptor* (p. 66). Lived in the Late Cretaceous. Found in Mongolia.

Inosaurus (ee-noh-SORE-us: "In lizard") A bipedal predator about 2m (6ft 6in) long: perhaps related to *Ornitholestes* (p. 78). Lived in the Early Cretaceous. Found in Niger. (*n.d.*)

Ischisaurus = *Herrerasaurus* (p. 40).

Ischyrosaurus = *Pelorosaurus.*

Itemirus (EE-tem-EE-rus: "Itemir lizard") A small, bipedal carnivore: perhaps related to the much larger *Tyrannosaurus* (p. 54). Lived in the Late Cretaceous. Found in Uzbekistan.

J **Janenschia** (YAN-ENSH-ee-a: "Janensch") A large, quadrupedal herbivore: a sauropod related to *Saltasaurus* (p. 106). Lived in the Late Jurassic. Found in Tanzania and Zimbabwe. Named in 1991.

Jaxartosaurus (jak-SART-oh-SORE-us: "Jaxartes lizard") A bipedal/quadrupedal herbivore 9m (29ft 6in) long: a hadrosaur related to *Corythosaurus* (p. 148). Lived in the Late Cretaceous. Found in Kazakhstan and China.

"Jiangjunmiaosaurus" (jyang-joon-mee-ow-SORE-us: "Jiang Jun-miao lizard") Informal name for a large carnivore not yet formally described: perhaps a primitive relative of *Allosaurus* (p. 52). Lived in the Late Jurassic. Found in China.

Jubbulpuria (jab-al-POOR-yah: "from Jabalpur") A bipedal carnivore 1.2m (4ft) long. Lived in the Late Cretaceous. Found in India. (*n.d.*)

Jurapteryx = *Archaeopteryx* (p. 74).

Jurassosaurus (joo-RAS-oh-SORE-us: "Jurassic lizard") A quadrupedal, armoured herbivore 3m (10ft) long: a primitive ankylosaur with protective plates. Lived in the Middle Jurassic. Found in China. Named in 1992.

K **"Kagasaurus"** (ka-ga-SORE-us: "Kaga lizard") Informal name for a large, bipedal carnivore: perhaps related to *Megalosaurus*. Lived in the Late Cretaceous. Found in Japan. Classification uncertain.

Kaijiangosaurus (kie-jang-oh-SORE-us: "Kaijang lizard") A large, bipedal carnivore. Lived in the Middle Jurassic. Found in China.

Kakuru (KA-ka-roo: "rainbow serpent") A bipedal carnivore about 2.4m (8ft) long, with slim shin bones. Lived in the late Early Cretaceous. Found in Australia. Classification uncertain.

Kangnasaurus (kang-na-SORE-us: "Kangna Ranch lizard") A small, bipedal plant-eater somewhat like *Hypsilophodon* (p. 136). Lived in the Early Cretaceous. Found in South Africa. Classification: Dryosauridae, Euornithopoda, Ornithopoda, Ornithischia. (*n.d.*)

"Katsuyamasaurus" (kat-soo-yah-mah-SORE-us: "Katsuyama lizard") Informal name for a large, bipedal carnivore: perhaps related to *Allosaurus* (p. 52). Lived in the Early Cretaceous. Found in Japan.

Kelmayisaurus (kel-a-MAY-ee-SORE-us: "Kelmayi lizard") A poorly known, large, bipedal carnivore. Lived in the Early Cretaceous. Found in China. Classification uncertain. (*n.d.*)

Kentrosaurus (KEN-troh-SORE-us) See p. 118.

Kentrurosaurus = *Kentrosaurus* (p. 118).

"Kitadanisaurus" (kit-ah-dan-ee-SORE-us: "Kitadani lizard") Informal name for a small, bipedal carnivore known from a tooth: perhaps related to *Deinonychus* (p. 70). Lived in the Early Cretaceous. Found in Japan.

"Klamelisaurus" (kla-mel-ee-SORE-us: "Klameli lizard") Informal name for a large, quadrupedal herbivore: a sauropod perhaps related to *Mamenchisaurus* (p. 104). Lived in the Late Jurassic. Found in China.

Koreasaurus (koh-ree-oh-SORE-us: "Korean lizard") A small, bipedal carnivore: perhaps *Deinonychus* (p. 70). Lived in the Cretaceous. Found in South Korea. (*n.d.*)

Kotasaurus (KOH-ta-SORE-us: "Kota lizard") A large, quadrupedal herbivore: a sauropod perhaps related to *Cetiosaurus* (p. 92). Lived in the Early Jurassic. Found in India.

Kritosaurus (KRITE-oh-SORE-us: "noble lizard") A large, bipedal/quadrupedal herbivore: a hump-nosed hadrosaur related to *Maiasaura* (p. 146). Lived in the Late Cretaceous. Found in western North America, and remains attributed to it have been found in Argentina.

Kunmingosaurus (KOON-MING-oh-SORE-us: "Kunming lizard") A large, quadrupedal herbivore: a primitive sauropod. Lived in the Early Jurassic. Found in China. Classification: Vulcanodontidae, Sauropoda, Sauropodomorpha, Saurischia.

Hypacrosaurus   *Iguanodon*   *Kentrosaurus*   *Lambeosaurus*

Labocania (la-boh-KAY-nee-ah: "La Bocana") A large, bipedal carnivore: perhaps related to *Tyrannosaurus* (p. 48). Lived in the Late Cretaceous. Found in Mexico.

Labrosaurus = *Allosaurus* (p. 52).

Laelaps = *Dryptosaurus*.

Laevisuchus (LEE-VEE-syoo-kus: "slender crocodile") A bipedal carnivore 2m (6ft 6in) long: perhaps like *Calamospondylus*. Lived in the Late Cretaceous. Found in India. (*n.d.*)

Lambeosaurus (LAMB-ee-oh-SORE-us) See p. 150.

Lametasaurus (la-met-a-SORE-us: "Lameta lizard") Named from mixed fossils, some from a big, quadrupedal herbivore: a sauropod related to *Saltasaurus* (others from a carnivorous dinosaur and a crocodile). Lived in the Late Cretaceous. Found in India. (*n.d.*)

Lanasaurus (lahn-ah-SORE-us: "wool lizard") A small, bipedal/quadrupedal herbivore: an ornithopod related to *Heterodontosaurus* (p. 134). Lived in the Early Jurassic. Found in South Africa.

Lancangjiangosaurus (lan-kang-jyang-oh-SORE-us: "Lancangjian lizard") A large, quadrupedal herbivore: a sauropod perhaps related to *Cetiosaurus* (p. 92). Lived in the Middle Jurassic. Found in Tibet. (*n.d.*)

Lancangosaurus = *Datousaurus*.

Laosaurus (LAY-oh-SORE-us: "fossil lizard") A small, bipedal herbivore: an ornithopod perhaps related to *Hypsilophodon* (p. 136). Lived in the Late Jurassic. Found in Wyoming, USA. (*n.d.*)

Laplatasaurus = *Titanosaurus*.

Lapparentosaurus (la-pa-rent-oh-SORE-us: "Lapparent's lizard") A huge, quadrupedal herbivore: a sauropod related to *Brachiosaurus* (p. 94). Lived in the Middle Jurassic. Found in Madagascar.

Leaellynasaura (LEE-EL-IN-a-SORE-a: "Leaellyn's lizard") A small, bipedal herbivore: an ornithopod related to *Hypsilophodon* (p. 136). Lived in the Early Cretaceous. Found in Australia. Named in 1989.

Leipsanosaurus = *Struthiosaurus*.

Leptoceratops (lep-toh-SERRA-tops: "slim horned face") A mainly quadrupedal herbivore 2.4m (8ft) long: a ceratopsian related to *Protoceratops* (p. 158). Lived in the Late Cretaceous. Found in Alberta, Canada, and Wyoming, USA.

Leptospondylus = *Massospondylus* (p. 88).

Lesothosaurus (le-SOO-too-SORE-us) See p. 132.

Lexovisaurus (lex-OH-vi-SORE-us: "Lexovii lizard") A quadrupedal, plated herbivore 6m (19ft 6in) long: a stegosaur akin to *Kentrosaurus* (p. 118). Lived in the Middle Jurassic. Found in England and France.

Liliensternus (LIL-ee-en-SHTERN-us: "Lilienstern") A bipedal carnivore 5m (16ft 6in) long: a ceratosaur. Lived in the Late Triassic. Found in Germany.

Limnosaurus = *Telmatosaurus*.

Lisboasaurus (leesh-voh-a-SORE-us: "Lisbon lizard") A crow-sized, bipedal carnivore: a "lizard" redescribed in 1991 as a theropod perhaps related to *Troodon* (p. 68) or *Archaeopteryx* (p. 74). Lived in the Late Jurassic. Found in Portugal.

Loncosaurus (LON-koh-SORE-us: "lance head lizard") A bipedal carnivore: a theropod based on a tooth. Lived in the Late Cretaceous. Found in Argentina. (*n.d.*)

Longosaurus (lon-goh-SORE-us: "Long's lizard") A bipedal carnivore 3m (10ft) long: perhaps *Coelophysis* (p. 46). Lived in the Late Triassic. Found in New Mexico, USA. (*n.d.*)

Lophorhothon = *Prosaurolophus*?

Loricosaurus = *Neuquensaurus*?

Lufengocephalus = *Lufengosaurus*.

Lufengosaurus (loo-FUNG-oh-SORE-us) See p. 89.

Lukousaurus (loo-kow-SORE-us: "Lukou lizard") A small, bipedal carnivore: probably a theropod, but of unknown family. Lived in the Late Triassic/Early Jurassic. Found in China.

Lusitanosaurus (LOOZ-i-TANE-oh-SORE-us: "Lusitania lizard") A quadrupedal, armoured herbivore related to *Scelidosaurus* (p. 112). Lived in the Early Jurassic. Found in Portugal.

Lycorhinus (LIE-koh-RINE-us: "wolf snout") A small, bipedal, tusked herbivore: an ornithopod like *Heterodontosaurus* (p. 134). Lived in the Early Jurassic. Found in South Africa.

Macrophalangia = *Chirostenotes*.

Macrurosaurus (mak-ROO-roh-sore-us: "long-tailed lizard") A large, quadrupedal herbivore: a sauropod possibly related to *Saltasaurus* (p. 106). Lived in the Early Cretaceous. Found in England. (*n.d.*)

"Madsenius" (mad-SEN-ee-us: "Madsen") A large, bipedal carnivore still to be described: a relative of *Allosaurus* (p. 52).

Magnosaurus = *Megalosaurus*?

Magyarosaurus = *Titanosaurus*?

Maiasaura (MY-ah-SORE-ah) See p. 146.

Majungasaurus (mah-JOON-gah-SORE-us: "Majunga lizard") A large, bipedal carnivore: perhaps related to *Carnotaurus* (p. 48). Lived in the Late Cretaceous. Found in Madagascar and perhaps Egypt and India.

Majungatholus (mah-JOON-ga-THOH-lus: "Majunga dome") A bipedal herbivore about 1.4m (4ft 6in) long: a bone-headed ornithischian related to *Pachycephalosaurus* (p. 154). Lived in the Late Cretaceous. Found in Madagascar.

Maleevosaurus (mah-LAY-ev-oh-SORE-us: "Maleev's lizard") A large, bipedal carnivore related to *Tyrannosaurus* (p. 54). Lived in the Late Cretaceous. Found in Mongolia. Named in 1992.

Maleevus (mah-LAY-ev-us: "Maleev") A large, quadrupedal, armoured dinosaur: an ankylosaur related to *Euoplocephalus* (p. 128). Lived in the Late Cretaceous. Found in Mongolia.

Mamenchisaurus (mah-MEN-chee-SORE-us) See p. 104.

Mandschurosaurus (mand-CHOO-roh-SORE-us: "Manchurian lizard") A large, bipedal/ quadrupedal herbivore: a hadrosaur resembling *Gilmoreosaurus*. Lived in the Late Cretaceous. Found in China.

Manospondylus = *Tyrannosaurus* (p. 54).

Marmarospondylus = *Bothriospondylus*.

Marshosaurus (MARSH-oh-SORE-us: "Marsh's lizard") A bipedal carnivore resembling various kinds of theropods including *Coelurus*. Lived in the Late Jurassic. Found in Utah, USA.

Massospondylus (MAS-oh-SPON-die-lus) See p. 88.

Megacervixosaurus (MEG-a-SER-vix-oh-SORE-us: "big neck lizard") A large, quadrupedal herbivore: a sauropod related to *Diplodocus* (p. 100). Lived in the Late Cretaceous. Found in Tibet. (*n.d.*)

Megadactylus = *Anchisaurus* (p. 84).

Megadontosaurus = *Microvenator*.

Megalosaurus (MEG-a-loh-SORE-us) See p. 51.

Melanorosaurus (MEL-an-or-oh-SORE-us: "black mountain lizard") A quadrupedal herbivore 7.5m (24ft) long: a prosauropod related to *Riojasaurus* (p. 90). Lived in the Late Triassic. Found in South Africa.

Metriacanthosaurus (MET-REE-a-kan-thoh-SORE-us: "moderately spined lizard") A bipedal carnivore 8m (26ft) long. Lived in the Early Jurassic. Found in England. Classification uncertain.

Lufengosaurus   *Maiasaura*   *Megalosaurus*   *Melanorosaurus*

Microceratops (mik-roh-SERRA-tops: "tiny horned faced") A mainly bipedal, horned dinosaur under 80cm (2ft 8in) long: a ceratopsian related to *Protoceratops* (p. 158). Lived in the Late Cretaceous. Found in China and Mongolia.

Microcoelus (mik-roh-SEEL-us: "tiny hollow") A large, quadrupedal herbivore: perhaps the sauropod *Saltasaurus* (p. 106). Lived in the Late Cretaceous. Found in Argentina.

Microdontosaurus (mik-roh-DONT-oh-SORE-us: "tiny tooth lizard") A large, quadrupedal herbivore: a prosauropod or sauropod. Lived in the Middle Jurassic. Found in Tibet. Classification uncertain. (*n.d.*)

Microhadrosaurus (mik-roh-HAD-roh-SORE-us: "tiny *Hadrosaurus*") A bipedal herbivore 2.4m (8ft) long: a hadrosaur. Lived in the Late Cretaceous. Found in China. (*n.d.*)

Micropachycephalosaurus (mik-roh-pak-ee-SEF-a-loh-SORE-us: "tiny thick-headed lizard") A tiny, bipedal herbivore 50cm (20in) long: a pachycephalosaur of unknown family. Lived in the Late Cretaceous. Found in China.

Microsaurops = *Microcoelus*.

Microvenator (mik-roh-ven-AH-tor: "tiny hunter") A small, bipedal carnivore: perhaps related to *Chirostenotes*. Lived in the Early Cretaceous. Found in Montana, USA.

"Mifunesaurus" (mih-FOON-e-SORE-us: "Mifune lizard") Informal name of a large, bipedal carnivore based on a tooth. Lived in the Late Cretaceous. Found in Japan. Identity uncertain.

Minmi (min-MY) See p. 126.

Mochlodon = *Rhabdodon*.

Mongolosaurus (mon-gol-oh-SORE-us: "Mongolian lizard") A large herbivore that might be a sauropod or a segnosaur. Lived in the Early Cretaceous. Found in China. (*n.d.*)

Monkonosaurus (mon-kon-oh-SORE-us: "Monko lizard") A large, quadrupedal, plated herbivore perhaps related to *Tuojiangosaurus* (p. 120). Lived in the Early Cretaceous. Found in Tibet.

Monoclonius (mon-oh-KLOH-ni-us: "single stem") A quadrupedal, horned herbivore: a ceratopsian related to *Centrosaurus* (p. 160). Lived in the Late Cretaceous. Found in Alberta, Canada, and Montana, USA.

Monolophosaurus (mon-oh-loaf-oh-SORE-us: "single ridge lizard") A large, bipedal carnivore: a theropod perhaps related to *Allosaurus* (p. 52) or *Eustreptospondylus* (p. 50). Lived in the Middle Jurassic. Found in China.

Montanoceratops (mon-tan-oh-SERRA-tops: "Montana horned face") A quadrupedal, horned dinosaur: a ceratopsian akin to *Protoceratops* (p. 158). Lived in the Late Cretaceous. Found in Montana, USA.

Morinosaurus = *Pelorosaurus*.

Morosaurus = *Camarasaurus* (p. 96).

Moshisaurus = *Mamenchisaurus* (p. 104).

Mussaurus (mus-OR-us: "mouse lizard") A bipedal/quadrupedal herbivore 3m (10ft) long: a prosauropod related to *Plateosaurus* (p. 86). Lived in the Late Triassic. Found in Argentina.

Muttaburrasaurus (MUT-a-BUR-a-SORE-us) See p. 140.

N **Nanosaurus** (nan-oh-SORE-us: "dwarf lizard") A bipedal herbivore 90cm (3ft) long: an ornithopod perhaps like *Hypsilophodon* (p. 136). Lived in the Late Jurassic. Found in Colorado and Utah, USA.

Nanotyrannus (NAN-oh-tie-RAN-us: "tiny tyrant") A bipedal carnivore 5m (16ft 6in) long, related to *Tyrannosaurus* (p. 54). Lived in the Late Cretaceous. Found in Montana, USA.

Nanshiungosaurus (nan-SHOONG-oh-SORE-us: "Nanshiung lizard") A heavy-bodied carnivore or herbivore, probably related to *Segnosaurus* (p. 108) and *Therizinosaurus*. Lived in the Late Cretaceous. Found in China.

Nemegtosaurus (nem-EG-toh-SORE-us: "Nemegt lizard") A large, quadrupedal herbivore: a sauropod with a low head. Lived in the Late Cretaceous. Found in Mongolia and China. Classification: Dicraeosauridae, Sauropoda, Sauropodomorpha, Saurischia.

Neosaurus = *Parrosaurus*.

Neosodon = *Pelorosaurus*.

Neuquensaurus (NYOO-kyen-SORE-us: "Neuquén lizard") A large, quadrupedal herbivore: a sauropod related to *Saltasaurus* (p. 106). Lived in the Late Cretaceous. Found in Argentina.

Ngexisaurus (n-gay-shee-SORE-us: "Ngexi lizard") A small, bipedal carnivore related to *Ornitholestes* (p. 78). Lived in the Middle Jurassic. Found in Tibet. (*n.d.*)

Nipponosaurus (nip-ON-oh-SORE-us: "Japanese lizard") A bipedal/quadrupedal herbivore: a small hadrosaur related to *Corythosaurus* (p. 148). Lived in the Late Cretaceous. Found on Sakhalin Island (now in Russia).

Noasaurus (noh-ah-SORE-us: "north-west Argentina lizard") A bipedal carnivore 2.4m (8ft) long, with a switchblade toe-claw. Lived in the Late Cretaceous. Found in Argentina. Classification: Noasauridae, Ceratosauria, Theropoda, Saurischia.

Nodosaurus (no-doh-SORE-us: "node lizard") A large, quadrupedal, armoured herbivore: an ankylosaur related to *Edmontonia* (p. 122). Lived in the Late Cretaceous. Found in Kansas and Wyoming, USA.

Notoceratops (NOH-TOH-SERRA-tops: "southern horned face") A poorly known, quadrupedal herbivore: perhaps related to the ceratopsians. Lived in the Late Cretaceous. Found in Argentina. (*n.d.*)

Nouerosaurus = *Nurosaurus*.

Nurosaurus (NYOO-roh-SORE-us: "Nur lizard") A huge, quadrupedal herbivore 26m (85ft) long: a sauropod related to *Mamenchisaurus* (p. 104). Lived in the Early Cretaceous. Found in China. Named in 1991.

Nuthetes (nyoo-THEE-teez: "monitor") A small, bipedal carnivore: perhaps a juvenile related to *Megalosaurus*. Lived in the Early Cretaceous. Found in England. (*n.d.*)

Nyasasaurus (nie-as-a-SORE-us: "Nyasa lizard") A bipedal/quadrupedal herbivore 2m (6ft 6in) long: possibly like *Anchisaurus* (p. 84). Lived in the Middle Triassic. Found in Tanzania.

O **Ohmdenosaurus** (OHM-den-oh-SORE-us: "Ohmden lizard") A quadrupedal herbivore 4m (13ft) long: a primitive sauropod. Lived in the Early Jurassic. Found in Germany. Classification: Vulcanodontidae, Sauropoda, Sauropodomorpha, Saurischia.

Oligosaurus = *Rhabdodon*.

Omeisaurus (oh-my-EE-SORE-us: "Omei lizard") A quadrupedal herbivore 20m (66ft) long: a sauropod probably related to *Mamenchisaurus* (p. 104). Lived in the Late Jurassic. Found in China.

Omosaurus = *Dacentrurus*.

Onychosaurus = *Rhabdodon*.

Opisthocoelicaudia (oh-PIS-thoh-SEEL-i-KOW-dee-a: "tail vertebrae cupped behind") A quadrupedal herbivore 12m (39ft) long: a sauropod related to *Camarasaurus* (p. 96). Lived in the Late Cretaceous. Found in Mongolia.

Microceratops   *Minmi*   *Ornithomimus*   *Orodromeus*   *Ouranosaurus*

Oplosaurus = *Pelorosaurus.*

Orinosaurus = *Euskelosaurus.*

Ornatotholus (OR-nat-oh-THOH-lus: "ornate dome") A bipedal herbivore 2.4m (8ft) long: a bone-headed relative of *Pachycephalosaurus* (p. 154). Lived in the Late Cretaceous. Found in Alberta, Canada.

Ornithodesmus (OR-nith-oh-DEZ-mus: "bird ligament") Probably a small, bipedal carnivore: perhaps like *Troodon* (p. 68). Once thought to be "pterosaur", but redefined in 1993. Lived in the Early Cretaceous. Found in England.

Ornithoides = *Saurornithoides.*

Ornitholestes (OR-nith-oh-LES-teez) See p. 78.

Ornithomerus = *Rhabdodon.*

Ornithomimoides (OR-nith-oh-MEE-moy-deez: "bird-form mimic") A poorly known, large, bipedal carnivore. Lived in the Late Cretaceous. Found in India. (*n.d.*)

Ornithomimus (OR-ni-thoh-MEE-mus: "bird mimic") A bipedal omnivore up to 3.5m (11ft 6in) long: an ostrich dinosaur similar to *Struthiomimus* (p. 64). Lived in the Late Cretaceous. Found in western North America.

Ornithopsis = *Pelorosaurus.*

Ornithotarsus = *Hadrosaurus.*

Orodromeus (OR-oh-DROH-mee-us: "mountain runner") A bipedal herbivore 2m (6ft 6in) long: an ornithopod like *Hypsilophodon* (p. 136). Lived in the Late Cretaceous. Found in Montana, USA.

Orosaurus = *Euskelosaurus.*

Orthogoniosaurus (OR-thoh-GON-ee-oh-SORE-us: "straight angle lizard") A large, bipedal carnivore known from an unusual tooth. Lived in the Late Cretaceous. Found in India. (*n.d.*)

Orthomerus (OR-thoh-MER-us: "with straight parts") A large, poorly known, bipedal/quadrupedal herbivore: a hadrosaur perhaps like *Maiasaura* (p. 146). Lived in the Late Cretaceous. Found in the Netherlands, and maybe Spain and the Ukraine. (*n.d.*)

Oshanosaurus (oh-SHAN-oh-SORE-us: "Oshan lizard") A large, quadrupedal herbivore: a sauropod perhaps like *Cetiosaurus* (p. 92). Lived in the Early Jurassic. Found in China. (*n.d.*)

Othnielia (oth-ni-EL-ee-a: "Othniel") A bipedal herbivore up to 4m (13ft) long: an ornithopod related to *Hypsilophodon* (p. 136). Lived in the Late Jurassic. Found in Colorado, Utah, and Wyoming, USA.

Ouranosaurus (OO-ran-oh-SORE-us) See p. 142.

Oviraptor (OHV-ih-RAP-tor) See p. 66.

Ovoraptor = *Velociraptor.*

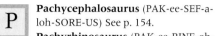

P **Pachycephalosaurus** (PAK-ee-SEF-a-loh-SORE-US) See p. 154.

Pachyrhinosaurus (PAK-ee-RINE-oh-SORE-us) See p. 163.

Pachysauriscus = *Plateosaurus* (p. 86).

Pachysaurops = *Plateosaurus* (p. 86).

Pachysaurus = *Plateosaurus* (p. 86).

Pachyspondylus = *Massospondylus* (p. 88).

Palaeopteryx (PAL-ee-OP-ter-ix: "ancient wing") A poorly known, small, bipedal carnivore: perhaps related to *Archaeopteryx* (p. 74) or *Troodon* (p. 68). Lived in the Late Jurassic. Found in Colorado. (*n.d.*)

Palaeoscincus (PAL-ee-oh-SKINK-us: "ancient skink") A large, quadrupedal, armoured herbivore: a nodosaur based on teeth. Lived in the Late Cretaceous. Found in Montana, USA. (*n.d.*)

Panoplosaurus (pan-OP-loh-SORE-us: "armoured lizard") A quadrupedal, armoured herbivore 7m (23ft) long: an ankylosaur related to *Edmontonia* (p. 122). Lived in the Late Cretaceous. Found in western North America.

Paraiguanodon = *Bactrosaurus.*

Paranthodon (PAR-AN-thoh-don: "beside *Anthodon*") A quadrupedal, plated herbivore: a stegosaur 5m (16ft 6in) long, related to *Kentrosaurus* (p. 118). Lived in the Early Cretaceous. Found in South Africa.

Parasaurolophus (par-a-SORE-oh-LOAF-us: "beside *Saurolophus*") A bipedal/quadrupedal herbivore 10m (33ft) long: a hadrosaur related to *Corythosaurus* (p. 148). Lived in the Late Cretaceous. Found in western North America, perhaps including Alaska.

"Parhabdodon" = *Rhabdodon.*

Parksosaurus (PARX-oh-SORE-us: "Parks's lizard") A bipedal herbivore 2.4m (8ft) long: an ornithopod related to *Hypsilophodon* (p. 136). Lived in the Late Cretaceous. Found in Alberta, Canada.

Paronychodon (par-on-EYE-koh-don: "beside the nail (or claw) tooth") A bipedal carnivore 2m (6ft 6in) long: perhaps like *Deinonychus* (p. 70). Lived in the Late Cretaceous. Found in Montana, USA. (*n.d.*)

Parrosaurus (PAHR-oh-SORE-us: "Parr's lizard") A poorly known, large, quadrupedal herbivore: a sauropod. Lived in the Late Cretaceous. Found in Missouri, USA.

Patagosaurus (PAT-a-goh-SORE-us: "Patagonian lizard") A large, quadrupedal herbivore: a sauropod related to *Cetiosaurus* (p. 92). Lived in the Late Jurassic. Found in Argentina.

Pectinodon = *Troodon* (p. 68).

Peishansaurus (PAY-shan-SORE-us: "Mount Pei lizard") Perhaps a quadrupedal, armoured herbivore, but poorly known. Lived in the Late Cretaceous. Found in China. (*n.d.*)

Pelorosaurus (PEL-oh-roh-SORE-us: "monstrous lizard") A huge, quadrupedal herbivore: a sauropod related to *Brachiosaurus* (p. 94). Lived in the Early Cretaceous. Found in England and France.

Peltosaurus = *Sauropelta* (p. 124).

Pentaceratops (PEN-ta-SERRA-tops: "five-horned face") A quadrupedal, horned herbivore: a ceratopsian related to *Triceratops* (p. 164). Lived in the Late Cretaceous. Found in New Mexico, USA.

Phaedrolosaurus (FEED-rol-oh-SORE-us: "gleaming lizard") A bipedal carnivore: perhaps similar to *Deinonychus* (p. 70). Lived in the Early Cretaceous. Found in China. (*n.d.*)

Phyllodon (FIL-oh-don: "leaf tooth") A bipedal herbivore, perhaps only 90cm (3ft) long: maybe like *Hypsilophodon* (p. 136). Lived in the Late Jurassic. Found in Portugal.

Piatnitzkysaurus (pee-at-NITS-kee-SORE-us: "Piatnitzky's lizard") A bipedal carnivore 4.3m (14ft) long: perhaps related to *Allosaurus* (p. 52). Lived in the Middle Jurassic. Found in Argentina.

Pinacosaurus (pin-AK-oh-SORE-us: "plank lizard") A quadrupedal, armoured herbivore: an ankylosaur 5m (16ft 6in) long related to *Euoplocephalus* (p. 128). Lived in the Late Cretaceous. Found in China and Mongolia.

Pisanosaurus (pee-SAN-oh-SORE-us: "Pisano's lizard") A bipedal herbivore 90cm (3ft) long: a primitive ornithischian. Lived in the early Late Triassic. Found in Argentina. Classification uncertain.

Piveteausaurus (PEEV-eh-toh-SORE-us: "Piveteau's lizard") A bipedal carnivore perhaps 11m (36ft) long: possibly related to *Megalosaurus.* Lived in the Middle Jurassic. Found in France.

Plateosauravus = *Euskelosaurus.*

Plateosaurus (PLAT-ee-oh-SORE-us) See p. 86.

Pleurocoelus (PLEW-roh-SEEL-us: "hollow side") A large, quadrupedal herbivore: a sauropod related to *Brachiosaurus* (p. 94). Lived in the Early Cretaceous. Found in Maryland and Texas, USA, and England.

Parasaurolophus   *Pinacosaurus*   *Plateosaurus*

Pleuropeltus = *Struthiosaurus*.

Podokesaurus (po-DOH-kee-SORE-us: "swift-footed lizard") A bipedal carnivore 90cm (3ft) long: perhaps related to *Coelophysis* (p. 46). Lived in the Early Jurassic. Found in Connecticut, USA.

Poekilopleuron (peek-il-oh-PLEW-ron: "varying side") A bipedal carnivore 9m (29ft 6in) long, with short, strong arms: perhaps related to *Megalosaurus*. Lived in the Middle Jurassic. Found in France. Classification uncertain.

Polacanthoides = *Hylaeosaurus*.

Polacanthus (pol-a-KAN-thus: "many spines") A quadrupedal, armoured herbivore related to *Sauropelta* (p. 124). Lived in the Early Cretaceous. Found in the Isle of Wight, England, and South Dakota, USA.

Polyodontosaurus = *Troodon* (p. 68).

Polyonax = *Triceratops* (p. 164).

Prenocephale (pren-oh-SEF-a-lee: "sloping head") A bipedal herbivore 2.4m (8ft) long: a bone-headed relative of *Pachycephalosaurus* (p. 154). Lived in the Late Cretaceous. Found in Mongolia.

Priconodon (PRY-kon-oh-don: "serrated conical tooth") A large, quadrupedal, armoured herbivore, perhaps like *Sauropelta* (p. 124). Lived in the Early Cretaceous. Found in Maryland, USA. (*n.d.*)

Priodontognathus (PRY-oh-dont-oh-NAY-thus: "saw-toothed jaw") A quadrupedal, armoured herbivore, perhaps like *Sauropelta* (p. 124). Lived in the Late Jurassic. Found in England.

Probactrosaurus (PROH-BAK-troh-SORE-us: "before *Bactrosaurus*") A bipedal/quadrupedal herbivore: an ornithopod related to *Iguanodon* (p. 138) and the hadrosaurs. Lived in the Late Cretaceous. Found in China and Mongolia.

Proceratops = *Ceratops*.

Proceratosaurus (PROH-ser-AT-oh-SORE-us: "before *Ceratosaurus*") A medium-sized, bipedal carnivore with a single nose horn. Lived in the Middle Jurassic. Found in England. Classification uncertain.

Procerosaurus (PRO-SER-oh-SORE-us: "first horned lizard") A bipedal or quadrupedal herbivore: perhaps *Iguanodon* (p. 138), known only from a single, incomplete bone. Lived in the Late Cretaceous. Found in Czech Republic. (*n.d.*)

Procheneosaurus = *Corythosaurus* (p. 148) and *Lambeosaurus* (p. 150).

Procompsognathus (PROH-KOMP-soh-NAY-thus: "before *Compsognathus*") A bipedal carnivore 1.2m (4ft) long: an early theropod related to *Coelophysis* (p. 46). Lived in the Late Triassic. Found in Germany.

Prodeinodon (PROH-DINE-oh-don: "before *Deinodon*") A large, bipedal carnivore: perhaps *Alectrosaurus*. (*n.d.*)

Prosaurolophus (PROH-sore-oh-LOAF-fus: "before *Saurolophus*") A bipedal/quadrupedal herbivore: a hadrosaur related to *Edmontosaurus* (p. 144). Lived in the Late Cretaceous. Found in Alberta, Canada, and Montana, USA.

Protiguanodon = *Psittacosaurus* (p. 156).

Protoavis (PROH-TOH-AY-vis: "first bird") A small, bird-like carnivore of uncertain relationships. Lived in the Late Triassic. Found in Texas, USA. Described in 1991.

Protoceratops (PROH-toh-SERRA-tops) See p. 158.

Protognathosaurus (PROH-toh-NAY-thoh-SORE-us: "early jaw lizard") A large, quadrupedal herbivore: a sauropod related to *Cetiosaurus* (p. 92). Lived in the Middle Jurassic. Found in China. Named in 1991. (*n.d.*)

Protognathus = *Protognathosaurus*.

Protorosaurus = *Chasmosaurus*.

Psittacosaurus (Si-TAK-oh-SORE-us) See p. 156.

Pteropelyx (ter-oh-PEL-ix: "wing pelvis") A large, bipedal/quadrupedal herbivore: a hadrosaur, possibly *Corythosaurus* (p. 148) or *Hypacrosaurus*. Lived in the Late Cretaceous. Found in Montana, USA. (*n.d.*)

Pterospondylus (ter-oh-SPON-di-lus: "winged vertebrae") A small, bipedal carnivore: perhaps a ceratosaur. Lived in the Late Triassic. Found in Germany. (*n.d.*)

Q **Quaesitosaurus** (ky-sit-oh-SORE-us: "unusual lizard") A large, quadrupedal herbivore: a sauropod that might be *Nemegtosaurus*. Lived in the Late Cretaceous. Found in Mongolia.

R **Rapator** (RAP-ah-tor: "plunderer") A bipedal carnivore 10m (33ft) long: perhaps a relative of *Carnotaurus* (p. 48). Lived in the Early Cretaceous. Found in Australia.

Rebbachisaurus (reb-BATCH-i-SORE-us: "Rebbachi lizard") A large, quadrupedal herbivore: a sauropod related to *Dicraeosaurus*. Lived in the Early Cretaceous. Found in Morocco, Tunisia, Niger, Mali, and Algeria.

Regnosaurus (REG-noh-SORE-us: "royal lizard") A quadrupedal herbivore (a sauropod or, more likely, an ankylosaur), known from a piece of jaw. Lived in the Early Cretaceous. Found in England. (*n.d.*)

Revueltosaurus (rev-WEL-toh-SORE-us: "Revuelto lizard") A small, bipedal herbivore, perhaps like *Lesothosaurus* (p. 132). Lived in the Late Triassic. Found in New Mexico, USA. Named in 1989. (*n.d.*)

Rhabdodon (RAB-doh-don: "rod tooth") A bipedal herbivore 4m (13ft) long: an ornithopod with features seen in *Hypsilophodon* (p. 136) and *Iguanodon* (p. 138). Lived in the Late Cretaceous. Found in Spain, France, Austria, and Romania.

Rhodanosaurus = *Struthiosaurus*.

Rhoetosaurus (reet-oh-SORE-us: "Rhoetos lizard") A quadrupedal herbivore over 15m (49ft) long: a sauropod related to *Cetiosaurus* (p. 92). Lived in the Middle Jurassic. Found in Australia.

Ricardoestesia (ri-KARD-oh-es-TEEZ-i-a: "Richard Estes") A small, bipedal carnivore known only from teeth and bits of lower jaw. Lived in the Late Cretaceous. Found in Alberta, Canada, and Montana and Wyoming, USA. Named in 1990. Classification uncertain.

Richardoestesia = *Ricardoestesia*.

Rioarribasaurus = *Coelophysis* (p. 46).

Riojasaurus (ree-O-ha-SORE-us) See p. 90.

Roccosaurus = *Melanorosaurus*.

S **Saichania** (sigh-CHAN-ee-a: "beautiful") A quadrupedal, armoured herbivore 6.6m (22ft) long: an ankylosaur like *Euoplocephalus* (p. 128). Lived in the Late Cretaceous. Found in Mongolia.

Saltasaurus (Sal-te-SORE-us) See p. 106.

Saltopus (SALT-oh-pus: "leaping foot") A tiny, bipedal carnivore 60cm (2ft) long: a ceratosaur. Lived in the Late Triassic. Found in Scotland. (*n.d.*)

"Sanchusaurus" (san-choo-SORE-us: "Sanchu lizard") Informal name for a bird-like, bipedal carnivore (or omnivore): an ostrich dinosaur like *Gallimimus* (p. 62). Lived in the Late Cretaceous. Found in Japan.

"Sangonghesaurus" (san-gong-eh-SORE-us: "Sangonghe lizard") A quadrupedal, armoured herbivore: an ankylosaur like *Euoplocephalus* (p. 128). Lived in the Late Cretaceous. Found in China. (*n.d.*)

Sanpasaurus (san-pa-SORE-us: "Sanpa lizard") Named from mixed-up fossils of a sauropod and an ornithopod. Lived in the Middle Jurassic. Found in China. (*n.d.*)

Prosaurolophus   *Riojasaurus*   *Saltasaurus*   *Saurolophus*

Sarcolestes (sar-koh-LES-teez: "flesh robber") A quadrupedal, armoured herbivore: an early ankylosaur related to *Sauropelta* (p. 124). Lived in the Middle Jurassic. Found in England.

Sarcosaurus (SAR-koh-sore-us: "flesh lizard") A bipedal carnivore 3.5m (11ft 6in) long: a ceratosaur of unknown family. Lived in the Early Jurassic. Found in England.

Sauraechinodon = *Echinodon.*

Saurolophus (SORE-oh-LOAF-us: "ridged lizard") A bipedal/quadrupedal herbivore 9m (29ft 6in) long: a hadrosaur related to *Edmontosaurus* (p. 144). Lived in the Late Cretaceous. Found in Alberta, Canada; California, USA, and Mongolia.

Sauropelta (SORE-oh-PEL-ta) See p. 124.

Saurophagus = *Allosaurus* (p. 52).

Sauroplites (SORE-op-LITE-eez: "lizard hoplite") A quadrupedal, armoured herbivore: an ankylosaur perhaps like *Euoplocephalus* (p. 128). Lived in the Early Cretaceous. Found in China.

Saurornithoides (sore-OR-nith-OID-eez: "bird-like lizard") A bipedal carnivore 2m (6ft 6in) long: like *Troodon* (p. 68). Lived in the Late Cretaceous. Found in Mongolia.

Saurornitholestes (sore-OR-nith-oh-LES-teez: "bird-robbing lizard") A bipedal carnivore 1.8m (6ft) long: like *Deinonychus* (p. 70). Lived in the Late Cretaceous. Found in Alberta, Canada.

Scelidosaurus (skel-IDE-oh-SORE-us) See p. 112.

Scolosaurus = *Euoplocephalus* (p. 128).

Scutellosaurus (skoo-TEL-oh-SORE-us) See p. 113.

Secernosaurus (si-KER-noh-SORE-us: "severed lizard") A bipedal/quadrupedal herbivore 3m (10ft) long: probably a primitive hadrosaur. Lived in the Late Cretaceous. Found in Argentina.

Segisaurus (SAY-hee-SORE-us: "Segi [Canyon] lizard") A bipedal carnivore 1m (3ft 3in) long: a ceratosaur perhaps like *Coelophysis* (p. 46). Lived in the Early Jurassic. Found in Arizona, USA.

Segnosaurus (SEG-noh-SORE-us) See p. 108.

Seismosaurus (SIZE-moh-SORE-us: "earth-shaking lizard") A huge, quadrupedal herbivore reportedly 40m (130ft) long (the longest known dinosaur): a sauropod related to *Diplodocus* (p. 100). Lived in the Late Jurassic. Found in New Mexico, USA. Described in 1991.

Sellosaurus (SEL-oh-SORE-us: "saddle lizard") A bipedal/quadrupedal herbivore 6.5m (21ft) long: a prosauropod related to *Plateosaurus* (p. 86). Lived in the Late Triassic. Found in Germany.

Shamosaurus (SHAM-oh-SORE-us: "Gobi [Desert] lizard") A large, quadrupedal, armoured herbivore: an ankylosaur like *Euoplocephalus* (p. 128). Lived in the Early Cretaceous. Found in Mongolia.

Shanshanosaurus (shan-SHAN-oh-SORE-us: "Shanshan lizard") A bipedal carnivore 2.4m (8ft) long: perhaps related to *Aublysodon.* Lived in the Late Cretaceous. Found in China.

Shantungosaurus (shan-TUNG-oh-SORE-us: "Shantung lizard") A bipedal/quadrupedal herbivore 15m (49ft) long: a hadrosaur like *Edmontosaurus* (p. 144). Lived in the Late Cretaceous. Found in China.

Shunosaurus (SHOON-oh-SORE-us) See p. 93.

Shuosaurus = *Shunosaurus* (p. 93).

Siamosaurus (sigh-AM-oh-SORE-us: "Siam lizard") A large, bipedal, carnivore, perhaps like *Spinosaurus* (p. 60). Lived in the Late Jurassic. Found in Thailand.

Silvisaurus (SIL-vih-SORE-us: "forest lizard") A quadrupedal, armoured herbivore 4m (13ft) long: an ankylosaur related to *Sauropelta* (p. 124). Lived in the Early Cretaceous. Found in Kansas, USA.

Sinocoelurus (SINE-oh-seel-YEW-rus: "Chinese *Coelurus*") A small, bipedal carnivore only known from teeth. Lived in the Late Jurassic. Found in China. (*n.d.*)

"Sinornithoides" (sine-ORN-ith-OID-eez: "Chinese bird-like") A small, bipedal carnivore like *Troodon* (p. 60), not yet formally described. Lived in the Early Cretaceous. Found in China.

Sinosaurus (SINE-oh-SORE-us: "Chinese lizard") A bipedal carnivore 2.4m (8ft) long, perhaps like *Herrerasaurus* (p. 40). Lived in the Early Jurassic. Found in China. (*n.d.*)

Sphenospondylus = *Iguanodon* (p. 138).

Spinosaurus (SPINE-oh-SORE-us) See p. 60.

Spondylosoma (SPON-di-loh-SOH-ma: "vertebra body") A poorly known, bipedal carnivore: perhaps a primitive theropod related to *Staurikosaurus.* Lived in the early Late Triassic. Found in Brazil.

Staurikosaurus (stor-IK-oh-SORE-us: "[Southern] Cross lizard") A bipedal carnivore 2m (6ft 6in) long: a primitive theropod somewhat similar to *Herrerasaurus* (p. 40). Lived in the early Late Triassic. Found in Brazil. Classification: Staurikosauridae, Theropoda, Saurischia.

Stegoceras (ste-GOS-er-as) See p. 155.

Stegopelta = *Nodosaurus.*

Stegosauroides (STEG-oh-sore-OIDE-eez: "stegosaur form") A quadrupedal, armoured herbivore: an ankylosaur perhaps like *Euoplocephalus* (p. 128). Lived in the Late Cretaceous. Found in China. Classification uncertain. (*n.d.*)

Stegosaurus (STEG-oh-SORE-us) See p. 114.

Stenonychosaurus = *Troodon* (p. 68).

Stenopelix (STEN-oh-PEL-ix: "narrow pelvis") A bipedal herbivore 1.5m (5ft) long: perhaps a primitive pachycephalosaur. Lived in the Early Cretaceous. Found in Germany.

Stenotholus = *Stygimoloch.*

Stephanosaurus = *Lambeosaurus* (p. 150).

Stereocephalus = *Euoplocephalus* (p. 128).

Sterrholophus = *Triceratops* (p. 164).

Stokesosaurus (STOKES-oh-SORE-us: "Stokes's lizard") A bipedal carnivore 4m (13ft) long: perhaps related to *Allosaurus* (p. 52). Lived in the Late Jurassic. Found in Utah, USA. Classification uncertain.

Strenusaurus = *Riojasaurus* (p. 90).

Struthiomimus (STRUTH-ee-oh-MEEM-us) See p. 64.

Struthiosaurus (STRUTH-ee-oh-SORE-us: "ostrich lizard") A quadrupedal, armoured dinosaur 1.8m (6ft) long: an ankylosaur related to *Sauropelta* (p. 124). Lived in the Late Cretaceous. Found in Austria and Romania. Formal redescription pending. (*n.d.*)

Stygimoloch (STIJ-i-MOH-lok: "[River] Styx demon") A bipedal herbivore: a bone-headed relative of *Pachycephalosaurus* (p. 154). Lived in the Late Cretaceous. Found in Montana and Wyoming, USA.

Styracosaurus (sty-RAK-oh-SORE-us) See p. 162.

"Sugiyamasaurus" (SOO-gee-YAH-mah-SORE-us: "Sugiyama lizard") Informal name for a large, quadrupedal herbivore: a sauropod known only from teeth. Lived in the Late Cretaceous. Found in Japan. Not yet formally described.

Supersaurus (SUE-per-SORE-us: "super lizard") A huge, quadrupedal herbivore 30m (98ft) long: a sauropod related to *Diplodocus* (p. 100). Lived in the Late Jurassic. Found in Colorado, USA.

Symphyrophus = *Camptosaurus.*

Syngonosaurus = *Acanthopholis*?

Syntarsus (sin-TAR-sus: "fused ankle") A bipedal carnivore 3m (10ft) long: related to *Coelophysis* (p. 46). Lived in the Early Jurassic. Found in South Africa, Zimbabwe, and Arizona, USA.

Syrmosaurus = *Pinacosaurus.*

Scelidosaurus   *Shantungosaurus*   *Shunosaurus*   *Spinosaurus*

Szechuanosaurus (sich-WAN-oh-SORE-us: "Szechuan lizard") A bipedal carnivore 8m (26ft) long: related to *Allosaurus* (p. 52). Lived in the Late Jurassic. Found in China.

Talarurus (tal-a-ROO-rus: "basket tail") A quadrupedal, armoured herbivore 6m (19ft 6in) long: an ankylosaur like *Euoplocephalus* (p. 128). Lived in the Late Cretaceous. Found in Mongolia.

Tanius (TAN-i-us: "of the Tan") A bipedal/quadrupedal herbivore: probably a primitive hadrosaur. Lived in the Late Cretaceous. Found in China.

Tanystrosuchus = *Halticosaurus*.

Tarascosaurus (TA-RAS-koh-SORE-us: "Tarasque lizard") A bipedal carnivore: a relative of *Carnotaurus* (p. 48). Lived in the Late Cretaceous. Found in France. Named in 1991.

Tarbosaurus (TAR-boh-SORE-us: "alarming lizard") A bipedal carnivore 10m (33ft) long: like *Tyrannosaurus* (p. 54). Lived in the Late Cretaceous. Found in China and Mongolia.

Tarchia (TAR-kee-a: "brain") A quadrupedal, armoured herbivore 8.5m (28ft) long: an ankylosaur related to *Euoplocephalus* (p. 128). Lived in the Late Cretaceous. Found in Mongolia.

Tatisaurus (DAH-DEE-SORE-us: "Ta-Ti lizard") A quadrupedal, armoured or plated dinosaur: perhaps related to *Scelidosaurus* (p. 112) or *Huayangosaurus*. Lived in the Early Jurassic. Found in China.

Taveirosaurus (ta-VEE-roh-SORE-us: "Taveiro lizard") A bipedal herbivore known only from teeth. Thought to be a bone-headed ornithischian dinosaur, perhaps related to *Homalocephale*. Lived in the Late Cretaceous. Found in Portugal. Named in 1991.

Tawasaurus = *Lufengosaurus*.

Technosaurus (TEK-noh-SORE-us: "Texas lizard") A small, bipedal herbivore: a primitive ornithischian perhaps much like *Lesothosaurus* (p. 132). Lived in the Late Triassic. Found in Texas, USA. (*n.d.*)

Teinurosaurus (TEYN-you-roh-SORE-us: "extended lizard") A small, bipedal carnivore, known only from one tail bone. Lived in the Late Jurassic. Found in France. Classification uncertain. (*n.d.*)

Telmatosaurus (tel-mat-oh-SORE-us: "marsh lizard") A large, bipedal/quadrupedal herbivore: a primitive hadrosaur. Lived in the Late Cretaceous. Found in Romania.

Tenantosaurus = *Tenontosaurus*.

Tenchisaurus = *Tianchisaurus*.

Tenontosaurus (TEH-NON-toh-SORE-us: "sinew lizard") A bipedal/quadrupedal herbivore up to 7.5m (24ft) long: an ornithopod with features seen in *Dryosaurus* and *Iguanodon* (p. 138). Lived in the Early Cretaceous. Found in Montana, Oklahoma, Texas, and Utah, USA.

Tetragonosaurus = *Lambeosaurus* (p. 154).

Thecocoelurus = *Calamospondylus*.

Thecodontosaurus (THEEK-oh-DON-toh-SORE-us: "socket-toothed lizard") A bipedal herbivore 2.4m (8ft) long: the most primitive of the prosauropods. Lived in the Late Triassic. Found in England. Classification: Thecodontosauridae, Prosauropoda, Sauropodomorpha, Saurischia.

Thecospondylus (THEEK-oh-SPON-di-LUS: "socket vertebrae") A dinosaur known only from a fragmentary fossil. Lived in the Early Cretaceous. Found in England. Classification uncertain. (*n.d.*)

Therizinosaurus (THER-ih-ZINE-oh-SORE-us: "scythe lizard") A bipedal or bipedal/quadrupedal carnivore, insectivore, or herbivore up to 12m (39ft) long, named from scythe-like claws. Perhaps related to *Segnosaurus* (p. 108). Lived in the Late Cretaceous. Found in Mongolia.

Therosaurus = *Iguanodon* (p. 138).

Thescelosaurus (thes-kel-oh-SORE-us: "wonderful lizard") A bipedal/quadrupedal herbivore 3.4m (11ft) long: an ornithopod somewhat like *Hypsilophodon* (p. 136). Lived in the Late Cretaceous. Found in western USA and Alberta, Canada.

Thespesius = *Edmontosaurus*? (p. 144).

Thotobolosaurus (thoh-toh-boh-loh-SORE-us: "Thotobolo lizard") A large, quadrupedal herbivore: probably a prosauropod related to *Riojasaurus* (p. 90). Lived in the Late Triassic. Found in Lesotho.

Tianchisaurus (ti-an-chih-SORE-us: "Tianchi lizard") A quadrupedal, armoured herbivore: an ankylosaur perhaps like *Euoplocephalus* (p. 128). Lived in the Middle Jurassic. Found in China. (= *Jurassosaurus*?)

Tianchungosaurus = *Dianchungosaurus*?

Tichosteus (tik-os-TEE-US: "walled bone") A poorly known, large, bipedal/quadrupedal herbivore: perhaps like *Hypsilophodon* (p. 136). Lived in the Late Jurassic. Found in Colorado, USA. (*n.d.*)

Tienshanosaurus (tyen-shan-oh-SORE-us: "Tienshan lizard") A quadrupedal herbivore up to 12m (39ft) long: a sauropod related to *Camarasaurus* (p. 96) or *Mamenchisaurus* (p. 104). Lived in the Late Jurassic. Found in China.

Titanosaurus (tie-TAN-oh-SORE-us: "titanic lizard") A quadrupedal herbivore 12m (39ft) long: a sauropod related to *Saltasaurus* (p. 106). Lived in the Late Cretaceous. Found in India. (Name also used in the past for *Atlantosaurus*.)

Tochisaurus (toe-chee-SORE-us: "Tochi lizard") A small, bipedal carnivore related to *Troodon* (p. 68). Lived in the Late Cretaceous. Found in Mongolia. Named in 1991.

Tomodon = *Diplotomodon*.

Tornieria (tor-NEAR-ee-a: "Tornier") A large, quadrupedal herbivore: a sauropod related to *Diplodocus* (p. 100). Lived in the Late Jurassic. Found in Tanzania. (=*Barosaurus*?)

Torosaurus (tor-oh-SORE-us: "bull lizard") A quadrupedal, horned dinosaur 7.5m (24ft) long with the largest head of any known land animal: a ceratopsian related to *Triceratops* (p. 164). Lived in the Late Cretaceous. Found in western North America.

Torvosaurus (tor-voh-SORE-us: "savage lizard") A bipedal carnivore up to 10m (33ft) long, with short, strong arms: related to *Megalosaurus*. Lived in the Late Jurassic. Found in Colorado, USA. Classification uncertain.

Trachodon (TRAK-oh-don: "rough tooth") A large, bipedal/quadrupedal herbivore: a hadrosaur known only from fragments including teeth. Lived in the Late Cretaceous. Found in Montana, USA, and England. Classification uncertain. (*n.d.*)

Triceratops (try-SERRA-tops) See p. 164.

Trimucrodon (try-MEW-kroh-don: "three-grooved tooth") A small, bipedal herbivore, perhaps related to *Lesothosaurus* (p. 132). Lived in the Late Jurassic. Found in Portugal. (*n.d.*)

Troodon (TROH-oh-don) See p. 68.

Tsintaosaurus (chin-TAY-oh-sore-us: "Tsintao lizard") = *Tanius* mixed up with other fossils.

Tugulusaurus (TOO-goo-loo-SORE-us: "Tugulo lizard") A bipedal carnivore about 3m (10ft) long: perhaps like *Ornitholestes* (p. 78). Lived in the Early Cretaceous. Found in China.

Tuojiangosaurus (toh-HWANG-oh-SORE-us) See p. 120.

Turanoceratops (too-RAHN-oh-SERRA-tops: "Turan horned face") A quadrupedal, horned dinosaur: a ceratopsid. Lived in the Late Cretaceous. Found in Uzbekistan. Named in 1989.

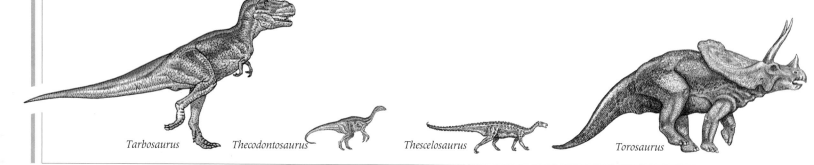

Tarbosaurus   *Thecodontosaurus*   *Thescelosaurus*   *Torosaurus*

Tylocephale (tie-loh-SEF-ah-lee: "swollen head") A bipedal herbivore 2m (6ft 6in) long: a pachycephalosaur related to *Pachycephalosaurus* (p. 154). Lived in the Late Cretaceous. Found in Mongolia.

Tylosteus = *Pachycephalosaurus* (p. 154).

Tyrannosaurus (tie-RAN-oh-SORE-us) See p. 54.

Udanoceratops (oo-dan-oh-SERRA-tops: "Udan horned face") A large, quadrupedal herbivore: a ceratopsian related to *Protoceratops* (p. 158). Lived in the Late Cretaceous. Found in Mongolia. Named in 1992.

Ugrosaurus = *Triceratops*? (p. 164).

Uintasaurus = *Camarasaurus* (p. 96).

Ultrasauros (ult-ra-SORE-os: "ultra lizard") A huge, quadrupedal herbivore up to 27m (89ft) long: a sauropod like *Brachiosaurus* (p. 94) but even larger. Lived in the Late Jurassic. Found in Colorado, USA. Name respelled in 1991 to avoid duplication of previously published *Ultrasaurus*.

Ultrasaurus (ult-ra-SORE-us: "ultra lizard") A quadrupedal herbivore like *Brachiosaurus* (p. 94), but smaller. Lived in the Early Cretaceous. Found in South Korea. Named in 1983. (*n.d.*)

Umarsaurus = *Barsboldia*.

Unquillosaurus (un-keel-yo-SORE-us: "Unquillo lizard") A bipedal carnivore 11m (36ft) long, known only from a hip bone. Lived in the Late Cretaceous. Found in Argentina. Classification uncertain.

"Utahraptor" (YOO-tah-RAP-tor: "Utah plunderer") A bipedal carnivore 6m (19ft 6in) long, not yet formally described: akin to *Deinonychus* (p. 70). Lived in the Late Jurassic. Found in Utah, USA.

Valdoraptor (VAL-doh-RAP-tor: "Wealden plunderer") A large, bipedal carnivore, perhaps like *Allosaurus* (p. 52). Lived in the Early Cretaceous. Found in England. Named in 1991.

Valdosaurus (VAL-doh-SORE-us: "Wealden lizard") A bipedal herbivore 3m (10ft) long: an ornithopod like *Hypsilophodon* (p. 136). Lived in the Early Cretaceous. Found in England, Romania, and Niger. Classification: Dryosauridae, Euornithopoda, Ornithopoda, Ornithischia.

Vectensia = *Hylaeosaurus*?

Vectisaurus (VEK-ti-SORE-us: "Isle of Wight lizard") A large, bipedal/quadrupedal herbivore: like *Iguanodon* (p. 138). Lived in the Early Cretaceous. Found in England.

Velocipes (vel-O-si-peez: "quick foot") A small, bipedal carnivore known from part of one bone. Perhaps a ceratosaur. Lived in the Late Triassic. Found in Germany. (*n.d.*)

Velociraptor (vel-O-si-RAP-tor: "quick plunderer") A bipedal carnivore 1.8m (6ft) long: similar to *Deinonychus* (p. 70). Lived in the Late Cretaceous. Found in China and Mongolia.

Velocisaurus (vel-O-si-SORE-us: "quick lizard") A small, bipedal carnivore with unusual upper foot bones. Lived in the Late Cretaceous. Found in Argentina. Named in 1991. Classification: Velocisauridae, Ceratosauria, Theropoda, Saurischia.

Volkheimeria (VOLK-hie-mer-i-a: "Volkheimer's") A large, quadrupedal herbivore: a sauropod related to *Brachiosaurus* (p. 94). Lived in the Middle Jurassic. Found in Argentina.

Vulcanodon (vul-KAN-oh-don: "volcano tooth") A quadrupedal herbivore 6.5m (21ft) long: a small, primitive sauropod. Lived in the Early Jurassic. Found in Zimbabwe. Classification: Vulcanodontidae, Sauropoda, Sauropodomorpha, Saurischia.

Wakinosaurus (wah-keen-oh-SORE-us: "Wakin lizard") A large, poorly known, bipedal carnivore, perhaps like *Allosaurus* (p. 52). Lived in the Early Cretaceous. Found in Japan. Named in 1992. (*n.d.*)

Walgettosuchus = *Rapator*?

Walkeria (wauk-EAR-i-a: "Walker's") A bipedal carnivore about 1.2m (4ft) long: possibly related to *Herrerasaurus* (p. 40). Lived in the Late Triassic. Found in India. Classification uncertain.

Wannanosaurus (wan-an-oh-SORE-us: "Wannan lizard") A tiny, bipedal herbivore (one of the smallest dinosaurs) about 60cm (2ft) long: a flat-headed pachycephalosaur related to *Goyocephale*. Lived in the Late Cretaceous. Found in China.

Wuerhosaurus (WER-oh-SORE-us: "Wuerho lizard") A quadrupedal, plated herbivore 6m (19ft 6in) long, related to *Stegosaurus* (p. 114). Lived in the Early Cretaceous. Found in China.

Xenotarsosaurus (zen-oh-tar-soh-SORE-us: "strange-ankle lizard") A large, bipedal carnivore related to *Carnotaurus* (p. 48). Lived in the Late Cretaceous. Found in Argentina.

Xiaosaurus (SHEE-ah-o-SORE-us: "Xiao lizard") A bipedal herbivore 1.5m (5ft) long: perhaps an ornithopod related to *Hypsilophodon* (p. 136). Lived in the Middle Jurassic. Found in China. (*n.d.*)

Xuanhanosaurus (shwan-HAN-oh-SORE-us: "Xuanhan lizard") A bipedal/quadrupedal carnivore 6m (19ft 6in) long, with sturdy arms. Lived in the Middle Jurassic. Found in China. Classification uncertain.

Xuanhuasaurus (SHWAN-hwah-SORE-us: "Xuanhua lizard") A small, bipedal herbivore: a pachycephalosaur related to *Chaoyangosaurus*. Lived in the Late Jurassic. Found in China. (*n.d.*)

Yaleosaurus = *Anchisaurus* (p. 84).

Yandusaurus (YAN-doo-SORE-us: "Yandu lizard") A bipedal herbivore 2m (6ft 6in) long: an ornithopod related to *Hypsilophodon* (p. 136). Lived in the Middle Jurassic. Found in China. (See also *Yubasaurus*.)

Yangchuanosaurus (yang-choo-AHN-oh-SORE-us: "Yangchuan lizard") A bipedal carnivore 9m (29ft 6in) long: maybe related to *Eustreptospondylus* (p. 50). Lived in the Late Jurassic. Found in China. Classification uncertain.

Yaverlandia (YAV-er-land-ee-ah: "of Yaverland") A bipedal herbivore or a quadrupedal, armoured herbivore: possibly a pachycephalosaur, but maybe an ankylosaur, perhaps related to *Hylaeosaurus*. Lived in the Early Cretaceous. Found in England. (*n.d.*)

Yaxartosaurus = *Jaxartosaurus*.

Yingshanosaurus (ying-SHAN-oh-SORE-us: "Mt. Ying lizard") A quadrupedal, plated herbivore: a stegosaur probably related to *Tuojiangosaurus* (p. 120). Lived in the Jurassic. Found in China.

Yubasaurus = *Yandusaurus* (or vice versa, if *Yubasaurus* was named first).

Yunnanosaurus (yoo-NAN-oh-SORE-us: "Yunnan lizard") A bipedal/quadrupedal herbivore 7m (23ft) long: a prosauropod with self-sharpening, spoon-shaped teeth. Lived in the Early Jurassic. Found in China. Classification: Yunnanosauridae, Prosauropoda, Sauropodomorpha, Saurischia.

Zapsalis = *Paronychodon*.

Zephyrosaurus (ZEF-ear-o-SORE-us: "west wind lizard") A bipedal herbivore 1.8m (6ft) long: an ornithopod like *Hypsilophodon* (p. 136). Lived in the Early Cretaceous. Found in Montana, USA.

Zigongosaurus = *Omeisaurus*.

Zizhongosaurus (zeez-HONG-oh-SORE-us: "Zizhong lizard") A quadrupedal herbivore 9m (29ft 6in) long: a primitive sauropod perhaps like *Vulcanodon*. Lived in the Early Jurassic. Found in China.

Velociraptor *Wuerhosaurus* *Yandusaurus* *Yangchuanosaurus*

GLOSSARY

Acetabulum The hip socket.

Ankylosaurs Quadrupedal, armoured thyreophoran ornithischians.

Antorbital fenestra A hole in the skull in front of each eye: a hallmark of the archosaurs.

Archosaurs A group of reptiles that includes dinosaurs, crocodilians, pterosaurs, and "thecodonts".

Armoured dinosaurs Dinosaurs with bodies protected by bony plates or studs. They included ankylosaurs. Some sauropods were also armoured in a similar fashion.

Bipedal Walking on hind legs only.

Bone-headed dinosaurs The pachycephalosaurs.

Braincase Bones of the skull containing and guarding the brain.

Carnivore A meat-eating animal.

Carnosaurs Big bipedal theropods: a group of tetanurans formally named the Carnosauria.

Carpals The bones of the wrist.

Caudal vertebrae Tail bones.

Cenozoic Era The geological time span covering the last 65 million years: "Age of Mammals". It comprises the Tertiary and Quaternary periods.

Cerapoda A great group of related ornithischian dinosaurs comprising the ornithopods and the marginocephalians.

Ceratopsians Bipedal and quadrupedal marginocephalians comprising psittacosaurids (parrot lizards) and neoceratopsians.

Ceratosaurs One of two major groups of theropods.

Cervical vertebrae Neck bones.

Chevron bones Bones projecting down from the caudal vertebrae (tail bones).

Clade A group of organisms (such as dinosaurs) that share uniquely evolved anatomical features.

Class A group of organisms consisting of one or more related orders (sometimes grouped in subclasses). Classes traditionally include Aves (birds), Reptilia (reptiles), and Mammalia (mammals).

Cloaca A combined outlet for body wastes and sperm or eggs.

Coelurosaurs Mainly small, bipedal saurischian theropods forming a group called the Coelurosauria.

Cold-blooded Depending for body warmth upon heat from the sun.

Coracoid A short bone joined to a dinosaur's scapula that helps to form its shoulder girdle.

Coronoid process An upward projection of the mandible's dentary bone, anchoring the jaw muscles.

Cranium See **Braincase**.

Cretaceous Period The third and last part of the Mesozoic Era or "Age of Dinosaurs".

Dentary The main, tooth-bearing bone of the lower jaw.

Denticles Tiny, pointed projections such as those on the cutting edges of some dinosaurs' teeth.

Dinosaurs A great group of advanced, small to immense archosaurs, probably including the ancestors of birds.

Dorsal vertebrae Spinal bones supporting the back, between the cervical vertebrae and the sacrum.

Duckbilled dinosaurs A popular name for the large, flat-beaked ornithopods known as hadrosaurs.

Euornithopods Advanced ornithopods.

Family Related organisms comprising a genus or several genera. Formal family names end in -idae, as in Tyrannosauridae; informal family names end in -ids, as in tyrannosaurids.

Femur The thigh bone.

Fenestra "Window".

Fibula The calf bone in the leg.

Gastralia Belly ribs.

Genetic change Change to the minute hereditary units called genes found in living cells. Genes programme an individual's development. Generations of accumulating genetic changes cause new species to evolve.

Genus (plural: genera) A group of closely related organisms within a family. A genus consists of one or more species. In print, the name of a genus appears in italics with a capital first letter.

Gizzard A thick-walled, muscular bulge in the gut, with a tough, horny lining to grind up food. Occurs in birds and in some dinosaurs.

Gizzard stones (gastroliths) Stones that are swallowed to help grind up food in a gizzard.

Hadrosaurs Big ornithopods with duck-like beaks. They comprised two families, known as the Hadrosauridae and Lambeosauridae.

Herbivore A plant-eating animal. Ornithischians and sauropodomorphs were herbivorous dinosaurs.

Horned dinosaurs Big, quadrupedal ceratopsians forming the family Ceratopsidae. They had huge skull frills and a nose horn and/or brow horns.

Humerus The upper arm bone.

Ilium (plural: ilia) One of a pair of bones forming the top of the pelvis, blade-like or shelf-like in dinosaurs. Ilia anchored hind-limb muscles, also the spinal column's sacral vertebrae, so transferring body weight to the hind limbs.

Infraorder A major subdivision of an order.

Ischium (plural: ischia) One of a pair of rear, lower hip bones (ischia), rod-like in dinosaurs. The ischium anchored hind-limb muscles that pulled the leg in and back.

Jugal bone A bone below the eye. In ceratopsians it formed a flaring cheek bone.

Jurassic Period The second part of the Mesozoic Era or "Age of Dinosaurs".

Mandible The lower jaw.

Maniraptorans Small coelurosaurian theropods with a distinctive wrist design. Many scientists think maniraptorans gave rise to birds.

Marginocephalians Ornithischians with a skull ridge or shelf: the pachycephalosaurs and ceratopsians.

Maxilla (plural: maxillae) The upper jaw, and, in particular, one of its pair of main tooth-bearing bones.

Mesozoic Era The geological time span of 248–65 million years ago, also called "Age of Dinosaurs". It comprised three geological periods: Triassic, Jurassic, and Cretaceous.

Metacarpals The "palm" bones, situated between the wrist (carpus) and the fingers.

Metatarsals Bones of the upper foot, between the ankle bones and the toe bones.

Naris (plural: nares) Opening of the nasal passage(s).

Neoceratopsians Small to large, chiefly quadrupedal ceratopsians, many with huge, horned heads: the Protoceratopsidae and Ceratopsidae.

Neural spines Bones that project up from vertebrae.

Order A group of organisms below subclass level.

Ornithischians "Bird-hipped" dinosaurs: herbivores comprising one of the two major dinosaur groups.

Ornithodires The group of archosaurs including dinosaurs and pterosaurs (and arguably birds).

Ornithopods "Bird feet": small to very large, mainly bipedal, plant-eating ornithischians.

Pachycephalosaurs Bipedal marginocephalians with an immensely thick skull.

Palaeozoic Era The geological time span of 570–248 million years ago. Fishes, amphibians, and reptiles appeared during this time.

Parrot lizards The psittacosaurids: a family of small ceratopsians with parrot-like beaks.

Pelvis The hip, comprising a left and a right ilium, pubis, and ischium.

Phalanges (singular: phalanx) Toe bones or finger bones (excluding metacarpals and metatarsals).

Plated dinosaurs See **Stegosaurs**.

Predentary bone A toothless bone located at the tip of the lower jaw of ornithischians.

Preparator A scientist specializing in the removal of fossils from rock.

Prosauropods Mainly bipedal/quadrupedal and wholly quadrupedal, small to large, early sauropodomorphs.

Pterosaurs Warm-blooded flying reptiles related to dinosaurs.

Pubis (plural: pubes) One of a pair of front, lower hip bones, rod-like in dinosaurs. Some pubes had a long, forward extension, or prepubis. In many dinosaurs the pubis anchored a muscle that pulled a leg forwards.

Quadrupedal Walking on all fours.

Radius One of two forearm bones.

Reptiles "Cold-blooded", scaly vertebrates breeding on land. Some dinosaurs and pterosaurs were atypical.

Rostral bone A bone forming the tip of the upper jaw of ceratopsians.

Sacral vertebrae The bones of that part of the backbone or spinal column attached to the pelvis.

Sacrum Fused vertebrae that are joined to the pelvis.

Saurischians "Lizard-hipped" dinosaurs: herbivores and carnivores comprising one of the two major dinosaur groups.

Sauropodomorphs Mainly large to immense, long-necked, long-tailed, quadrupedal, herbivorous saurischian dinosaurs. They comprised the prosauropods and sauropods.

Sauropods Large to immense sauropodomorphs.

Scapula The shoulder blade. (See also **Coracoid**.)

Sclerotic ring A "pineapple ring" of bony plates supporting the eye; found in birds, dinosaurs, and other vertebrates.

Scutes Bony plates set in the skin to protect it against the teeth and jaws of predators. The outer surfaces of scutes were often horn-covered.

Segnosaurs A puzzling group of saurischian dinosaurs: perhaps bizarre theropods.

Skull The head's bony framework that protects the brain, eyes, ears, and nasal passages.

Species In the classification of living things, the level below genus. *Tyrannosaurus rex* is a species in the genus *Tyrannosaurus*.

Stegosaurs Quadrupedal thyreophoran ornithischians with two tall rows of plates and/or spines running down the neck, back, and tail.

Subclass The major subdivision of a class.

Suborder The major subdivision of an order.

Tarsals Ankle bones. In dinosaurs they included a distinctively shaped astragalus bone.

Tetanurans One of two major groups of theropods.

"Thecodonts" A mixed group of archosaurs that includes ancestors of dinosaurs, crocodilians, and pterosaurs.

Theropods Bipedal, carnivorous saurischian dinosaurs.

Thyreophorans The armoured ankylosaurs, plated stegosaurs, and their close relatives.

Tibia The shin bone.

Triassic Period The first part of the Mesozoic Era or "Age of Dinosaurs".

Ulna One of the two bones of the forearm.

Ungual phalanges Terminal toe or finger bones bearing claws, hooves, or nails.

Vertebrae Bones of the spinal column.

Vertebrates Backboned animals: fishes, amphibians, reptiles, birds, and mammals.

Warm-blooded Maintaining body warmth by turning food into heat inside the body.

INDEX

ACKNOWLEDGMENTS

Dorling Kindersley would like to thank:

Museums and other organizations: Mary Dawson, Pam Pochapin, and Betty Hill, The Carnegie Museum of Natural History, Pittsburgh, Pennsylvania, USA; Professor W.-D. Heinrich, Museum für Naturkunde, Humboldt-Universität, Berlin, Germany; Paul Howard and Stuart Ogilvy, Yorkshire Museum, York, UK; Margherita and Gilda Majani, Erizzo Editrice, Venice, Italy; John Martin, Leicestershire Museum, Leicester, UK; Dr Jaime E. Powell, Instituto Miguel Lillo, Universidad Nacional de Tucumán, Argentina; Dr Teresa Maryanska and Dr Wojciech Skarzynski, Polish Academy of Sciences, Warsaw, Poland; Mark Norell and Barbara Mathe, The American Museum of Natural History, New York, NY, USA; Kevin Padian, Museum of Paleontology, University of California at Berkeley, USA; Dr Philip Powell, Oxford University Museum, Oxford, UK; Dr Monty Reid, Royal Tyrrell Museum of Paleontology, Alberta, Canada; Dr G.W. Rougier, Museo Argentino de Ciencias Naturales, Buenos Aires, Argentina; Professor Rozanov and Dr S.M. Kurzanov, Palaeontological Institute, Moscow, Russia; Raymond Rye, Caroline Newman, Pamela Baker, and Chip Clark, National Museum of Natural History, Smithsonian Institution, Washington DC, USA; Dr Charles R. Schaff, Museum of Comparative Zoology, Harvard University, Massachusetts, USA; Bruce Selyem, Museum of the Rockies, Montana State University, Bozeman, USA; Mary Ann Turner, Lynnette Jordan, Eric Hoag, and Barbara Narendra, Peabody Museum, Yale University, New Haven, Connecticut, USA; Hiromi Yamazaki, Fuji Television Network Inc, Tokyo, Japan; Professor Dong Zhiming, Institute of Vertebrate Paleontology and Paleoanthropology, Beijing, China.

Additional palaeontology assistance: Tracy Ford, William Lindsay, Jack Macintosh, George Olshevsky

Additional design assistance: Paul Calver, Dirk Kaufman, Gwyn Lewis, Salim Qurashi, Chris Walker, Bryn Walls

Additional editorial assistance: Mike Darton, Paul Docherty, Ellen Dupont, Martyn Page, Mukul Patel, Cathy Rubinstein, Louise Tucker

Index: Sue Bosanko

Retouching: Roy Flooks, Selwyn Hutchinson, David Pugh

US research: Mary Ann Lynch

Special thanks to Susannah Massey for coordinating and interpreting in Russia

The Essential Dinosaur designed by Clare Shedden

ILLUSTRATORS

Simone Boni/L.R. Galante: 26–27, 152 tr, 160 cr, 162 tc, 166 bl
Roby Braun: 21 mr, 50–51, 60–61, 66–67, 77 c, 79 c, 104–105, 114–115, 150–151, 160–161
Simone End: 10 tr, 10 bl, 10 br, 24 tr, 39 bl, 64 bc, br, 78 cr, br, 83 tr, 84 bc, 86 tr, 88 br, 91 bc, 92 tr, 109 br, 111 tr, 116 c, 121 tr, 123 tc, 131 tr, 144 c, cra, 153 tl
John Holmes: 20 c, 59 br, 89 tr, 93 crb, 105 br, 120 tr
Dave Hopkins/Ian Fleming Associates: 56 tl, 164 tr
Andrew Hutchinson: 108–109 c, 110 tr, 112–113
Steve Kirk: 43 tl, 46 c, 60 tr, 65 b, 67 tl, tc, tr, cra, 74 tr, cr, br, 113 tc, 162 bc
Janos Marffy: cladograms, family trees, and skeletons and silhouettes for Fact File boxes, 44 tr, 79 br, 80 tr, 111 c, ca, bc, 143 tl, tr
Ikkyu Murakawa: 155 tl
Andrew Robinson: 40 bc, 77 tl, 106 br, 108 tr, 109 tl, tc

Colin Rose: 12 (main image), 53 tl, cla
Graham Rosewarne: 12 (small images), 13 (small images), 14 c, 17 tm, 19 tm, 46 tr, 60 c, 66 bl, 76 tr, 82 tr, 124 tr, 126 tr, 133 tl, 134 br, 158 tr, 161 tr, 161 br, 163 br
John Sibbick: 6 full page, 11 tr, 15 r, 17 r, 18 c, 19 r, 22 br, 23 tr, 38 tl, 40 tr, 42 bl, 47 tr, 62 bl, 68 cr, 70 bc, 82 bl, 95 tr, 102 br, 110 bl, 130 tr, 138 br, 139 tr, 142 tr, 150 bc, br, 151 bl, 152 tr
John Temperton: 50 tr, 51 bc, 60 br, 72 cl, bc, 88 tr, 90 bc, 93 ca, 96 tr, 102 tr, 106 tr, 118 tr, 154 tr

MODEL MAKERS

Roby Braun: 38 bl (*Allosaurus, Compsognathus*), 40–41, 44 c, 45 br, 48–49, 48tc, 49 tl, 52 mr, br, 53 br, 56 cr, 63 tl, 80–81, 81 r, 84–85, 84 cr, 85 br, 106–107, 116 t, bm, 117 c, 130 bl (*Iguanodon*), 132–133, 133 tr, 136–137, 140 t, 152 bl (*Styracosaurus*), 154–155, 162–163, 163 bl
Centaur Studios: 54 tr, 54–55, 58–59, 94 cr, 94–95, 98–99, 140–141, 148–149, 166–167
David Donkin: 14 tr, 16 tr, 18 tr
John Holmes: 34–35 (*Gallimimus* sequence), 38 bl (*Gallimimus*), 63 bc, 128–129, 130 bl (*Hypsilophodon*), 137 tc

SKELETAL AND FOSSIL MATERIAL

American Museum of Natural History, New York, NY, USA: 23 br, 32–33, 32 bl, cb, 33 cl, tr, 57 br, 98 tr, 149 tr, 157 tr, 158 br, 159 bc, 160 tr, 162 tr, 166 bc
Institute und Museum für Geologie und Paläontologie der Universität Tübingen, Germany: 86 bc, 86–87, 87 bc, 117 tc, tl, 118–119, 119 tl
Instituto Miguel Lillo, Universidad Nacional de Tucumán, Argentina: 40 cr, 41 tc, 90–91, 91 tc, 106 ca, 107 cra
Leicestershire Museum, Leicester, UK: 92–93
Museo Argentino de Ciencias Naturales, Buenos Aires, Argentina: 48 bc, 49 tr
Museum für Naturkunde, Humboldt-Universität, Berlin, Germany: 75 tr, 95 tl
The Natural History Museum, London, UK: 24 br, 26 br, 42 tr, 52–53, 58 tr, br, 59 tl, 82 cra, 88–89, 92 b, 92 bc, 100–101 c, 112 cr, br, 113 c, 120–121, 124 tr, 132 tr and bc, 136 t, 138–139, 144–145, 165 bc, 167 tc
Naturmuseum Senckenberg, Frankfurt, Germany: 55 br, 56–57, 100–101, 139 bc
Oxford University Museum, Oxford, UK: 50 c, cr, bc, 51 cl
Peabody Museum, Yale University, New Haven, Connecticut, USA: 70–71, 72 tl, 84 tc, 85 r, 102 cr
Queensland Museum, South Brisbane, Australia: 26 mr; Bruce Cowell (photographer) 127 tc, 140 bl
Royal Tyrrell Museum of Paleontology, Alberta, Canada: 20 tr, 21 tl, 21 br, 23 mr, 38 tr, cr, crb, 44–45, 47 bc, 55 cr, 56 tc, 64 ca, 64–65, 87 cra, 129 br, 131 cl, 135 cr, 146–147, 150 cra, tr, 152 bl, 155 tr, cr, 163 crb, 164–165
Section of Vertebrate Fossils, Carnegie Museum of Natural History, Pittsburgh, Pennsylvania, USA: 10 bm, 102–103, 103 cr, 115 tc
Smithsonian Institution, Washington DC, USA: 24 tl, 27 ml, 30–31, 42–43, 83 cla, 96–97, 97 tr, 100 tr, 145 tc, 148 tr, 165 tr
Staatliches Museum für Naturkunde, Stuttgart, Germany: 52 tr
Yorkshire Museum, York, UK and The Institute of Vertebrate Paleontology and Paleoanthropology, Beijing, China: 89 cra, 93 br, 120 c, 121 cr

PICTURE CREDITS

Courtesy Department of Library Services, American Museum of Natural History, New York, USA: 26 tl (Neg.no. 356084), 125 tc (Neg. no. 314802); 125 ca (Neg. no. 314803); 148 cl (Neg. no. 13547); 158 cla (Neg. no. 410764)
Stuart Baldwin, Witham, Essex, UK (from *Dinosaur Stamps of the World*): 9 tc, 37 tc, 169 tc
The Hulton Deutsch Collection: 166 cl
The Bridgeman Art Library: 100 br
Bristol City Museums and Art Gallery, Bristol: 112 ca, tr
Dr Eric Buffetaut, Laboratoire de Paléontologie des Vertèbres, Paris, France: 61 br
Bruce Coleman Limited/Jane Burton: 73 tc, 80 bl
Canadian Museum of Nature, Ottawa, Canada: 69 tr (model of *Dinosauroid* by Ron Séguin in collaboration with Dr Dale A. Russell)
Section of Vertebrate Fossils, Carnegie Museum of Natural History, Pittsburgh, Pennsylvania, USA: 31 tr (Neg. no. 8P25), cra (Neg. no. 18P26), 33 br (Neg. no. B376), 46 ba (Neg. no. 10P26); 78 tr (Neg. no. 1086); 98 cl (Neg. no. 1095); 99 bc (Neg. no. 1012); 99br (Neg. no. 170); 100 cl (Neg. no. C1058); 164 cl (Neg. no. 61)
Fuji Television Network Inc, Tokyo, Japan and Palaeontological Institue, Moscow, Russia: 76 cr, 156–157
Robert Harding Picture Library: 25 bl
Dr Ian Ievers and Dr Ralph E. Molnar, South Brisbane, Australia: 126 cb, bc
Dr S.M. Kurzanov/Palaeontological Institute, Moscow, Russia: 76 clb, bc
Ligabue Studies and Researches Centre Archive, Venice, Italy: 142 cla, cb, 142–143, 151 cr, 158 cr, 159 tc
Museo Argentino de Ciencias Naturales, Buenos Aires, Argentina: 29 bc
Museum für Naturkunde, Humboldt-Universität, Berlin, Germany: 75 cl, 94 cl, 118 c, cr
Museum of the Rockies, Montana, USA: Bruce Selyem (photographer) 146 tr
National Museum of Natural Science, Taichung, Taiwan: 34 tr, 75 tl
The National Museum of Wales, Cardiff, UK and The Institute of Vertebrate Paleontology and Paleoanthropology, Beijing, China: 29 tc, ca, 104 bc
The Natural History Museum Picture Library, London, UK: 35 c, cra, crb, 54 bc, 58 c, 72–73, 74 bl, 89 tr (John Holmes), 93 crb (John Holmes), 94 tr, 96 cl, 105 br (John Holmes), 120 tr (John Holmes), 122 c, tr, 123 br, 129 cra, crb, 134 c, 136 c, 137 cl, 138 tc, 139 tl, 144 bc, 166 tr
John Ostrom/Peabody Museum, Yale University, New Haven, Connecticut, USA: 28 tr, br, 73 cra, crb
Oxford Scientific Films: 25 br
Palaeontological Museum, Uppsala University, Sweden: Christer Bäck (photographer) 105 c, cr
Dr Jaime E. Powell, Instituto Miguel Lillo, Universidad Nacional de Tucumán, Argentina: 29 bc, 48 bl
Queensland Museum, South Brisbane, Australia: 140 bm
Wojciech Skarzynski, Institute of Palaeobiology, Polish Academy of Sciences, Warsaw, Poland: 30 bl, 30 tr, 62 tr
Smithsonian Institution, Washington DC, USA: 31 br
South African Museum, Cape Town, South Africa and Museum of Comparative Zoology, Harvard University, Massachusetts, USA: Al Coleman (photographer) 134–135